ACCOUNTING AND FINANCE FOR LAWYERS

IN A NUTSHELL

By

CHARLES H. MEYER

Director–Taxes and
Tax Counsel
GE Capital Aviation Services

ST. PAUL, MINN.
WEST PUBLISHING CO.
1995

COPYRIGHT © 1995 By WEST PUBLISHING CO.
610 Opperman Drive
P.O. Box 64526
St. Paul, MN 55164–0526
1–800–328–9352

Library of Congress Cataloging-in-Publication Data

Meyer, Charles H.
Accounting and finance for lawyers in a nutshell / by Charles H. Meyer.
p.   cm. — (Nutshell series)
Includes index.
ISBN 0–314–04763–8
1. Accounting. 2. Corporations—Finance. 3. Lawyers—Handbooks, manuals, etc. I. Title. II. Series.
HF5635.M5857   1995
657'.024344—dc20   94–39430
                                              CIP

ISBN 0–314–04763–8

TEXT IS PRINTED ON 10% POST CONSUMER RECYCLED PAPER

To
Joseph, Lisa, and Pat
In Memory of
Howard Meyer

*

FOREWORD

In the area of nonlegal disciplines, few bodies of knowledge have more widespread relevance and day-to-day impact for business and commercial lawyers than the areas of accounting and finance. Accounting and finance are important for attorneys working on many types of major acquisition and financing transactions Concepts from these areas frequently arise in a wide range of private and public contractual arrangements. Trial lawyers who work on securities litigation or accountants' malpractice cases are constantly exposed to accounting and auditing issues. Income tax laws employ numerous accounting and finance concepts such as depreciation and other accounting method issues and the application of the financial concept of time value of money as evidenced by the original issue discount rules and economic accrual concepts.

This book is intended to be a useful outline and reference tool for the law students who, in the author's opinion, are wise enough to take the typical accounting for lawyers course offered by most law schools. In addition, this book can serve as a useful learning tool for those lawyers who have not had the opportunity to pursue a formal course in accounting. Finally, this book should serve as a useful review tool for lawyers who have had training in accounting but wish to sharpen their skills and update themselves on the constantly shifting sands of "generally accepted accounting principles."

FOREWORD

The author is indebted to Wm. Douglas Kilbourn, Jr. for his inspiration and leadership in bringing the knowledge of accounting and finance to law students and the legal profession. I am also grateful for the assistance of Jan Harvey in the preparation of the manuscript for this Nutshell. Finally, I wish to acknowledge the valuable contribution of my family through their patience and support during the process of writing this Nutshell.

The selection of the material covered and the depth of analysis in this Nutshell are based on the author's experience with accounting and finance issues in private practice and as a corporate attorney. In addition, the author is the co-instructor of a one-day course on accounting for lawyers that has been presented in cities across the country and has also taught as an adjunct professor at the University of Minnesota Law School.

CHM

Shoreview, MN
November, 1994

OUTLINE

                                                    Page

FOREWORD -- V

**Chapter 1. The Basic Financial State-
    ments** --- 1
A. The Balance Sheet ------------------------------- 1
    1. Assets -- 2
    2. Liabilities ----------------------------------- 3
    3. Owners' Equity ----------------------------- 4
    4. The Balance Sheet Equation ------------ 5
    5. Balance Sheet Format -------------------- 6
B. The Income Statement ------------------------- 7
    1. Revenues and Gains ----------------------- 7
    2. Expenses and Losses ---------------------- 8
    3. Format of the Income Statement ------ 8
C. The Statement of Owners' Equity ----------- 10
D. Statement of Cash Flows ---------------------- 10
E. Additional Information ------------------------- 13
    1. Footnotes ----------------------------------- 13
    2. Supplemental Disclosures --------------- 14
    3. Audit Report -------------------------------- 14

Chapter 2. The Accounting Process ------- 16
A. Source Documents -------------------------------- 16
B. Journal Entries ------------------------------------ 17
C. Ledgers and Posting ---------------------------- 19

		Page
D.	Adjusting Entries	24
	1. Accrued Revenues and Expenses	25
	a. Accrued Revenues	26
	b. Accrued Expenses	27
	c. Accounting for Actual Receipt of Payment	28
	d. Reversing Entries	29
	2. Deferred Revenues and Expenses	30
	a. Deferred Revenues	31
	b. Prepaid Expenses	33
	3. Depreciation Expense	35
	4. Recognizing Cost of Goods Sold	37
E.	Revenue and Expense Accounts	39
F.	Closing the Books	42
G.	Preparation of Financial Statements	45

Chapter 3.　Generally Accepted Accounting Principles | | 46
A.	Official Sources of GAAP	47
	1. FASB Statements	48
	2. APB Opinions	49
	3. Accounting Research Bulletins	50
	4. Enforcement of Official Standards	50
B.	Other Sources of GAAP	51
C.	Governmental Regulation of Accounting	51
	1. SEC	51
	2. Regulatory Agencies	52
D.	Income Tax Accounting	53
E.	Some Fundamental Accounting Concepts	55
	1. Historical Cost	56
	2. The Going Concern Assumption	58
	3. Yearly Reporting	59
	4. Revenue Recognition and Matching	61

Page

E. Some Fundamental Accounting Concepts—Continued
   5. Conservatism 61
   6. Materiality and Cost–Benefit Analysis   63

Chapter 4. Recognition of Revenues and Expenses 65
A. Revenue Recognition 67
   1. Sale of Goods or Services 68
   2. Revenue From Services 69
     a. Specific Performance Method 69
     b. Proportional Performance Method   70
     c. Completed Performance Method .. 70
   3. Long Term Contracts 71
   4. Revenue Recognized With the Passage of Time 72
   5. Revenue Recognized Based on Receipt of Cash 73
   6. Completion of Production 74
   7. Changes in Market Value 74
   8. Asset Writedowns 76
B. Matching 77
   1. Direct Matching 78
   2. Immediate Write–Off 79
   3. Systematic and Rational Allocation ... 79

Chapter 5. Current Assets and Liabilities 81
A. Cash 82
   1. Cash Equivalents 82
   2. Restricted Cash 83
   3. Petty Cash 84
   4. Internal Controls 84
B. Marketable Securities 85

		Page
C.	Receivables	86
	1. Trade Receivables	86
	2. Other Receivables	88
	3. Reporting Receivables	89
	4. Bad Debts	89
	a. Percentage of Sales Method	90
	b. Aged Receivables Analysis	91
	5. Financing and Sales of Receivables	92
	6. Notes Receivable	94
	7. Imputing Interest	95
	8. Receivables From Related Parties	96
D.	Prepayments	96
E.	Accounts Payable	98
	1. Reporting Accounts Payable	98
	2. Imputing Interest	100
F.	Short Term Borrowings	100
	1. Interest on Notes Payable	100
	2. Currently Maturing Amounts of Long Term Debt	101
G.	Accrued Liabilities	103
H.	Deferred Revenues and Deposits	104
I.	Estimated Liabilities	106
J.	Contingent Liabilities	108
Chapter 6. Accounting for Inventories		112
A.	Determining Physical Quantities on Hand	113
	1. Periodic Inventory System	114
	2. The Perpetual Inventory System	116
B.	Determining Inventory Values	118
	1. Specific Identification	119
	2. Cost Flow Assumptions	119
	a. First In, First Out Method	120
	b. Last In, First Out	121

Page

B. Determining Inventory Values—Continued

    c. Average Cost 123

    d. Application to Perpetual Inventory Systems 124

    e. Retail Inventory Methods 125

C. Applying Lower of Cost or Market 125

    1. Determining Market 126

    2. Effect on Inventory and Cost of Goods Sold 127

D. Manufacturing Companies 128

Chapter 7. Property, Plant, and Equipment and Depreciation 130

A. Accounting at Acquisition 131

    1. General Rule 131

    2. Exchanges for Other Property 132

    3. Acquisitions of Multiple Assets 135

    4. Self–Constructed Assets 136

B. Accounting for Depreciation 138

    1. Useful Life 140

    2. Salvage Value 140

    3. Method of Depreciation 141

        a. Straight Line Method 141

        b. Sum-of-the-Years'-Digits Method 142

        c. Declining Balance Method 144

        d. Units of Production Method 146

        e. Depletion of Natural Resources ... 147

        f. Other Methods 148

C. Repairs and Improvements 149

D. Disposal of Fixed Assets 151

Chapter 8. Intangible Assets 153

A. Identifiable Intangible Assets 153

Page

A. Identifiable Intangible Assets—Continued
  1. Types of Identifiable Intangible Assets 153
     a. Patents 153
     b. Copyright 154
     c. Trademarks, Service Marks, and Trade Names 154
     d. Franchises 154
     e. Deferred Charges 154
  2. Accounting for Purchased Identifiable Intangible Assets 155
  3. Accounting for Internally Created Identifiable Intangible Assets 156
     a. Research and Development 157
     b. Computer Software Costs 157
B. Unidentifiable Intangible Assets 158

Chapter 9. Accounting for Investments 160
A. Investments in Bonds 160
  1. Acquisition of Bonds at Face Value ... 161
  2. Acquisition of Bonds at a Discount or Premium 164
     a. Straight Line Amortization of Bond Discount or Premium 164
     b. Effective Interest Method of Amortizing Bond Discount and Premium 167
  3. Changes in Value After Acquisition ... 170
B. Accounting for Stock Investments 172
  1. The Cost Method 172
     a. Dividend Income 173
     b. Changes in Value After Acquisition 174

Page

B. Accounting for Stock Investments—Continued
      c. Stock Splits and Stock Dividends   175
    2. The Equity Method 176
    3. Consolidated Financial Statements 179
C. Other Investments 183
    1. Land 183
    2. Cash Value of Life Insurance 184
    3. Sinking Funds and Other Permanent
       Funds 185

**Chapter 10. Accounting for Long Term
    Debt** 186
A. Forms of Long Term Debt 186
B. Accounting for Long Term Debt Issued at
    Par Value 187
    1. Issuance on an Interest Payment
       Date 187
    2. Issuance of Bonds Between Interest
       Payment Dates 189
C. Accounting for the Issuance of Bonds at
    Other Than Par Value 190
    1. Bonds Issued at a Discount 191
    2. Bonds Issued at a Premium 192
D. Bond Issuance Costs 193
E. Retirement of Bonds Prior to Maturity 194
    1. Actual Retirements 194
    2. In–Substance Defeasance 196
F. Restructuring of Long Term Debt 197
    1. Restructuring With No Gain or Loss   199
    2. Restructuring With Recognition of
       Gain 200
G. Convertible Debt 201
    1. Conversion—Book Value Method 201

Page

G. Convertible Debt—Continued
  2. Conversion—Market Value Method --- 202
  3. Induced Conversions............................ 203
  4. Debt Issued With Stock Warrants 204

Chapter 11. Accounting for Leases 206
A. Introduction 206
B. Characterizing and Accounting for Leases 208
  1. Accounting by the Lessee.................... 209
  2. Accounting by the Lessor.................... 214
C. Special Rules 217
  1. Leveraged Leases 217
  2. Leases Involving Real Estate 218
  3. Sale/Leasebacks................................ 218
D. Disclosures Regarding Leases 221

Chapter 12. Accounting for Other Long Term Liabilities 222
A. Accounting for Income Taxes..................... 222
  1. Temporary Differences....................... 223
    a. Types of Temporary Differences .. 225
    b. Deferred Tax Liabilities................ 226
    c. Deferred Tax Assets..................... 228
    d. Analysis of Deferred Taxes 229
    e. Multiple Period Effects................ 230
  2. Net Operating Losses 233
  3. Valuation Allowances on Deferred Tax Assets.. 234
  4. Reporting Deferred Tax Liabilities and Assets in the Balance Sheet 236
  5. Intraperiod Tax Allocation 237
  6. Permanent Tax Differences................. 239

Page

B. Accounting for Retirement Plans ----------- 241
    1. Defined Contribution Plans ------------- 241
    2. Defined Benefit Plans ----------------------- 244
        a. Components of Pension Expense   245
            (i)   Current Service Cost ----------- 245
            (ii) Interest Cost --------------------- 245
            (iii) Amortization of Transition
                  Cost ------------------------------ 246
            (iv) Prior Service Cost -------------- 246
            (v)   Actuarial Gains and Losses   247
            (vi) Expected Return on Plan
                  Assets ---------------------------- 248
        b. Pension Assets and Liabilities ----- 249
        c. Minimum Liability --------------------- 250
        d. Disclosures ------------------------------ 252
C. Accounting for Other Post–retirement
    Benefits --- 253

**Chapter 13. Accounting for Stock and
    Stockholders' Equity** ----------------------- 256
A. Contributions to Capital ----------------------- 256
    1. Contributed Capital Accounts ----------- 256
    2. Issuing Stock for Cash --------------------- 257
    3. Issuing Stock for Noncash Property -- 258
    4. Stock Subscriptions ------------------------ 259
    5. Stock Issuance Costs ---------------------- 260
B. Accounting for Retained Earnings ---------- 262
C. Accounting for Dividends and Other Dis-
    tributions --- 263
    1. Key Dates Related to Dividends -------- 263
    2. Cash Dividends ------------------------------ 264
    3. Property Dividends-------------------------- 265
    4. Stock Dividends ----------------------------- 266

Page

C. Accounting for Dividends and Other Distributions—Continued
    5. Distributions of Stock Rights 267
    6. Stock Splits 268
D. Other Adjustments to Retained Earnings ... 269
    1. Prior Period Adjustments 269
    2. Appropriations 270
E. Accounting for Treasury Stock 270
    1. The Cost Method 270
    2. The Par Value Method 272
F. Convertible Stock 274
G. Compensatory Stock Options and Stock Appreciation Rights 275
    1. Stock Options 275
    2. Stock Appreciation Rights 278
    3. Disclosures 281

Chapter 14. Partnership Accounting 282
A. Capital Accounts 282
B. Defining a Partner's Interest in Profits and Losses 284
    1. Allocating Individual Items of Income or Loss 284
    2. Recognizing Different Forms of Partner Contributions 285
       a. Salary for Services 286
       b. Interest on Capital 286
       c. Residual Income and Loss Sharing Ratios 287
C. Admission of New Partners 288
    1. Transfer of Partnership Interests 288
       a. No Adjustments to Partnership Net Assets 289

Page

C. Admission of New Partners—Continued
    b. Adjusting Partnership Net Assets 289
  2. Contribution to the Partnership 290
    a. No Adjustment to Partnership Capital Accounts 291
    b. The Goodwill Method 292
    c. The Bonus Method 293
D. Retirements of Partners 294
  1. Goodwill Method 295
  2. Bonus Method 296

Chapter 15. Accounting for Business Combinations 298

A. Purchase and Pooling Methods 299
  1. Overview 299
  2. Determining Which Method Applies 300
    a. Autonomy 301
    b. Independence 301
    c. Single Transaction 302
    d. Voting Common Stock as Consideration 302
    e. No Equity Restructuring 304
    f. Limitation on Treasury Stock 304
    g. Maintaining Shareholder Ratios 304
    h. Full Voting Rights 304
    i. No Contingencies 305
    j. Absence of Planned Transactions 305
  3. Application of Purchase Accounting 306
    a. Recording the Acquisition 307
    b. Effects of the Purchase Method on the Income Statement 310
    c. Accounting for Acquisition Costs 311
  4. Application of Pooling Accounting 311

Page

A. Purchase and Pooling Methods—Continued

    a. Recording the Acquisition Using Pooling 312

    b. The Income Statement Under the Pooling Method 313

    c. Costs Under the Pooling Method 313

  5. Application to Acquisitions of Stock .. 314

Chapter 16. Earnings Per Share and Financial Ratios 315

A. Earnings Per Share 315

  1. EPS in a Simple Capital Structure.... 316

  2. EPS in a Complex Capital Structure 319

    a. Effect of Stock Options 320

    b. Effect of Convertible Securities ... 322

B. Financial Ratios 326

  1. Measures of Liquidity 328

    a. Current Ratio 328

    b. Quick Ratio 329

  2. Measures of Leverage 329

    a. Debt–Equity Ratio 330

    b. Debt to Asset Ratio...................... 330

    c. Times Interest Earned 331

    d. Times Fixed Charges Earned 331

  3. Activity Ratios 332

    a. Asset Turnover.............................. 332

    b. Receivables Turnover 333

    c. Inventory Turnover 333

  4. Measures of Profitability.................... 334

    a. Profit Margin 334

    b. Return on Assets 334

    c. Return on Equity 335

    d. Earnings per Share........................ 336

Page

B. Financial Ratios—Continued
    e. Price/Earnings Ratio 336
    f. Payout Ratio 337
    g. Dividend Yield 337

Chapter 17. Special Reporting Issues 338
A. Separately Reported Components of Income 338
    1. Extraordinary Items 339
    2. Discontinued Operations 340
    3. Effects of a Change in Accounting Principle 341
    4. Income Statement Reporting 344
B. Segment Reporting 345
    1. Reporting on Industry Operations 346
    2. Reporting on Foreign Operations and Export Sales 348
    3. Information About Major Customers ... 349
C. Interim Financial Statements 350

Chapter 18. Corporate Finance—Valuation 353
A. Valuation of Securities 353
    1. Valuation of Bonds 354
      a. Mechanics of Bond Value Calculations 354
      b. Determining Market Interest Rates 356
        (i) Credit Risk 356
        (ii) Term to Maturity 357
      c. Bonds With Additional Features .. 358
    2. Valuation of Preferred Stock 359
      a. Nonredeemable Preferred Stock .. 359

OUTLINE

Page

A. Valuation of Securities—Continued
    b. Redeemable Preferred Stock 360
    c. Rate of Return for Preferred Stock 360
    d. Preferred Stock With Additional Features 361
  3. Valuation of Common Stock 362
    a. Constant Dividends 362
    b. Dividends Growing at a Constant Rate 363
    c. Present Value Analysis 363
    d. Price/Earnings Multiples 366
    e. Determining the Required Rate of Return 366
B. Cost of Capital 369
  1. Determining a Company's Cost of Capital 369
  2. Use of Cost of Capital in Capital Budgeting 371
C. Valuation of a Business 372
  1. Discounted Cash Flow Analysis 372
    a. Estimate the Cash Flows for a Projection Period 372
    b. Terminal Cash Flow 374
    c. Determination of Discount Rate .. 375
    d. Computation of the Value of the Firm 375
    e. Example 376
  2. Multiples Analysis 378
  3. Asset Values 380

OUTLINE

	Page
Appendix: Time Value of Money	383
INDEX	409

*

XXI

ACCOUNTING AND FINANCE FOR LAWYERS

IN A NUTSHELL

*

CHAPTER 1

THE BASIC FINANCIAL
STATEMENTS

The main subject matter of this Nutshell is financial accounting. Financial accounting involves the process of recording transactions in the accounting records of a business and periodically extracting, sorting, and summarizing the recorded transactions to produce a set of financial statements. Financial statements are the primary means by which businesses communicate financial information to various users. When a business issues a complete set of financial statements, there are four individual statements that are typically prepared. This chapter will introduce and describe the basic financial statements. Various items and concepts introduced briefly in this chapter will be discussed in more detail in later chapters. A general familiarity with the output of the financial accounting process should assist in understanding the accounting process and the issues that arise in the preparation of the financial statements.

A. THE BALANCE SHEET

The balance sheet, also called the statement of financial position, sets forth the assets, liabilities, and owners' equity (the investment of the owners) of a business as of a particular point in time (typically, the end of the fiscal year). The balance sheet is a snapshot as of the date it is issued. A sample balance sheet is shown in Exhibit 1.1. In a typical balance sheet, the assets are listed on the left hand side. On the right hand side are listed the liabilities of the business and the owners' equity accounts.

Exhibit 1.1

Balance Sheet

Cash	$ 20,000	Accounts Payable	$ 40,000
Accounts Receivable	40,000	Accrued Liabilities	30,000
Inventory	60,000	Notes Payable	10,000
Current Assets	120,000	Current Liabilities	80,000
Land	50,000	Bonds Payable	80,000
Buildings and		Pension Liability	40,000
Equipment	140,000	Total Liabilities	200,000
Less: Accumulated		Owners' Equity	100,000
Depreciation	(10,000)	Total Liabilities	
Total Assets	$300,000	and Equity	$300,000

1. Assets

The assets of a business as shown on the balance sheet are of two basic types. One type of asset is a tangible or intangible property interest or legal right of the business, something that one normally expects in response to the question, "What do you own?" Examples of this type of asset are cash (*e.g.*, currency, coins, bank balances), receivables, whether represented by formal notes or not, inventories, land, buildings and equipment, patents, trademarks, copyrights, etc. The other type of asset listed on a balance sheet is a "deferred expense" or "deferred charge." The concept of deferral will be discussed in Chapter 2. For now, it is sufficient to note that a deferred expense or deferred charge is a cost incurred by a business where the business expects to benefit from that cost over a period of time beyond the current year. An example would be a prepaid subscription to a business periodical the cost of which will be recognized as an expense over the subscription period.

Some items listed in the assets section of the balance sheet fall in both of the above categories. A building represents tangible property owned by the business. At the same time, the cost of the building represents a type of prepaid or deferred expense that will be recognized and deducted in computing net income over the life of the building through a process called depreciation accounting (discussed in Chapter 7).

2. Liabilities

Liabilities represent the obligations of a business to persons other than the owners of the business (although owners may also be creditors, particularly in the case of a corporation). Liabilities may be actual cash obligations payable at some time in the future, such as accounts payable, notes payable, bonds, and mortgages. These liabilities may be recognized by formal, written instruments such as promissory notes or they may be based on oral agreements or other informal understandings.

Liabilities may also be created in several other ways. Some liabilities represent prepaid revenues (also called deferred income or deferred revenue). This type of liability arises where money has been collected in advance of rendering a service or delivering goods. Until that revenue is "earned" and included in the computation of income or loss for the period, the amount collected is shown as a liability. Accrued liabilities are created when a business recognizes currently an expense even though no actual legal obligation exists as of the balance sheet date. An example would be the recognition of the salaries and wages earned by employees through a balance sheet date that falls in the middle of a payroll period. "Contingent liabilities" are recognized for possible future obligations of a business where there is no current obligation and it is not even clear that there ever will be an actual obligation of the business (for example, recognizing a contingent liability for possible future litigation claims).

3. Owners' Equity

Owners' equity is the residual claim of the owners of the business on its assets after recognition of the liabilities of the business. Owners' equity represents the amounts contributed by the owners to the business, plus the accumulated income of the business since its formation, less any amounts that have been distributed to the owners.

The manner in which owners' equity is reported in the balance sheet depends on the legal form of the business (sole proprietorship, partnership, corporation, etc.). For corporations, the accounts in owners' equity typically include capital stock, representing the par or stated value of stock that has been issued, additional paid-in-capital, representing the amount paid for stock in excess of its par or stated value, and retained earnings, representing the cumulative or running balance of the net income of the business less any distributions of dividends to the owners. Certain specialized accounting procedures may also require recognition of amounts that are treated as additions to, or subtractions from, owners' equity.

4. The Balance Sheet Equation

There is a fundamental relationship that exists among the three components of the balance sheet. That relationship is expressed as follows:

Assets = Liabilities + Owners' Equity

This is a very useful relationship to remember when trying to understand how a transaction will affect the financial statements. If you know, for example, that a transaction will cause an asset to increase, then one or more of the following must also occur to maintain the balance sheet equation: another asset will be decreased, a liability will be increased, or owners' equity will be increased. Thus, an increase in cash could result from the disposition of another asset such as the collection of a receivable, the creation of a liability such as a note payable to a bank, or an increase in owners' equity as the result of, for example, an additional contribution by the owners.

5. Balance Sheet Format

Balance sheets are typically prepared in a classified format like the one shown in Exhibit 1.1. In a classified balance sheet, the assets are grouped in two categories. The current assets are listed first. Current assets are those assets that will generally be converted into cash or consumed by the business within the coming year. They include cash, marketable securities, receivables, inventories, and prepaid expenses. The long term or noncurrent assets are shown next. Long term assets include property, plant, and equipment, long term intangible assets such as patents, long term investments, and miscellaneous deferred charges.

In the liabilities section of the balance sheet, current liabilities are generally shown first. Current liabilities are those liabilities that will be paid within the coming year. They include accounts payable, short term notes payable, accrued expenses, and the portion of long term debt that will mature in the next year. The long term liabilities are listed next. Long term liabilities include long term notes, bonds, and mortgages. Preparation of the classified balance sheet facilitates financial analysis by segregating the short term or current assets and liabilities from the long term assets and liabilities. As we will see, a number of frequently used financial analysis techniques involve computations that segregate the current and long term assets and liabilities.

B. THE INCOME STATEMENT

The income statement, also called the statement of results of operations, sets forth the primary components of net income or loss for the year. It is a "flow statement" in that it reports the income for a period of time, typically one year, ending on the date of the related balance sheet. The primary components of the income statement are revenues, expenses, gains, and losses. A sample income statement is shown in Exhibit 1.2.

Exhibit 1.2

Income Statement

Revenues	$125,000
Expenses	
Cost of Goods Sold	(50,000)
Depreciation Expense	(20,000)
Compensation Expense	(30,000)
Income Tax Expense	(10,000)
Net Income	$ 15,000

1. Revenues and Gains

Revenues include the primary source of earnings of the business, such as the proceeds from sales of products for manufacturers or merchandising operations and the revenues received for services rendered by service-type businesses. Also included in revenues are miscellaneous items such as dividends and interest from investments (of course, interest and dividends may be the primary source of income for financial companies). Although usage varies, the term "gains" is typically used to refer to the results of transactions that occur other than in the ordinary course of business. Gains represent the amounts realized on sales of assets in excess of the book value of the assets sold. Book value refers to the amount at which the assets are carried in the financial records. For example, if a machine having a book value of $30,000 is sold for $75,000, there is a gain of $45,000. These types of gains may or may not be shown separately from the other revenues of the business depending on the amount and nature of the gains.

2. Expenses and Losses

Expenses are the costs incurred and consumed by the business in generating the revenues of the business. The principal expenses of most businesses include such items as cost of goods sold, salaries and wages, depreciation (the cost of fixed assets like furniture and fixtures treated as consumed in the current period), rent, interest, and income taxes. The term "losses" usually refers to losses from sales of property or other events (*e.g.,* litigation or fires) not in the ordinary course of business.

3. Format of the Income Statement

The revenues and gains for the year, less the expenses and other losses, equals the net income or loss of the business for the year. Most businesses simply show all the revenues and gains as a single amount and then subtract all the expenses and losses grouped into several major categories to compute the net income or loss for the year. This is referred to as the single step form of income statement. Exhibit 1.2 is a single step income statement. Some businesses calculate various subtotals before computing the final net income or loss. Thus, the income statement may first subtract costs of goods sold from sales and report the resulting amount of gross profit or gross margin. Next, operating expenses are subtracted to produce a subtotal called operating margin, or net operating margin. Then, other revenues, gains, expenses, and losses are shown and the final net income or loss number is computed. This is referred to as a multiple step income statement. For internal or management reporting purposes, there will be extensively more detailed categorization and breakdown of revenues and expenses. The use of the single step or multiple step formats are optional.

Certain unusual or nonrecurring amounts, if material, must be separately reported in the income statement. The amounts that must be shown separately are any "extraordinary gains or losses," the operating results and gain or loss from certain discontinued operations, and the effect on income of certain changes in accounting methods. A more detailed discussion of these items can be found in Chapter 17. If any of these items exist, the income statement will first show the net income or loss before these items. The items requiring separate disclosure will next be separately stated reduced by any income tax effect associated with these items (see Chapter 17 for how to determine the tax attributable to these items). Finally, net income or loss will be computed.

The income statement normally shows certain earnings per share calculations based on the income for the year. The earnings per share amount is frequently used by analysts in reviewing stock values of companies. For companies with complicated capital structures, these earnings per share calculations can become quite complex. Earnings per share calculations are discussed in greater detail in Chapter 16.

C. THE STATEMENT OF OWNERS' EQUITY

The statement of owners' equity summarizes the changes in the owners' equity accounts for the period covered by the income statement. The beginning balance of owners' equity is set forth followed by any additional amounts invested by the owners, the net income or loss of the business for the period, and any distributions to the owners that reduce the owners' equity. These amounts are then totalled to produce the ending balance of owners' equity.

D. STATEMENT OF CASH FLOWS

The last major financial statement is a statement of cash flows that provides detail about the changes in the business' cash balance for the period covered by the income statement. As will be discussed below, income does not equal cash. A business can have a strong earnings record and yet be suffering from a shortage of cash because all of the income has not been converted into cash and because of the need to use the available cash to replace assets or expand the business. The statement of cash flows is designed to give additional information about the sources from which cash is derived and how the cash is used.

The statement of cash flows is divided into three main parts. The first section shows cash flow from operating activities. This includes the cash generated by the primary income producing activities of the business (cash received from the sale of products or services less the cash paid out for ordinary expenses incurred in generating the sales as well as interest and tax payments) plus interest and dividends received on miscellaneous investments.

In the section setting forth cash provided by operations, the statement of cash flows typically starts with net income and makes two adjustments. First, noncash expenses such as depreciation expense are added back to income. The depreciation deducted in computing net income does not involve any current payment of cash. It is simply an accounting allocation. Adding back the depreciation (and other similar noncash expenses and revenues) is necessary to convert net income to a cash flow figure.

The second adjustment modifies income for changes in certain current assets and liabilities. For example, net income includes all sales for the year. But not all sales are immediately collected in cash. If the business extends credit to its customers, some sales will be represented by accounts receivable (cash to be received in the future). If the balance in accounts receivable has increased during the period covered by the financial statements, this increase must be subtracted from net income to convert the sales component of net income to an amount reflecting the actual *collections* on account of sales, which is the correct amount to include in the cash flow from operations. Similar adjustments are made for changes in inventory, accounts payable, and other current asset and liability accounts.

The second section in the statement of cash flows is the cash flow from investing activities. This includes the cash flow from the purchase and sale of operating assets (buildings, machinery, patents, etc.) and the purchase and sale of investments (buying and selling stocks and bonds, making loans, and receiving repayment on loans).

The third section is the cash flow from financing activities. This includes amounts received from issuing debt instruments or selling stock and amounts paid out to repay loans or repurchase stock. It also includes amounts paid out as dividends on a corporation's stock, but not the amount paid as interest on loans, which is included in computing the cash flow from operating activities.

A simple form of cash flow statement is shown in Exhibit 1.3.

Exhibit 1.3

Statement of Cash Flows

Net Income	$20,000	
Add: Depreciation Expense	15,000	
Less: Changes in Net Current Assets and Liabilities Resulting from Operations	(25,000)	
Total Cash Provided by Operations		$10,000
Purchase of Building	($80,000)	
Sale of Excess Land	40,000	
Total Cash Used in Investing Activities		(40,000)
Sale of Additional Common Stock	$50,000	
Retirement of Bonds	(30,000)	
Total Cash Provided by Financing Activities		20,000
Net Cash Used During the Year		($10,000)

E. ADDITIONAL INFORMATION

1. Footnotes

In addition to the actual financial statements described above, a complete set of financial statements includes certain additional information. Financial statements include a number of footnotes. One critical footnote describes the significant accounting policies adopted by the issuer of the financial statements. As we will see in many of the chapters in this nutshell, there are a number of areas where alternative accounting treatments are available for material items included in the financial statements. The footnote on accounting policies alerts the readers to the alternative accounting procedures that have been adopted by the issuer in question.

In addition, the footnotes set forth additional detail about certain components of the financial statements and also set forth information that cannot be included on the face of the financial statements. Examples include detailed discussions about a company's obligations under long term leases, the company's retirement plans, and contingent liabilities. The footnotes should be carefully studied by anyone reviewing financial statements.

2. Supplemental Disclosures

Certain supplemental disclosures are also made by the issuer. For example, full financial statements are typically provided for two or sometimes three years in order to permit analysis of trends over time. In addition to the full financial statements, an issuer will include a supplementary table that sets forth certain key items from the financial statements for a longer period of five, ten, or twenty years.

3. Audit Report

Finally, the audit report is a key element of audited financial statements. When financial statements are audited, the auditor must include with the financial statements a report or opinion. This report does three things. It sets forth the scope of the audit work conducted and indicates whether there were any limitations on the scope of the audit procedures performed by the auditor. The report also sets forth certain inherent limitations in any audit and puts the reader on notice that the existence of an audit does not guarantee that the financial statements are accurate in all respects. The audit report then sets forth the auditor's opinion about whether the financial statements are presented fairly in accordance with "generally accepted accounting principles." To the extent that any problems were uncovered by the audit and were not corrected by management, the report sets forth information about the items that the auditor believes should be handled differently and, if possible, the effect that the items have on the financial statements.

CHAPTER 2

THE ACCOUNTING PROCESS

Having described in Chapter 1 the end result of
the financial accounting process, the basic financial
statements, Chapter 2 will now describe the accounting process itself. What follows is a summary
of the major steps in the accounting process of a
typical business. This discussion will include the
steps through which the underlying transactional
information is entered into the financial records
and eventually makes its way to the financial statements. This chapter will also discuss the concept of
accrual accounting and the special accounting entries and procedures required by accrual accounting.

A. SOURCE DOCUMENTS

The first step in the accounting process is the
collection of the raw data reflecting the transactions
of the business and economic events affecting the
business. This raw data comes in a variety of
forms often evidenced by source documents.
Source documents are documents generated either
externally or internally that provide information
necessary to recording accounting information.
They may be by-products of transactions or they

may be specially created to facilitate the accounting process.

For example, a business will receive a number of checks as well as currency and coin representing the proceeds from current or past sales. At the end of the day, the checks and cash amounts are deposited in the bank. In addition to the actual cash and checks, the business will typically receive "remittance advices" accompanying collections received through the mail (*e.g.*, the copies of invoices or monthly statements mailed with the checks) and will generate some type of cash register tape for sales made on the premises. The remittance advices, cash register tapes, and bank deposit slips all represent source documents that are used by the accounting department to record in this case information about sales and collections.

Similarly, in the case of purchases, there will be purchase orders, receiving reports, invoices, and the check register that will provide information about purchases of materials and supplies and the payment for such items. Other types of transactions of a business will each have their own set of source documents.

B. JOURNAL ENTRIES

Once the accounting department has collected all of the appropriate source documents, the transactions are recorded in the accounting records. Traditionally, the initial recording of these transactions occurs in a journal. The journal is a chronological record of the business transactions recorded in the accounting records. In making these accounting entries in the journal, accountants employ a system called "double-entry bookkeeping." In double entry bookkeeping, every transaction recorded by the business involves one or more "debit" entries and one or more "credit" entries. The debit entries must always equal the credit entries for each transaction recorded. More will be said about debits and credits below.

To illustrate a journal entry, assume that a business purchases land for a total purchase price of $100,000 with $25,000 being paid immediately in cash and $75,000 being paid by the business issuing its note payable in that amount. The journal entry for this transaction would be as follows:

Land (Debit)	$100,000	
Cash (Credit)		$25,000
Notes Payable (Credit)		$75,000

The references to "Land," "Cash," and "Notes Payable" are to different "accounts" maintained by the business. A separate account is established for each principal asset, liability, and component of owners' equity of the business. Accounts also exist for the principal categories of revenues and expenses. The journal entry thus identifies the accounts affected by a transaction and the dollar amounts to be entered in these accounts.

Note that the debit items equal the credit items. This must always be true. The convention is that the debit entries are offset to the left of the credit entries in the journal. An actual journal entry would also have associated with it the date of the entry and in some cases, a description of the transaction that produced the entry. In a similar manner, all of the other transactions of the business and other events affecting the accounting records would be recorded in the journal with the debits always equalling the credits. This format for journal entries will be used throughout this nutshell to illustrate accounting for different events and transactions.

A very small business might use one general journal to record all of its transactions. For most businesses, however, it is necessary to use a series of specialized journals each of which records transactions of a similar nature that recur frequently. Thus, a business might have a cash receipts journal, a cash payments journal, a sales journal, a purchases journal, and a general journal (the general journal being used to record all of the transactions that do not fit in any of the special journals). Although the actual format of the special journals varies from that of the general journal, the underlying concept of the journal entries remains the same.

C. LEDGERS AND POSTING

Periodically, the transactions that have been recorded in the journals are "posted" to various ledger books. A separate ledger page is maintained for each account that the business has. The ledger is used to consolidate all of the accounting entries that have been made in each of the accounts of the business. Thus, the ledger for the cash account includes all the entries increasing or decreasing the cash account. For illustrative purposes, the separate ledgers for each account are frequently represented by "T-accounts." The land purchase transaction recorded above would be posted to the ledger (as represented here by T-accounts) as follows:

Land		Cash	
$100,000			$25,000

Notes Payable	
	$75,000

With the help of the T-accounts representing the ledger, we can now expand on the concepts of debits and credits and explain the significance of posting the journal entry on either the left or right hand side of the T-account (the left and right hand sides of the T-accounts represent two columns in the ledger—one for the debit entries and one for the credit entries). The terms debit and credit are merely labels that are used in describing the process of recording accounting transactions. A debit entry is a left-side entry and a credit entry is a right-side entry. In the journal entry for the land purchase, the debit entry is set off slightly to the left of the credit entry and the credit entry is similarly to the right of the debit entry. In posting this journal entry to the ledger, the debit entry to the Land account for $100,000 has been posted to the left hand side of the Land T-account. The credit entries for Cash and Notes Payable have been posted to the right hand side of those T-accounts.

By convention, debit or left-hand entries are used to show an increase in an asset account or a decrease in a liability or owners' equity account. The debit entry to Land means that the Land account has been increased, which would be the expected result of a purchase of land. Credit or right-hand entries are used to show a decrease in an asset account or an increase in a liability or owners' equity account. The credit entry to Cash, an asset account, means that the Cash account has been decreased. The credit entry to Notes Payable, a liability account, means that Notes Payable has been increased as result of the purchase of the land.

In order to further the understanding of accounting entries and debits and credits, the accounting entries for several common business transactions by a corporation (Company J) follow:

Company J sells 10,000 shares of its common stock ($1 par value) for $50,000.

Cash	$50,000	
Capital Stock		$10,000
Additional Paid-in-Capital		$40,000

The debit entry increases cash and the credit entries increase the owners' equity accounts. The stockholders' equity accounts in a corporation will be discussed in Chapter 15. For now it is sufficient to note that the capital stock account represents the par or stated value of the stock issued and the additional paid-in-capital account represents the proceeds from issuances of stock for amounts in excess of par or stated value.

Company J purchases inventory on open account credit for $20,000.

Inventory	$20,000	
Accounts Payable		$20,000

The debit entry increases the inventory asset account and the credit entry increases a liability called accounts payable.

Rent for the current month in the amount of $1,000 is paid.

Rent Expense	$1,000	
Cash		$1,000

The debit to rent expense represents an increase in the rent expense for the year, which is also a decrease in owners' equity. The use of temporary accounts for revenues and expenses and their relationship to the balance sheet accounts for owners' equity will be discussed below.

Company J sells inventory that was originally purchased for $5,000. It is sold on open account for $8,000. Two entries are needed to record this transaction.

Accounts Receivable	$8,000	
Sales		$8,000

This debit entry increases accounts receivable, an asset. The credit entry increases the sales revenue account, which also represents an increase in owners' equity. This entry illustrates a feature of "accrual accounting." In accrual accounting, revenues are recorded when they are earned and expenses are recorded when they are incurred without regard to whether any present cash receipt or payment is occurring. As will be discussed below, GAAP requires the use of accrual accounting.

The second entry related to the sale is as follows:

Cost of Goods Sold	$5,000	
Inventory		$5,000

The credit decreases the inventory asset account and the debit increases the expense account called cost of goods sold. The increase in cost of goods sold is also a decrease in owners' equity that offsets the increase in owners' equity resulting from the revenue on the sale transaction (*i.e.,* the profit on the sale is the difference between the sales revenue and the cost of the goods sold).

Company J pays a portion of its accounts payables.

Accounts Payable	$10,000	
Cash		$10,000

The liabilities account called accounts payable is reduced by the debit entry and the asset account for cash is reduced by the credit entry.

To a significant extent, the physical recording and posting procedures described above have been extensively changed by the use of computers and particularly the use of database software. There is less reliance on formal source documents in a number of cases. In addition, accounting entries are frequently made directly into a computerized accounting database one time. If the business needs a chronological listing of transactions similar to a journal, the computer can prepare a report providing such information. If a listing of all transactions affecting an account, *i.e.*, a ledger report, is needed, the computer prepares such a report. Nevertheless, the basic concepts underlying the development of the database for the accounting information and the process that the computer uses to prepare various reports is essentially the same as the concepts underlying the manual accounting procedures described above and illustrated in later chapters of this book.

D. ADJUSTING ENTRIES

The accounting entries that are illustrated above are all triggered by some type of transaction or event usually involving a third party. In addition to these types of transactions, there are also a number of entries in the books that must be made without an external transaction to trigger the recording process. These types of entries are called adjusting entries. Adjusting entries are usually made at the end of the period for which financial statements will be prepared. The adjusting entries are required because without them, the balances in a number of accounts would not show the correct amounts at year-end. There are several classes of adjusting entries that share similar characteristics.

1. Accrued Revenues and Expenses

One type of adjusting entry results from the need to "accrue" certain revenues and expenses in order to compute net income of a business on the accrual basis. The accrual method, as distinguished from the cash receipts and disbursements method of accounting, reports revenues when they are earned even though no cash may have been received and reports expenses when they have been incurred even though no payment of cash has been made in connection with such expenses. The recording of the sales revenue and the related accounts receivable illustrated in section C. above is one example of the use of accrual accounting. Revenue is recognized when a sale is made, not when the cash is collected.

"Accrued revenues and expenses" are examples of the use of the accrual method of accounting that also necessitate adjusting entries. The accrual of a revenue or expense at the end of an accounting period is the recognition of a revenue or expense even though there has been no receipt or payment and no prior recording of the transaction. The recognition of sales revenue and a related receivable (asset) at the time of a sale is an accrual of revenue that is recorded during the accounting period at the time of a transaction. However, the use of the term accrual is usually applied to revenues and expenses that are not normally recognized in the financial books until the end of the accounting period.

a. *Accrued Revenues*

To illustrate the accrual of revenue, assume that a Company J holds a $50,000 note receivable (an asset) bearing interest at a rate of ten per cent per annum payable annually. The note is dated July 1, 199x, and interest is payable on each July 1 during the term of the note. The business maintains its books on a calendar year basis. At December 31, 199x, no interest has been received on the note. However, as of that date, the holder of the note has earned interest of approximately $2,500, one half of the $5,000 interest payment that will be made on July 1 of the following year. Therefore, the holder of the note will "accrue" $2,500 of interest revenue on December 31, 199x, to reflect the revenue that has been earned but not yet received. This interest revenue is accrued revenue. The adjusting entry that would be made on December 31, 199x, would be as follows:

Accrued Interest Receivable	$2,500	
Interest Revenue		$2,500

This entry "adjusts" the financial records to recognize the accrued interest revenue and create a corresponding asset. Similar accruals of revenue may be necessary for such things as rent and other types of revenue that are earned with the passage of time.

b. Accrued Expenses

Certain expenses are incurred with the passage of time even though such expenses have not yet been paid. These expenses must be recognized as they are incurred. The recognition of these expenses that have been incurred but not yet paid involves the accrual of the expense and typically the creation of a related liability.

Assume that a business pays its employees every other Friday. On December 31, 199x, the employees have worked one of the two weeks in their current payroll period. If the total payroll that will be paid on December 31 is $25,000, then the business should accrue compensation expense on December 31 in the amount of $12,500. That is, the business should recognize the compensation expense that has been earned by its employees on December 31 even though that compensation is not payable until the next Friday. (Note that payroll taxes and similar items related to payroll would be accrued as well but this illustration will be limited to the basic payroll.) The necessary adjusting entry to record the accrued compensation would be as follows:

Compensation Expense	$12,500	
Accrued Salaries & Wages Payable		$12,500

The debit entry records the appropriate amount of the accrued expense and the credit entry increases a corresponding liability account for the amount that will be paid. Other types of expenses for which accrual-type adjusting entries are often made include interest expense, rent expense, certain taxes (property taxes that accrue over time and income taxes that must be accrued as of year-end even though they are not payable for several months), and estimated liabilities (for example, the estimated exposure on outstanding warranties of businesses that extend warranties in connection with the sale of products).

c. *Accounting for Actual Receipt of Payment*

The adjusting entries that are illustrated above must be kept in mind when the actual receipt of cash or payment of cash later occurs in order to avoid misstating the relevant revenues or expenses. For example, when the interest payment on the note receivable discussed above is received, the full $5,000 will not be reported as revenue. Rather, the entry to record the receipt of the interest would be as follows (assuming no further accrual of interest revenue on the note has occurred during the current year):

Cash	$5,000	
Accrued Interest Receivable		$2,500
Interest Revenue		$2,500

The total interest revenue earned for the first full year of the note ($5,000) now has been recognized but through the use of the adjusting entry to accrue interest revenue in 199x, the revenue has been appropriately allocated between the two years.

Similarly, when the payroll discussed above is paid in the subsequent year, the correct entry would be as follows:

Compensation Expense	$12,500	
Accrued Salaries & Wages Payable	$12,500	
Cash		$25,000

As in the case of the interest revenue, the total compensation expense associated with the payroll has been appropriately allocated to 199x and the following year through the use of the adjusting entry at the end of 199x.

d. Reversing Entries

In actual practice, many businesses employ an additional procedure known as a "reversing entry" to simplify the accounting for an actual cash receipt or payment after an adjusting entry has been made to accrue revenue or expense. This process makes it much simpler for the appropriate accounting personnel who handle the routine transaction recording to ignore the adjusting entry process. To illustrate, assume that the books for 199x have been closed (a process that will be described below) and it is now the first day of business in the following year. For many of the adjusting entries that were made at the end of 199x, "reversing entries" will be made to eliminate the accrued revenue or expense and the related asset or liability.

Thus, for the interest revenue that was accrued in 199x, a reversing entry would be recorded in the next year as follows:

Interest Revenue	$2,500	
Accrued Interest Receivable		$2,500

This eliminates the interest receivable (asset) account. Immediately after this entry, interest revenue for the new year will actually show a negative (debit) balance of $2,500. When the interest payment is actually received on July 1, the appropriate accounting clerk can record the normal entry for receipt of interest as follows:

Cash	$5,000	
Interest Revenue		$5,000

When the $5,000 credit entry is made to the interest revenue account, the balance in the account immediately following the cash receipt will be $2,500, the $5,000 credit less the $2,500 that was debited to the account in the reversing entry process. A similar procedure could be followed for the accrual of compensation expense and for other accrued revenues and expenses.

2. Deferred Revenues and Expenses

Another type of adjusting entry involves the opposite of the accrual of revenue or expense. These entries create deferred revenues and expenses. In some situations, cash is paid before an expense has been incurred or cash is received before revenue has been earned. This results in prepaid (deferred) revenue or expense and usually necessitates an entry to defer the recognition of the revenue or expense to some point in time later than the receipt or payment of cash.

a. Deferred Revenues

To illustrate deferred revenue, assume that a business receives, on December 1, 199x, a semiannual rent payment of $30,000 giving the payor the right to use the rented property for the period from December 1, 199x, through May 31 of the following year. On the date of receipt, none of the rental revenue associated with the $30,000 payment has been earned, it is prepaid rent. There are two approaches for dealing with this prepaid rent.

Under one approach, the following entry would be made at the time of receipt of the $30,000 payment:

Cash	$30,000	
Deferred Rental Income		$30,000

The deferred rental income account is a liability account. Since the business has not earned the rent revenue on the date of payment, the liability account is a mechanism that permits deferral of the revenue. In effect, the business is recognizing its obligation to make the property available for the next six months. The liability account is used in this fashion even though there may be no legal obligation to return the cash to the lessee because the use of the property has been interrupted for some reason.

If this approach to recording prepaid revenues is taken, then an appropriate amount of rent revenue must be recognized as it is earned. On December 31, 199x, one-sixth of the $30,000 will have been earned. On that date, the following adjusting entry would be made to recognize the rent earned in December:

Deferred Rental Income	$5,000	
Rental Income (or Revenue)		$5,000

A similar entry or entries would have to be made during the first five months of the following year to transfer the remaining deferred rental income from the liability account to the revenue account as it is earned.

An alternative approach for the prepaid revenue would be to ignore the prepayment feature at the time of cash receipt and record the rent receipt as follows:

Cash	$30,000	
Rental Income		$30,000

This, of course, would overstate the rental income for 199x. Therefore, at December 31, 199x, an adjusting entry to defer the appropriate portion of the revenue would be made as follows:

Rental Income	$25,000	
Deferred Rental Income		$25,000

This entry reduces the revenue for the year to $5,000, which is the correct result. It also establishes the liability account that is used to defer recognition of the revenue related to the following year. If this approach is used, then a reversing entry could be made at the beginning of the next year as follows:

Deferred Rental Income	$25,000	
Rental Income		$25,000

No further entries would be necessary, unless, of course, monthly financial statements are prepared, in which case one of the procedures described above would be necessary at each month end.

b. *Prepaid Expenses*

Prepayments and the requirement for deferral also occur in connection with expenses. Assume that a business has taken out a three-year fire insurance policy covering the three-year period beginning September 1, 199x. The business pays the full cost of the policy ($90,000) on September 1, 199x. Because this policy covers a three-year period, the full premium does not represent an expense of 199x. The premium paid is a prepaid expense and the recognition of the expense in the income statement must be deferred.

One way to account for the actual payment of the insurance premium is as follows:

Prepaid Insurance	$90,000	
Cash		$90,000

Prepaid insurance is an asset sometimes called a deferred charge or deferred expense account. At the end of 199x, the following adjusting entry would be made:

Insurance Expense	$10,000	
Prepaid Insurance		$10,000

This transfers from the asset to an expense account the portion of the insurance premium that relates to coverage in 199x. The total premium is being amortized over the period covered by the policy. Similar entries would be made in the next three years to recognize as expense an appropriate amount of the balance of the premium.

An alternative approach would be to record the entire premium as expense when paid:

Insurance Expense	$90,000	
Cash		$90,000

At the end of 199x, an adjusting entry would be made to reclassify the deferred portion of the insurance premium and record it in the prepaid insurance current asset account:

Prepaid Insurance	$80,000	
Insurance Expense		$80,000

The combination of these two entries leaves an asset (prepaid insurance) of $80,000 and expense for the year of $10,000. At the beginning of the next year, a reversing entry would be made as follows:

Insurance Expense	$80,000	
Prepaid Insurance		$80,000

At the end of the next year, an adjusting entry would be made to recognize as an asset the then unexpired portion ($20/36$) of the premium:

Prepaid Insurance	$50,000	
Insurance Expense		$50,000

The entries to the insurance expense account for the year following 199x would be a debit of $80,000 and a credit of $50,000, leaving a net debit balance of $30,000. This is the correct amount of the insurance premium to be recognized as an expense in that year ($90,000/3).

3. Depreciation Expense

The next type of adjusting entry to be discussed is the recognition of depreciation expense. When a business purchases an asset such as a machine, furniture, or a building, the cost of the asset is "capitalized" and recorded as an asset. "Capitalizing" and "capitalization" are terms used frequently as a short hand way of saying that a payment by a business will not be recorded immediately as an expense but will initially be recorded as an asset and will eventually be recognized as an expense through the depreciation (or amortization) process to be described below.

Assuming that the asset in question has a limited useful life (which is usually the case except for certain assets with unlimited lives such as land), the cost of the asset must be recognized as expense over the expected useful life of the asset. For tangible property, the recognition of this expense is called depreciation.

To illustrate, assume that a building is purchased during 199x for $100,000. The purchase of the building would be recorded as follows:

| Buildings | $100,000 | |
| Cash | | $100,000 |

This entry transfers $100,000 from one asset, cash, to another asset, buildings. The methods and procedures used to calculate depreciation will be discussed in Chapter 7. Assume for now that the depreciation on this building for 199x is determined to be $5,000. At the end of 199x, the following adjusting entry would be necessary:

| Depreciation Expense | $5,000 | |
| Accumulated Depreciation | | $5,000 |

The expense of $5,000 will be included in the determination of net income for the year. The accumulated depreciation account is an example of a "contra account." A contra account is an offsetting account to some other account. In this case, the accumulated depreciation account is a contra account to the buildings account. To determine the remaining carrying cost or book value of the buildings owned by the business, you subtract the amount in the accumulated depreciation account from the amount in the buildings account. Thus, the remaining book value of the building purchased in 199x on the December 31, 199x, balance sheet would be $95,000 ($100,000 minus $5,000). Contra accounts are used in this situation to retain in the financial records the original cost of an asset and to record separately the portion of the original cost that has been transferred to expense through the depreciation process.

Similar adjusting entries are made to recognize depreciation expense for the year on all of the tangible property of the business. In like manner, the cost of long-lived intangible assets are also transferred to expense through an allocation process. The expense related to intangible assets is often called amortization expense rather than depreciation expense. In the case of intangible assets, it is less common to use a contra account for the accumulated amortization expense. If no contra account is used, the amortization expense recognized is credited directly to, and reduces the amount of, the related asset account.

4. Recognizing Cost of Goods Sold

For some businesses, an adjusting entry is necessary at the end of the year to recognize the cost of goods sold for the year. Businesses that sell products from inventory can use one of two methods to determine cost of goods sold. If a business maintains a perpetual inventory record, the cost of goods sold is determined each time a sale occurs and the appropriate amount is transferred from inventory to the cost of goods sold account (a form of expense account). Under this approach, no adjusting entry would be necessary at the end of the year.

Some businesses use a periodic inventory system. In this system, the cost of items sold is not determined at the time of each sale. The cost of all goods sold is determined at the end of the year (or other appropriate period). Assume that at the beginning of 199x, it is determined that a business has inventory of $75,000. During the year, purchases are made in the total amount of $500,000. A summary of the entries to record purchases occurring throughout the year would be:

Purchases	$500,000	
Accounts Payable		$500,000

At the end of the year, the business conducts an inventory and determines that the goods remaining on hand at the end of the year have a cost of $110,000. (The methods of determining the cost of inventory on hand will be discussed in Chapter 6.) The total cost of goods available for sale would be $575,000 (the sum of the beginning inventory of $75,000 and the purchases during the year of $500,-000). Since there is inventory on hand at the end of the year of $110,000, the cost of the items sold would be $465,000 (the goods available for sale of $575,000 less the remaining inventory of $110,000). The adjusting entry to record the cost of goods sold and to correct the amount in the inventory account would be as follows:

Inventory—Ending	$110,000	
Cost of Goods Sold	$465,000	
Purchases		$500,000
Inventory—Beginning		$ 75,000

Note first that the debits equal the credits in this compound entry. The inventory account (an asset account) is now $110,000, which is the correct amount remaining in inventory. The purchases account has been reduced to zero. The expense account (cost of goods sold) reflects the actual cost of the items sold during the year.

With the expansion of computerized inventory systems, fewer and fewer businesses use the periodic inventory approach to computing cost of goods sold. Even those businesses that use a periodic inventory system conduct periodic physical inventories to determine if the actual inventory on hand agrees with the amount shown by the periodic system.

E. REVENUE AND EXPENSE ACCOUNTS

Before examining how the accounting process proceeds from the recording and posting of accounting entries to the preparation of the financial statements, a discussion of the special nature of revenue and expense accounts is appropriate.

Revenue and expense accounts are subaccounts within owners' equity. They are used to record separately the many types of revenues and expenses that a business has. Obtaining information about individual components of revenues and expenses would be extremely difficult if all revenue and expense entries were made directly to retained earnings or even to a separate net income (loss) account for each year. Accordingly, a separate account is maintained for each revenue and expense item that the business wants to monitor on a separate basis. In fact, a large business literally has hundreds or even thousands of accounts when you consider the fact that most businesses want to segregate various revenue and expense items not only by their functional nature (compensation, depreciation, rent, interest, etc.) but also on the basis of a number of other classifications, including by geographic location, by department within the business, and by line of business.

Earlier it was pointed out that owners' equity accounts generally have credit (or right hand) balances. This is also true of revenue accounts. Since an increase in revenue also represents an increase in owners' equity, it would be expected that the revenue accounts would also have credit balances.

The expense accounts, on the other hand, will normally have debit balances. Each entry recording an expense will involve a debit to the appropriate expense account and normally a credit to some asset or liability account depending on the nature of the expense. Since expenses represent a reduction of owners' equity, this debit balance treatment is appropriate. If the expenses were entered directly into a single owners' equity account, they would be entered as a debit in order to reduce the amount of owners' equity. As we will see below, when the expense accounts are eventually closed out at the end of the year, the debit balance in these accounts will become a debit entry to the appropriate owners' equity account (retained earnings for a corporation).

The other unique feature of the revenue and expense accounts is that they are temporary accounts that exist for a certain period (usually one year) and are then closed out at the end of the year. Balance sheet accounts (the accounts for assets, liabilities, and the permanent owners' equity accounts) are permanent accounts. While the balances in these permanent accounts are computed at the end of the year and entered in the balance sheet, the next year's entries are made in the same accounts. There may be physical changes in that the business starts making entries in the permanent accounts on a new page, or a new book, or a new computer file, but continuity is maintained because each permanent (balance sheet) account starts with the balance in that account as of the end of the immediately preceding period. Thus, if the cash account, after all the debit and credit entries for 199x has a debit balance on December 31, 199x, of $40,000, then the cash account for the next year will begin with a balance on January 1 of $40,000 before any transactions in the new year have been recorded.

In contrast, each revenue and expense account will be closed out at the end of each year through the process described below. The balance in each account just prior to the closing will be computed and that balance will represent the net amount of all the entries to the account for that year. This balance will then be transferred to the permanent owners' equity accounts and the revenue and expense accounts will have zero balances. Since there will be no balances to carry forward to the next year, each revenue and expense account will start fresh at the beginning of each year with a zero balance.

F. CLOSING THE BOOKS

At the end of each year, the process of closing the books begins. The first step is the preparation of a trial balance. The balance in all of the accounts (both permanent accounts and the revenue and expense accounts) is computed and listed on a worksheet in separate columns for the accounts with debit balances and the accounts with credit balances. A preliminary check is made to confirm that the total of the accounts with debit balances equals the total of the accounts with credit balances. A corollary to the requirement that for each accounting entry the debit entries must equal the credit entries is the similar requirement that the total amount in the accounts with debit balances equals the total amount in the accounts with credit balances.

Assuming that the debits equal the credits in the trial balance, the next step in the process is the recording of the adjusting entries that are made at the end of the year, as discussed above. At that point, a second, "adjusted" trial balance is prepared and again the total of the debit balances is compared to the total of the credit balances. This confirms that the process of recording and posting the adjusting entries has not caused the accounts to become out of balance. To illustrate the remainder of the closing process, assume that a simplified adjusted trial balance appears as follows:

	Debit	Credit
Cash	$ 15,000	
Receivables	$ 30,000	
Inventory	$ 40,000	
Property, Plant, and Equipment	$150,000	
Accumulated Depreciation		$ 50,000
Accounts Payable		$ 20,000
Accrued Liabilities		$ 25,000
Long Term Debt		$ 60,000
Capital Stock		$ 10,000
Additional Paid-in-Capital		$ 30,000
Retained Earnings—Beginning of the Year		$ 20,000
Sales Revenue		$100,000
Cost of Goods Sold	$ 50,000	
Compensation Expense	$ 10,000	
Depreciation Expense	$ 5,000	
Interest Expense	$ 5,000	
Income Tax Expense	$ 10,000	
	$315,000	$315,000

Several things should be noted here. The total of the debit balances in the adjusted trial balance equals the total of the credit balances. Although accumulated depreciation has a credit balance, it is not a liability account. It is a contra account to property, plant, and equipment and, in the balance sheet, will be deducted from the property, plant, and equipment balance to give the net book value of that asset. Finally, the balance in retained earnings is the amount as of the beginning of the year. No entries have yet been made in retained earnings during the current year.

The next step in closing the books is to close out the revenue and expense accounts. The revenues and expenses could be closed directly to (entered into) the retained earnings account. Most businesses, however, close the revenues and expenses to another temporary account used solely in the closing process. This account is frequently called income summary. Assuming that this procedure is used, the closing entry would be as follows:

Revenues	$100,000	
Cost of Goods Sold		$50,000
Compensation Expense		$10,000
Depreciation Expense		$ 5,000
Interest Expense		$ 5,000
Income Tax Expense		$10,000
Income Summary		$20,000

As was discussed above, this entry has the effect of closing out (creating a zero balance in) the revenue and expense accounts. For example, the sales revenues account had a credit balance of $100,000. The $100,000 debit in the closing entry reduces the sales revenue account to zero. The same is true of the expense accounts. The net of all the revenue and expense accounts, $20,000, is now a credit balance in the income summary account.

The next closing entry would transfer the net income from the temporary income summary account to the permanent retained earnings account. The entry would be as follows:

Income Summary	$20,000	
Retained Earnings		$20,000

This closes out the final temporary account for 199x and brings the retained earnings account up to date as of the end of the year.

G. PREPARATION OF FINANCIAL STATEMENTS

The financial statements can now be prepared from the foregoing information. The income statement would be prepared using the balances in the revenue and expense accounts immediately before the closing entries are recorded. It might appear as follows (in single step format):

Income Statement

Sales Revenue		$100,000
Less:	Cost of Goods Sold	(50,000)
	Compensation	(10,000)
	Depreciation	(5,000)
	Interest	(5,000)
	Income Tax	(10,000)
Net Income		$20,000

The balance sheet as of the end of the year would be prepared on the basis of the balances in the accounts after completion of the closing process.

Balance Sheet

Cash	$ 15,000	Accounts Payable	$ 20,000
Receivables	30,000	Accrued Liabilities	25,000
Inventory	40,000	Current Liabilities	45,000
Current Assets	85,000	Long Term Debt	60,000
Property, Plant, and		Total Liabilities	105,000
Equipment	150,000	Capital Stock	10,000
Less: Accumulated		Additional	
Depreciation	(50,000)	Paid-in-Capital	30,000
		Retained Earnings	$ 40,000
Total Assets	$185,000	Total Equities	$185,000

CHAPTER 3

GENERALLY ACCEPTED ACCOUNTING PRINCIPLES

Reference is frequently made in the accounting area to "generally accepted accounting principles" or to the acronym "GAAP." In an auditors' report or opinion on financial statements, the auditor will state, *inter alia,* that the financial statements are presented in accordance with GAAP. In contracts containing negative covenants or other provisions related to financial statement or accounting matters, there will frequently be language requiring that one of the parties must prepare financial statements in accordance with GAAP or must make various calculations (*e.g.,* with respect to financial ratios or book value calculations) on the basis of financial statements prepared in accordance with GAAP.

Actually, usage of the term GAAP can vary depending on the speaker, the audience, and the context. In general, however, GAAP are a set of accepted accounting procedures and rules that are used in the preparation of financial statements. When an auditor's report makes reference to GAAP, GAAP means:

the conventions, rules, and procedures necessary to define accepted accounting practice at a particular time. It includes not only broad guidelines of general application, but also detailed practices and procedures.... Those conventions, rules, and procedures provide a standard by which to measure financial presentations.

Codifications of Statements on Auditing Standards, AU § 411.02, p. 315, AICPA (1994). (All references in this nutshell to an "SAS" are to the foregoing publication.) Of particular relevance to the lawyer are the sources to which accountants and auditors turn when they are trying to determine GAAP for a particular type of transaction or event (*i.e.*, guidance for how to record a transaction or event and report that transaction or event in the financial statements).

A. OFFICIAL SOURCES OF GAAP

The accounting profession has established a hierarchy of sources to be consulted when determining GAAP for a particular transaction or event. The items composing the first level in the hierarchy are the official statements that are promulgated from time to time by the organization designated by the accounting profession as the official body to determine the appropriate accounting treatment for various transactions and events. Currently, that official body is the Financial Accounting Standards Board or the FASB.

1. FASB Statements

The FASB is an independent body that was created to establish and improve standards for financial accounting and reporting. The FASB's seven members are selected by the Financial Accounting Foundation, which also provides the funding for the FASB. The members of the FASB represent a cross-section of accountants and users of financial statements. Its members must relinquish their private employment while serving as members of the Board in order to enhance the independence of the Board.

The principal guidance provided by the FASB is in the form of statements that are periodically issued setting forth the appropriate accounting for different types of transactions or events. These statements may cover narrow topics (Statement 85 covers one detailed aspect of the calculation of earnings per share) or may have extremely broad scope and application (Statement 13 and various amendments thereto cover the general topic of accounting for leases). As of April 30, 1994, the FASB had promulgated 117 statements.[1] In addition, the FASB publishes interpretations that may modify or extend the application of existing accounting stan-

1. Throughout this nutshell, references will be made to individual statements issued by the FASB (*e.g.*, FASB Statement No. 5) and to opinions issued by the Accounting Principles Board (*e.g.*, APB Opinion No. 20). These statements and opinions can be found in the two volume work entitled *Original Pronouncements—Accounting Standards as of June 1, 1993*, published by the Financial Accounting Standards Board (1993).

dards. Through April 30, 1994, the FASB had promulgated forty interpretations.

In developing statements and interpretations, the FASB goes through a process that it refers to as due process. Essentially, the development of a new statement or interpretation involves the identification of an issue on which guidance is needed, a review of that issue by the staff of the FASB, the gathering of input from various interested parties, the development of a tentative standard and the solicitation of oral and written comments on the proposal (including a public hearing), and finally the adoption of the statement or interpretation by a supermajority vote of five of the FASB's seven members.

2. APB Opinions

Prior to the formation of the FASB in 1973, the body responsible for issuing official accounting guidance was the Accounting Principles Board (APB). The APB was a creature of the American Institute of Certified Public Accountants and all of its members (18 to 21) were CPAs. One of the reasons for its disbandment was the domination of the APB by the accounting profession. During the period from 1959 through 1973, the APB issued 31 Opinions. Many of the APB Opinions are still in force and some of them cover pervasive accounting issues (*e.g.,* Opinion No. 15 dealing with the computation of earnings per share and Opinion No. 16 dealing with accounting for business combinations (acquisitions)).

3. Accounting Research Bulletins

Before the APB, official guidance on accounting came from the Committee on Accounting Procedure, which was also a part of the AICPA. From 1939 to 1959, the Committee issued 51 Accounting Research Bulletins (ARBs), a number of which are still in force as the official guidance on the topics covered.

4. Enforcement of Official Standards

As noted above, the FASB Statements and Interpretations, the APB Opinions, and the Accounting Research Bulletins fall into the first hierarchy in the sources of GAAP. Any auditor that is a member of the AICPA, in performing an audit, is bound to follow the guidance in these sources and can not issue an unqualified opinion on the financial statements being audited if those financial statements contain a material departure from the guidance in these sources. Compliance is not required if application of the accounting standards would in a particular case make the financial statements misleading. *SAS*, AU § 411.05(a), page 316, referencing Rule 203 of the AICPA Code of Professional Conduct. Further, many states have effectively incorporated this same requirement to follow the official accounting pronouncements in their rules of ethics governing CPAs licensed in those states. See, *e.g.*, Minn. R. 1100.4800 (1993), requiring licensed CPAs in Minnesota to comply with the auditing standards promulgated by the AICPA.

B. OTHER SOURCES OF GAAP

The next three categories in the hierarchy of accounting principles are composed of other types of pronouncements issued by the FASB and the AICPA as well as industry accounting practices that are widely recognized and prevalent. *SAS*, AU § 411.-05, p. 316. Attorneys are not normally exposed to these additional sources unless they are involved in a highly technical analysis of accounting rules (*e.g.,* in a lawsuit involving a dispute about the technically correct accounting for un unusual matter not covered by the official statements). If none of these sources provide guidance on an issue, then the accountants or auditors may look to a catchall category of other accounting literature including various professional pronouncements as well as accounting textbooks, handbooks, and articles. *SAS*, AU § 411.07, p. 317.

C. GOVERNMENTAL REGULATION OF ACCOUNTING

1. SEC

Notice that none of the sources of GAAP listed above are governmental in nature. The Securities and Exchange Commission ("SEC"), which regulates the sale of securities and the securities markets in the United States, obviously has a significant interest in the development of accounting principles since issuers of securities subject to the jurisdiction of the SEC must file audited financial statements with the SEC. For the most part, however, the SEC has elected to leave the development of accounting principles to the private sector accounting bodies described above. The exception to this has occurred when the SEC has determined that the accounting profession is not acting fast enough in a particular area. On those occasions, the SEC has issued its own guidance on accounting principles for financial statements filed with the SEC. The usual response has been prompt action by the private sector with the SEC then withdrawing its own pronouncement. The SEC thus acts as a catalyst in these situations.

The SEC has issued extensive regulatory guidance on the financial statements that are filed with it, primarily in the form of Regulation S–X. This regulatory guidance primarily relates to additional detailed disclosures in the footnotes to the financial statements and classification or format issues for the financial statements as opposed to the accounting principles to be followed in the preparation of the basic financial statements.

2. Regulatory Agencies

Another governmental source of accounting principles are the rules and regulations of various federal and state regulatory agencies that require financial statements to be filed with them. In some cases, these agencies have established accounting rules or procedures for issues that have not been addressed by the official private sector accounting standard setting bodies and to this extent, the regulatory rules can be an additional source of guidance for GAAP. However, these agencies frequently issue their own accounting procedures and rules that in some cases are actually in conflict with GAAP. In those cases, the companies subject to the jurisdiction of the regulatory agencies will often prepare one set of financial statements for filing with the regulatory agencies and another set of financial statements prepared in conformity with GAAP for use by shareholders, creditors, and other users. It may not be possible for an auditor to give an opinion that the financial statements prepared for filing with the regulatory agencies have been prepared in accordance with GAAP. The auditor can, however, express an opinion that the statements filed with the agency have or have not been prepared in accordance with the special accounting rules applicable to statements filed with the agency.

D. INCOME TAX ACCOUNTING

Governments that impose an income tax, particularly the federal government, have statutory and regulatory rules that determine how companies must compute their taxable income. As in the case of regulatory agencies, the taxing authorities may have addressed certain accounting issues that are not the subject of official guidance under GAAP and their approach to these issues may be considered by analogy for the purposes of financial accounting. The policies underlying an income tax system differ, however, from the policies underlying the preparation of general purpose financial statements. Many of the rules adopted for income tax accounting are inappropriate for financial accounting purposes. Take the case of deferred (prepaid) revenues discussed in Chapter 2. Because of the objective of collecting taxes when the cash is available, for federal income tax purposes, it is common to require businesses to report as current taxable income amounts of cash received that would be treated as deferred revenue under GAAP. Thus, while many small businesses may prepare their financial statements on the same basis as is used for determining taxable income, such statements are not generally treated as prepared in accordance with GAAP.

One unusual effect of income tax rules on GAAP relates to inventory accounting. For financial accounting purposes, a business may elect one of several methods for determining the cost of inventory on hand at the end of the year when that inventory has been acquired at different prices (see Chapter 6). For federal income tax purposes, if a business elects to use the "LIFO" method for determining inventory, a method that is frequently advantageous for tax purposes, the business must use the LIFO method for determining inventory in its general purpose financial statements issued to shareholders, creditors, etc.

E. SOME FUNDAMENTAL ACCOUNTING CONCEPTS

The foregoing discussion of GAAP relates primarily to how accountants determine whether a specific accounting treatment must be used for a particular transaction or event. From time to time, the accounting profession has also tried to establish a broader set of fundamental accounting principles (sometimes referred to as concepts, pervasive principles, conventions, postulates, axioms, etc.) that could be used primarily in two ways. These fundamental principles serve as the conceptual basis for the official standard-setting bodies when they are considering adopting a new accounting standard. A new standard is expected to be in conformity with the underlying, fundamental principles. Alternatively, when an accountant is trying to determine the accounting for a specific transaction or event and there is no guidance in any of the sources described above, the accountant should presumably be guided by the fundamental underlying principles in developing a solution to the particular accounting issue.

The most recent effort in the development of fundamental accounting principles has been that of the FASB. In addition to its Statements, Interpretations, and other specific guidance, the FASB has issued six Statements of Financial Accounting Concepts that address such issues as the purpose of financial statements, the nature of assets and liabilities, the kind of information that is useful to users of financial statements, and the fundamental rules for recognizing income. Other groups have also addressed these fundamental issues and the work of the FASB has built on these earlier efforts.

For the purposes of this nutshell, the most relevant portion of these conceptual discussions is the identification and explanation of certain guiding principles that actually have a practical, day-to-day application in determining how financial statements are prepared. The following material describes key concepts and how they affect the preparation of financial statements.

1. Historical Cost

Financial statements are prepared on the basis of the historical cost method of accounting. Financial statements do not purport to represent the current market value of a business or its assets. The historical cost concept relates primarily to the reporting of assets. When an asset is acquired, it is recorded at its cost on the date of acquisition and no adjustments are made to reflect changes in the market value of the asset over time. Even the process of recording depreciation of long lived assets discussed in Chapter 7 is a method of allocating the original or historical cost of assets to the periods that are benefitted by their use and not an attempt to report the assets at their market values. Thus, while the asset side of the balance sheet may reflect the market value of the business' assets at the time of formation, the balance sheet usually becomes quite out-of-date in market value terms, particularly where a business has large amounts of long lived or fixed assets. When using financial statements, users should not assume that they can determine directly the market value of a business from its balance sheet.

There are some exceptions to the use of historical cost. In the case of marketable securities, certain securities are now required to be adjusted to market value with recognition in income of the corresponding gain or loss. FASB Statement No. 115. In the case of inventory, GAAP requires that the inventory be valued at the lower of cost or market value at the balance sheet date. Also, long lived assets may be required to be written down to a value lower than book value where the loss in value is determined to be a permanent impairment in the value and not just a temporary loss in value due to temporary market conditions. Thus, the balance sheet actually is a mixture of historical cost amounts, market values in effect at some prior time but after the date of original acquisition, and current market values.

The other exception to the historical cost basis of accounting applies to certain specialized industries that report their primary assets on a market value basis. This applies primarily in the case of certain financial companies. Mutual funds, for example, report the assets in their investment portfolios at current market values.

For a period of time, companies were required to prepare alternative financial statements showing information about current costs of certain assets and information about the effect of changes in the general purchasing power of the dollar (inflation). This alternative reporting gave information about current costs of assets (*i.e.,* replacement costs), which would not necessarily be the same as "market values." Further, this information was included in supplementary disclosures and did not affect the basic financial statements. After a trial period, this supplemental reporting requirement was abandoned since the value of the additional information was not thought to be worth the cost of complying with the requirement.

2. The Going Concern Assumption

The value of a business' assets is affected by whether you view the business as an ongoing, viable operation as opposed to an entity about to be liquidated with assets being sold to pay off creditors and to make a final distribution to the owners. For example, the fact that inventory is carried at cost or even lower of cost or market value is a reflection of the going concern assumption. The resulting book value of the inventory is only valid on the assumption that the business will continue long enough to sell the inventory in the ordinary course of business. If the business were about to be liquidated, the inventory of most businesses would probably need to be written down substantially to reflect the amount that would likely be realized on a sale of the inventory on a bulk basis ("fire sale") or otherwise not in the ordinary course of business.

Another asset that is heavily dependent on the going concern assumption is goodwill. Goodwill is recognized in certain business combinations (acquisitions) and is the premium paid to acquire a business in excess of the fair market value of the individually identifiable assets of the acquired business (see Chapter 15). It is a reflection that the value of a business valued as a business is frequently greater than the sum of the values of the individual assets. The recognition of goodwill is only appropriate if you assume that the business is going to continue as a business and that the individual assets are not going to be sold off piecemeal.

Unless it is stated otherwise, all financial statements prepared in accordance with GAAP are prepared on the basis of the going concern assumption. If that assumption is not appropriate in a particular case, that fact should be disclosed and the book amounts of the assets and liabilities should be adjusted to reflect the amount likely to be realized on liquidation.

3. Yearly Reporting

Another feature of the accounting process is the practice of reporting financial information on a periodic basis. For external reporting purposes, the normal practice is to report on a yearly basis with somewhat less detailed information being reported on an interim basis during the year, typically quarterly.

Much of the complexity in the accounting process results from the need to report results of operations on a yearly basis. If the only reporting that occurred was at the beginning and the end of the life of a business, the process would be simple. At the end of its life, the business would sell off any remaining noncash assets. To evaluate how successful the business was, you would simply look at the initial cash invested and compare that to the cash distributed to the owners at the time of liquidation. The excess, with appropriate adjustments for any interim distributions to the owners or contributions of additional capital would tell how much the venture earned.

When businesses report on a yearly basis, there are numerous matters that are "in process." Revenue producing activities are in various states of completion. Many types of expenses have been incurred but must be estimated because complete information will not be available for days, weeks, months, or even years. Long term assets have been partially consumed but the future earning ability of those assets is unclear. All of this uncertainty creates the need to deal with the various adjusting entries that were described in Chapter 2 (such as the need to accrue revenue and expense or to defer prepaid items, the need to determine the amount of inventory on hand, and the need to depreciate assets). In addition, difficult questions about when revenue should be considered earned or otherwise recognizable must be addressed (this topic will be covered in Chapter 4). Notwithstanding all of the difficulties created, periodic reporting is a practical reality of accounting. Investors and other users of financial statements must make decisions during the course of a business' life such as whether to make an investment in the business or whether to terminate their investment in the business. These and other decisions require that accounting information be available prior to the end of the life of the business.

4. Revenue Recognition and Matching

The requirement for yearly reporting requires that a conceptual basis be developed for assigning revenue that may be earned through a continuous process to a particular accounting period. The "revenue recognition principle" is the conceptual basis for assigning revenue to particular accounting periods. Similarly, it is necessary to assign costs incurred in generating revenue as expenses to the appropriate accounting period. The conceptual approach to this issue is that expenses should be matched (recorded as expense) in the same period as the revenues to which they relate. Revenue recognition and the matching principle are the subject of Chapter 4.

5. Conservatism

In preparing financial statements, one of the concepts that frequently arises is the convention of conservatism. In the accounting area, conservatism basically means that when there is uncertainty about whether to record a particular transaction or how to value an asset, the uncertainty will be resolved with a "bias" in favor of understating income or assets. As an example, I have noted the requirement to report inventory at the lower of cost or market value. The determination of the "cost" of inventory can present some difficult issues but it is a fairly objective process. The determination of the market value of inventory is more subjective and requires the accountant to exercise a greater amount of judgment. By reporting the inventory at market only if lower than cost, the accountant avoids the potential for overstating the inventory. This is a reflection of conservatism. Similarly, FASB Statement No. 5 requires that certain contingent losses be accrued and recorded in the financial statements prior to the final determination of whether a loss has actually occurred see Chapter 5). That same statement prohibits the recognition of contingent gains. No contingent gain is recognized until any contingency is resolved.

The use of conservatism in accounting results from an assumption that users of financial statements are less likely to be misled to their detriment by understated assets or income than in the case of overstated assets or income. This may have been true when the primary external users of financial statements were banks and other creditors. It may also be a useful concept when the focus on equity participants is potential purchasers of stock. When consideration is given to the buying and selling that occurs in a publicly traded company's stock, the bias seems less appropriate since sellers could be led to sell their stock at an artificially low price because of a downward bias in the accounting statements. Whether or not the conservatism convention is appropriate, however, is virtually never debated in practice and users should simply understand that the convention exists and is employed.

6. Materiality and Cost–Benefit Analysis

The concept of materiality overrides all of the technical analysis related to accounting principles and their application. In preparing financial statements, accountants will frequently ignore the technically correct accounting treatment of a particular transaction or event if a determination is made that the item or items in question are not material to the financial statements. Even official pronouncements such as statements issued by the FASB expressly state that the requirements stated therein need not be applied if the failure to follow the requirements would not have a material effect on the financial statements.

As in the case of materiality in the law of fraud or securities regulation, there is no precise definition of materiality for accounting purposes. The concept is that an item is material if knowledge of the item would have an effect on the decision process of someone using the financial statements. There is usually thought to be an objective and subjective element to determinations of materiality. As to objective standards, materiality is normally considered in terms of the amount of an item expressed as a percentage of some base figure. The base figure might be total assets or some component thereof or the base figure may be net income or some component of net income. For example, certain items may not be considered material unless they represent more than 1% of net income or 5% of assets. While there are no standard percentages used to determine the materiality test, most companies and auditors will have there own tests for materiality.

With respect to the subjective element, some items will be deemed to be material regardless of their dollar magnitude because of some qualitative aspect of the items. For example, receivables from certain parties related to the issuer of financial statements must be separately disclosed regardless of the dollar amount of such items. Similarly, illegal activities may be deemed to be material even if the potential fines or penalties that may be imposed would not be material under the normal objective tests for materiality.

Closely related to the concept of materiality is the analytical technique of cost-benefit analysis. In some cases, even though a particular matter would be material, a determination may be made that the cost of implementing a technically correct accounting principle for that matter or providing additional information regarding a matter would exceed the additional benefits that could be derived. While this concept is understandable in theory, it is sometimes difficult to implement in practice because of the difficulty in determining the costs and particularly the benefits of a proposed application of accounting principles.

CHAPTER 4

RECOGNITION OF REVENUES AND EXPENSES

For most businesses, the process of generating revenue involves a number of steps and no clear basis for identifying exactly when the revenue should be treated as earned. Consider, for example, the production and sale of goods made to a customer's order. The revenue generation process for this type of activity begins with the receipt of an order from the customer. From this order, the production department is authorized to commence production of the goods to meet the order. Depending on the nature of the goods, this process could take anywhere from a matter of minutes to a matter of days or even longer. Upon completion of the production process, the goods are transferred to the shipping dock. The goods are then picked up by the customer or delivered by the manufacturer to the customer. At some point after delivery, an invoice will be generated and sent to the customer. Sometime later, depending on the terms of the invoice, the customer will make payment for the goods. Unless the producer has disclaimed all warranties, the producer will be under some type of continuing obligation with respect to the goods (*e.g.,* to repair or replace the goods if they are defective or to refund the sales price in some cases).

Theoretically, there are several points at which the revenue from this sale could be recognized for accounting purposes. Recognition of revenue could take place as early as the date on which the order is received. At the other extreme, revenue could be deferred until the expiration of all warranties and the risk of having to return the price of the goods to the buyer. The revenue could be recognized at some point between these two extremes. There is also the possibility of recognizing the total revenue from the transaction on a piecemeal basis with portions of the revenue being recognized at different points in the overall revenue-generating process.

It is also necessary to determine how to associate the expenses that are incurred by the business with the revenues that are recognized. Some costs or expenses may be easily identified with particular revenues. For example, the costs of the raw materials that were used in producing a particular order can be easily identified and associated with the appropriate revenue from that order. On the other hand, many expenses do not bear such a direct relationship to any particular revenue generating transaction and there is a need to determine when such expenses should be recognized for accounting purposes.

Two concepts have been developed to deal with these issues. The "revenue recognition principle" guides the determination of when to recognize for accounting purposes the revenue from the various transactions of a business. The "matching principle" determines when expenses should be recognized for accounting purposes.

A. REVENUE RECOGNITION

Conceptually, revenue recognition is generally determined on the basis of two factors: the existence of a "realization event" and the completion of the earnings process.

In the context of a revenue generating activity, an event of realization occurs when a business exchanges its goods or services or other assets for cash or a right to receive cash. (If a business exchanges its goods and services in exchange for some type of noncash property, realization will be deemed to occur even though there is no right to receive cash as long as their is an ability to determine within reasonable limits the fair market value of the property received.) The earnings process is determined to be complete when the business has delivered its goods, performed its services, or otherwise substantially completed the activities necessary to earn the revenues in question. Both of these criteria must normally be satisfied before revenue is recognized. In some cases, however, one or the other factor will be the primary consideration. Examples of the practical application of these two factors will help to clarify the meaning of these terms.

1. Sale of Goods or Services

The revenue associated with a sale of goods is generally treated as recognized when the goods are delivered to the customer. At this point in time, the revenue is earned because the seller has substantially completed all of its obligations with respect to the sale and realization has occurred as well because the seller has received the cash or has obtained by the terms of the sales contract the right to receive a fixed amount of cash in the future.

Where a continuing warranty obligation exists, it would be possible to delay recognition of all or a portion of the revenue from a sale until the warranty period expires. This approach is not generally applied in practice. Rather, as will be discussed below in connection with the matching principle, the estimated cost of honoring the warranties is recognized and recorded at the time of sale.

In many sales of goods, the buyer may have the right to return goods and recover the purchase price. Under FASB Statement No. 48, when the right of return exists, the recognition of revenue will be delayed until the right of return expires unless the following conditions are satisfied:

    a. The sales price is fixed or determinable.

    b. The buyer's obligation to pay for the goods is not contingent on resale by the buyer.

    c. The buyer's obligation to pay would not be changed because of theft or damage to the goods.

   d.   The buyer has economic substance independent of the seller.

   e.   The seller is not responsible for bringing about resale by the buyer.

   f.   Future returns can be reasonably estimated.

Even where sales revenue is recognized at the time of sale, it is often appropriate for the seller to accrue a liability and a corresponding offset to revenue for the amount of the returns or other allowances estimated to occur with respect to sales.

An argument might also be made for delaying recognition of the revenue on a credit sale until the cash is actually received. Under the accrual method required by GAAP, revenue is not deferred until receipt of the cash except in unusual cases, as described below at A.5. Normal uncertainty concerning the collection of the cash results in a computation of an estimate of the portion of the sales price that will not be collected and recognition of this expense at the time of the sale (see Chapter 5).

2. Revenue From Services

   Several methods of recognizing revenue from services are used in practice.

a. *Specific Performance Method*

The specific performance method is used to account for revenue when the revenue is earned by performance of a specific act. An example would be commissions that are earned upon completion of a specific act such as a sale of real estate by a broker, the performance of surgery by a doctor, or the repair of equipment. Under this method, no revenue is recognized as preparatory steps are completed but only when the critical function is performed.

b. *Proportional Performance Method*

Another method called the proportional performance method is sometimes used when services are performed over a period that includes more than one accounting period. A portion of the total revenue is recognized on the basis of some measure of the proportion of the service that has been performed. The appropriate proportion could be determined on the basis of costs incurred, the passage of time, or the number of acts completed when the service arrangement involves the performance of a set number of similar acts.

c. *Completed Performance Method*

The completed performance method is used when performance of the service involves a number of significant steps but the completion of a final step is so significant that no revenue can be treated as earned until that critical step is completed. This method is effectively used by law firms that perform litigation under a contingent fee arrangement. No revenue is recognized until the attorney collects a judgment or a settlement for the client. This would be in contrast to an attorney performing services under an arrangement with a client who will pay on the basis of time recorded, in which case service revenue would normally be recognized as bills are sent in the case of an accrual method business and on the basis of cash collected in the case of a cash basis business.

Where there is substantial uncertainty about the ability to collect service revenue that is earned, revenue may be recognized under a cash collection method where revenue would be recognized only as cash is collected. Note that recognition only when cash is collected by a business otherwise using the accrual method required by GAAP is different from a business that has decided to use the cash receipts and disbursements method of accounting.

3. Long Term Contracts

In the case of long term contracts such as construction contracts where the time to complete the delivery of the "goods" may extend out for two or more years, the normal rule, under which no revenue is recognized until "delivery" occurs, is modified. Assume for illustrative purposes that a contractor enters into a contract to construct a bridge for a total price of $1,000,000. At the end of 199x, when the bridge is 60% complete, costs of $480,000 have been incurred. It is estimated that the cost to complete the bridge in the following year will be an additional $320,000.

There are two methods that may be used to recognize the revenue on this project. Under the completed contract method, no revenue would be recognized until the contract is complete. No revenue and no income would be recognized in 199x. All of the revenue and the entire gross profit of

$200,000 ($1,000,000–$800,000) would be recognized in the following year.

The alternative method for accounting for this type of contract is the percentage of completion method. Under this method, an estimate is made at the end of 199x of the portion of the contract that has been completed at that point in time. That estimate is usually made on the basis of engineering analysis of the project or on the basis of the proportion of estimated total costs that have been incurred at the balance sheet date (in this example, both approaches indicate that the contract is 60% complete at the end of 199x). A corresponding portion of the total revenue on the project is recognized. Thus, $600,000 of the revenue would be recognized in 199x and the remaining $400,000 would be recognized in the next year. This approach also results in a recognition of a portion of the total gross profit on the contract in each of the two years.

The percentage of completion method is an exception to the normal rule of delaying recognition of revenue until the earning process is completed. Delaying recognition until completion of contracts usually would give a distorted picture of a business' efforts by lumping all the revenue and gross profit into the year of completion.

4. Revenue Recognized With the Passage of Time

In some cases, services (particularly services in the nature of the right to use assets) are deemed rendered continuously over time. Examples would include rentals and royalties from the use of property and interest from the use of money. In these situations the revenue is recognized with the passage of time, which normally corresponds to how these types of revenues are earned.

5. Revenue Recognized Based on Receipt of Cash

Even under the accrual method, revenue is not recognized until the receipt of cash in certain situations. Deferral of recognition occurs where there is more than the normal uncertainty about whether the revenue earned will actually be received in the form of cash. Two revenue recognition methods are in use in this situation. Under the installment method of reporting revenue where revenue is to be received in more than one installment, revenue would be recognized on a proportional basis as the cash is received. A similar proportion of the gross profit from the sale of goods would also be recognized. Thus, assume that a business sells goods for $300 to be paid in three installments of $100 each. The cost of the goods sold is $180 leaving a "gross profit" of $120. The installment method would report $100 of revenue as each installment is collected and would also recognize gross profit of $40 at the time of receipt of each installment.

If there were extreme uncertainty about the ability to collect the three installments, the business could use the "cost recovery method" of reporting the revenue and related gross profit. Under the cost recovery method of reporting, the business would report no revenue or gross profit from the sale until it has collected an amount equal to the cost of the goods sold. Thereafter, the entire collection would be reported as revenue and gross profit. Using the example from the previous paragraph, no revenue or gross profit would be reported at the time of the collection of the first installment. When the second installment is collected, the business would report revenue and gross profit of $20 since the total amount collected ($200) now exceeds the cost of goods sold ($180) by $20. The third installment would be reported as revenue and gross profit to the full extent of the collection, or $100.

6. Completion of Production

In rare situations, revenue may be recognized at the time of production of goods even though there is no sales transaction in place for the goods produced. This may happen in the case of the production of certain commodity type goods (for example, the mining of precious metals) where there are reported market prices for the goods and the nature of the markets is such that the producer knows that it can dispose of the goods at the quoted market price. Production of the goods essentially completes the earning process in this type of situation because of the known ability to dispose of all of the output at the market price.

7. Changes in Market Value

In some situations, revenue (usually in the form of gains or losses) is recognized solely on the basis of changes in market value of assets even in the absence of any transaction with a third party and even in the absence of any activity by the business that owns the assets. For example, businesses are now required to report certain marketable securities at the market value of those securities (see Chapter 9). Therefore, gains and losses are recognized as the market value of these securities goes up or down. This rule reflects the relatively reliable basis for determining market value of traded securities.

A similar rule is applied to inventory, which is required to be reported at the lower of cost or market value. This necessitates recognizing currently certain changes in the value of the inventory. The application of this principle to inventory is complicated because of the difficulty in determining the value of most inventory (with value being generally measured by replacement value, not resale value). The lower of cost or market rule for inventory is discussed in Chapter 6.

In some industries, the recognition of revenue (gains and losses) on the basis of mere changes in market value assumes much greater significance than the rather limited value recognition involved in the situations described above. For example, mutual funds generally revalue their entire portfolios of investment securities on a continuous basis and reflect the resulting changes in value in their income or loss for the year. In addition, businesses that deal in certain commodities (agricultural products, metals, financial products) for which there is an active market and continuous price quotations may value their inventories on a market value basis. This is, however, the exception rather than the rule.

8.　Asset Writedowns

In the limited cases described in the previous section, the recognition of changes in market value occurs regardless of the cause of the change. The changes could be the result of fundamental changes in the economy that have a particular effect on the business in question or they could be the result of the periodic swings in value in an active market as a response to miscellaneous factors that may be temporary in nature.

GAAP recognizes a more broadly applicable requirement to write down the book value of assets (and recognize a loss) in situations where a determination has been made that a permanent loss in value has occurred. For example, if the real estate market experiences periodic ups and downs, the resulting changes in the market value of a business' real estate would not be recognized for financial accounting purposes unless a sale or other realization event occurs. However, if circumstances arise that indicate that there has been a significant decrease in the value of real estate, that permanent loss in value will be recognized for accounting purposes. Similar rules apply to other long term or fixed assets of a business such as patents, machinery and equipment, and trademarks.

B. MATCHING

The revenue recognition principle establishes the rules and guidelines for determining when revenue should be recorded in the financial records of a business and reported in the financial statements. A similar set of guidelines are needed for the recognition of expenses. The matching principle sets forth the basic guidance on when to recognize expenses.

At this point, it is necessary to explain the difference between two terms that are the cause of some confusion in the financial accounting area—costs and expenses. "Cost" is the amount that must be paid to obtain goods or services. The amount paid to obtain a new machine is the cost of that machine. The interest paid on a loan is the cost incurred for the use of the money. The salary paid to a corporate officer is the cost of obtaining the officer's services. None of these cost items is necessarily an expense at the time it is incurred. This is easy to see with the machine. While a cost is incurred when the machine is purchased, no expense is recognized at that time. The cost of the machine will be recognized as an expense (depreciation) over the life of the machine. The cost associated with an officer's salary and the cost associated with interest are both normally treated as expenses when they are incurred. However, these costs would not be treated as expenses when paid if they are paid in advance of the service being rendered, in the case of the officer, or in advance of the use of the money in the case of the interest.

On the other hand, expenses may be recognized in some cases before any identifiable costs are actually incurred by the business. For example, when a business sells goods subject to a warranty, the normal practice is to report an estimated warranty expense at the time of the sale of the goods. The offsetting entry to the warranty expense (which is a debit entry) is a credit to a liability account for future warranty costs. The actual warranty costs will not be incurred until some later time. At that time, the warranty costs will be debited to the liability account rather than being deducted as an expense. Certain contingent expenses (such as the possible loss from litigation in which the business is a defendant) are also recognized as expenses prior to the actual resolution of the lawsuit. Thus, expense is recognized prior to any actual costs being incurred. It is the matching principle and the expense recognition rules derived therefrom that determine when "costs" are treated as "expenses" and deducted from revenues in the income statement to determine the net income of the business. There are three basic rules for recognizing expenses. These rules are the direct matching of expenses with related revenues, the immediate recognition of expense at the time that costs are incurred, and the systematic and rational allocation of costs as expense over an appropriate period.

1. Direct Matching

Certain types of costs can be directly related with revenue. These costs are recognized as expense when the related revenues are recognized. The cost of goods sold is an example of this approach to expense recognition. A retailer incurs costs in acquiring inventory that is held for sale. When the inventory is acquired, the cost is not treated as an expense but is reported in a current asset account called inventory. When sales occur and revenue is recognized, the appropriate cost of the items sold is removed from the inventory account and recognized as an expense called cost of goods sold.

2. Immediate Write–Off

Certain types of expenses cannot be traced to specific revenues. These types of costs are treated as expenses as they are incurred. Salaries and wages of employees working in the general administrative function of a business would be an example of this type of cost. These compensation costs provide benefit to the business as incurred but their connection with revenues is too remote to attempt to relate such items to any particular revenue. Interest expense associate with general working capital financing is treated as an expense as incurred, assuming that the interest is not being prepaid. (In some cases, interest associated with the construction of assets must be capitalized as part of the cost of the assets being constructed.)

3. Systematic and Rational Allocation

Some costs are not themselves directly connected with revenue but they are also not treated as expenses as incurred. These items provide a benefit that is associated with a period of time that runs beyond the current accounting year. These types of costs are allocated in a systematic and rational manner over the period that they are expected to benefit. The cost of a building, for example, is recognized as depreciation expense over the period that the building is expected to provide benefit to the business. Similarly, the cost of a three-year insurance premium for fire insurance would be recognized as expense over the three year period covered by the policy. If interest were prepaid on a loan, that interest would be treated as expense over the period for which interest was prepaid.

Some types of costs may be subject to more than one of the expense recognition procedures described above. The cost of manufacturing facilities, for example, would be recognized as depreciation over the expected useful life of the facilities. However, this depreciation would not be directly recognized as an expense. Rather, the depreciation would be treated as part of the cost of the products produced during the current year and would be transferred to inventory (another asset account). When the goods are taken out of inventory and sold, the inventory cost (including the portion attributable to depreciation) would be treated as an expense in the form of cost of goods sold under the direct recognition rule.

CHAPTER 5

CURRENT ASSETS AND LIABILITIES

This chapter will discuss accounting issues related to current assets and liabilities. Current assets are assets that are generally expected to be converted into cash or consumed in the business within the next year or within the operating cycle for businesses with an operating cycle greater than one year. The operating cycle is the length of time needed for a business to acquire raw materials or other inputs, produce and sell its goods or services, and collect the cash generated by the revenue-producing activities. For most businesses, the primary components of current assets are cash, marketable securities, receivables, inventories, and short term prepayments. Accounting for inventories will be discussed separately in Chapter 6.

Current liabilities are the liabilities of a business that will be paid or otherwise discharged through the use of current assets or by the creation of other current liabilities within the next year (or operating cycle). Current liabilities may be paid in cash within the coming year, may be satisfied by the delivery of goods or services within the coming year, or may be replaced by other current liabilities. Current liabilities include accounts payable, short term notes payable, accrued liabilities, deferred revenues, estimated liabilities, and contingent liabilities. Most current liabilities are reported on the balance sheet at their maturity amount (the amount expected to be paid to satisfy the liability).

The amount by which current assets exceed current liabilities is sometimes referred to as the working capital of the business. Working capital is a rough indicator of the liquidity of a business.

A. CASH

Cash is generally the first asset listed on the balance sheet of a business. Cash includes currency and coins held by the business, checking accounts of the business, savings accounts that are subject to withdrawal at any time, and negotiable checks not yet deposited or cashed. Certain amounts that might be thought of as cash, such as certificates of deposit and postdated checks, are not cash.

1. Cash Equivalents

The amount reported as cash in the balance sheet frequently includes additional items that are not strictly speaking cash but are close enough to cash to be included with the cash. These additional amounts are called cash equivalents and the caption in the balance sheet should then be "Cash and Cash Equivalents." Cash equivalents are generally short term, high quality, highly liquid money market instruments with a maturity of three months or less.

Examples of the types of items that might qualify as cash equivalents include commercial paper, treasury bills, and money market fund securities.

2. Restricted Cash

Certain amounts that would normally be treated as cash may not be included in the cash line in the balance sheet. For example, amounts may be set aside in bank accounts or otherwise restricted pursuant to contractual or other arrangements requiring the set aside of these funds for specific purposes. These amounts are not accessible for the normal cash needs of the business and they are generally reported in the "Other Assets" section of the noncurrent assets.

Another form of restriction on cash is a compensating balance arrangement. Banks that make loans or provide other services for customers may require the customers to maintain a minimum bank account balance. These minimum balances are called compensating balances. In addition to restricting the amount of cash actually available for use by a business, compensating balances also increase the effective interest rate on loans or the cost or other services in connection with which the balances are required to be maintained. The SEC requires that companies filing financial statements with the SEC report separately from the general cash balances the cash balances that are legally restricted under compensating balance arrangements.

3. Petty Cash

In order to facilitate payment of small dollar items (*e.g.,* small COD payments, postage stamps, taxi money), many businesses maintain one or more petty cash funds. A petty cash fund is established by withdrawing an amount from the company's bank account and placing the cash in a designated location. When payments are made from petty cash, a "voucher" is prepared setting forth the amount and nature of the expenditure. Periodically, the vouchers are sorted and summarized by category. A check is drawn on the company bank account to replenish the petty cash fund to its original balance. At this time, the various expenditures made from petty cash since the last replenishment are recorded as expenses or otherwise in the appropriate accounts. Technically, the petty cash fund should be replenished as of each balance sheet date to update all of the affected accounts.

4. Internal Controls

There are few accounting issues related to the cash account. Because of its highly liquid status and the exposure to theft, embezzlement, or other loss, the cash account is subject to extensive internal control procedures and stringent audit procedures to be certain that the amount of cash reported in the balance sheet is actually in existence and that cash is not being used for unauthorized purposes. Bank reconciliations are prepared on a regular basis to compare the company's reported cash in its bank accounts with the reported bank balances and to identify items that may have been entered directly into the bank accounts but for which accounting entries have not yet been made. Auditors will confirm with the banks the amounts reported in the accounts for those banks at the end of the year. At the same time, the auditors will confirm with the banks the absence of any unrecorded loans that may be used to conceal a cash shortage.

B. MARKETABLE SECURITIES

Marketable securities reported as current assets are generally highly liquid debt and equity securities that are held by a business as temporary investments of excess cash. These securities are held for sale or are available for sale to satisfy the need for additional cash that may arise. The investments are intended to generate a small return in lieu of having the cash sitting idle in bank accounts.

Most marketable securities in the current assets section of the balance sheet are now reported at their current market values. The rules for determining the amount to be reported in the balance sheet are discussed in Chapter 9 on Accounting for Investments.

If otherwise marketable securities are held as a long term investment with no present intention to sell the securities, these securities would be reported in the noncurrent assets section of the balance sheet. The intent to hold the securities may be pursuant to self-imposed limitations or may be the result of contractual or other arrangements requiring that certain marketable securities be set aside for specific purposes.

All marketable securities held as "trading securities" are classified as current assets. Marketable securities that are classified as "held to maturity" or as "available for sale" would be included in the current assets to the extent that they are expected to be converted into cash or otherwise sold or consumed within the next year. Other marketable securities would be reported in the investments portion of the noncurrent assets. The definitions of the categories of securities discussed in this paragraph are set forth in Chapter 9.

C. RECEIVABLES

Receivables are generally rights to receive cash in the future. In some cases, receivables may be satisfied by the receipt of other assets or services. Receivables may be represented by formal notes or they may simply result from oral or written contractual arrangements of the business.

1. Trade Receivables

Receivables may arise from several sources. For many businesses, the principal source of receivables is the result of sales or services rendered where the business agrees to defer the collection of the cash due for the sales or services. These receivables are called trade receivables. For example, a business may sell goods at a price of $100,000 with payment terms of $2/10$, net 30. When the business delivers the goods, accrual accounting recognizes the revenue from the sale and a corresponding account receivable is recognized (see Chapter 4 for a discussion of revenue recognition criteria). In this example, the buyer is entitled to reduce the purchase price by 2% if payment is made within 10 days. This is called a cash discount. Payment in full is due within thirty days. The seller may report the sale and the related receivable at an amount net of the cash discount (the "net method") as follows:

Accounts Receivable	$98,000	
Sales Revenue		$98,000

If the buyer pays within the discount period, the collection of the receivable is recorded as follows:

Cash	$98,000	
Accounts Receivable		$98,000

If the buyer does not pay within ten days and is not eligible for the cash discount, the seller records an item called "Cash Discounts Not Taken," which is a form of interest revenue. The entry would be:

Cash	$100,000	
Accounts Receivable		$98,000
Cash Discounts Not Taken		$ 2,000

The net method is the theoretically correct method.

Alternatively, the original sale can be reported under the gross method as follows:

Accounts Receivable	$100,000	
Sales Revenue		$100,000

In this case, if the buyer qualifies for the discount at the time of payment, the following entry would be made:

Cash	$98,000	
Cash Discounts Taken	$ 2,000	
Accounts Receivable		$100,000

The "Cash Discounts Taken" would be a reduction in the sales revenue otherwise reported in the income statement. If payment without discount is made, the collection would be recorded as follows:

Cash	$100,000	
Accounts Receivable		$100,000

2. Other Receivables

Receivables also arise in situations where revenue or income is earned with the passage of time with cash being payable periodically. The revenue accrued between payment dates is reported in the balance sheet as a receivable. An example of this type of receivable is interest on loans or notes receivable. As the interest accrues on these notes, a receivable is created. Similar accruals of income and related receivables are found in lease agreements where rent receivables may be created.

Additional sources of receivables are cash advances made by a business to employees, customers, and others. As in the case of receivables on credit sales, these receivables may be represented by formal notes or they may be on open account.

3. Reporting Receivables

Receivables are generally reported in the balance sheet at their net realizable values on the balance sheet date (*i.e.,* the net amount of cash expected to be received). In most situations, this means that the receivables will initially be recorded at their maturity amounts. If the seller is using the net method to record receivables eligible for cash discounts, that would necessitate an adjusting entry as of the balance sheet. On that date, it could be determined that some receivables recorded net of the cash discount are not eligible for the discount. An entry would be made to increase these receivables to the gross amount with a credit entry to Cash Discounts Not Taken.

4. Bad Debts

The other principal valuation issue for receivables relates to the collectibility of the receivables. Unless the risk of collection is extremely high, receivables are recorded at the time of sale notwithstanding some risk that the receivables may not be collected. In this situation, the business will estimate the amount of receivables that will not be collected and record an expense and an allowance for doubtful accounts in recognition of the fact that not all receivables will be collected. If, for example, a determination were made that $50,000 should be added to an allowance for doubtful accounts, the entry would be as follows:

Bad Debt Expense	$50,000	
Allowance for Doubtful Accounts		$50,000

The bad debt expense is reported in the income statement as an expense or as a reduction in the revenue from the sales that gave rise to the receivables. The allowance for doubtful accounts is a "contra account" that is deducted from the gross amount of receivables on the balance sheet to produce the net amount of receivables actually expected to be collected.

When a specific account is determined to be uncollectible, no additional bad debt expense is recorded. The identified account is removed from the receivables account and a like amount is removed from the allowance account with no net effect on income or on the balance sheet (since the net receivables reported in the balance sheet are unchanged). Thus, if a $5,000 receivable were determined to be uncollectible, the following entry would be made:

Allowance for Doubtful Accounts	$5,000	
Accounts Receivable		$5,000

a. *Percentage of Sales Method*

There are two approaches to determining the amount of bad debt expense and the related addition to the allowance for doubtful accounts. Under one approach, called the percentage of sales method, the company determines based on experience that a certain percentage of its credit sales will not be collectible. Each year, the company accrues additional bad debt expense based on the credit sales being made in the current year and adds the same amount to the allowance account. Thus, if a company has credit sales for the period of $3,000,000 and its history suggests that 6% of credit sales will not be collected, it would make an entry as follows:

Bad Debt Expense	$180,000	
Allowance for Doubtful Accounts		$180,000

Note that this entry was made without reference to the current balance in the allowance account.

b. *Aged Receivables Analysis*

The second approach for determining the bad debt expense for the period is the aged accounts receivable analysis. The accounts receivable are periodically divided into categories based on the age of the receivables. The amount in each aging category is examined and a determination is made, based on past experience, about how much of the receivables in each category will eventually be uncollectible. The total amount expected to be uncollectible is then computed and compared to the amount currently in the allowance account. The difference is recorded as an adjustment to bad debt expense and the allowance account. This aged accounts receivable analysis is also used as a periodic check on the amount computed under the percentage of sales method.

To illustrate the application of the aged receivables analysis, assume that a company completes an analysis and determines that the appropriate amount in the allowance account should be $300,000. The amount currently in the allowance ac-

count is $275,000. Additional bad debt expense in
the amount of $25,000 would be recorded as follows:

Bad Debt Expense	$25,000	
Allowance for Doubtful Accounts		$25,000

5. Financing and Sales of Receivables

Another accounting issue related to receivables
arises from the practice of converting receivables
into cash prior to collection either by borrowing
using the receivables as security for the loan or by
selling the receivables. If the receivables are assigned or pledged as collateral for a loan, the loan is
recorded as a liability and accounted for in the
normal manner. Generally, the assignor of the
receivables retains the responsibility for collecting
the receivables. The assigned receivables remain as
current assets, although they may be transferred to
an account called "Assigned Accounts Receivable"
to facilitate segregation of the assigned accounts
from accounts that have not been assigned. Thus,
assume that a business borrows $95,000 by assign-
ing accounts receivable in the amount of $100,000.
An interest bearing note is executed. This transaction would be recorded as follows:

Cash	$ 95,000	
Notes Payable		$ 95,000
Assigned Accounts Receivable	$100,000	
Accounts Receivable		$100,000

Interest expense on the note payable would be
recorded periodically. When the note is repaid and
the assignment of the receivables is terminated, the

remaining assigned accounts would be transferred back to the general accounts receivable.

Alternatively, the business may decide to sell or "factor" its receivables to raise cash. Assume that the business sells $100,000 in receivables in exchange for $80,000 with no recourse by the buyer of the receivables in the event of failure by the buyer to collect on the accounts. No loan would be recorded. The accounts receivable that were sold would be removed from the balance sheet and the difference between the book value of the receivables sold and the proceeds from the sale would be recorded in an expense account as a cost of financing, as follows:

Cash	$80,000	
Finance Charges	$20,000	
Accounts Receivable		$100,000

If the seller of the accounts retains any indemnity or other exposure on the accounts receivable that are sold, this contingent liability would be reported in the footnotes to the financial statements.

It is possible for a business to assign receivables with recourse (*i.e.,* with a right in the buyer of the receivables to recover from the seller of the receivables if the accounts are not collected) and still report the transaction as a sale of the receivables for accounting purposes, a form of off-balance sheet financing. In order to recognize a sale of receivables with recourse as a "sale" for accounting purposes, the following conditions must be met:

1.   The sale must transfer the "economic control" of the receivables (*e.g.,* the transferor may not retain an option to reacquire the receivables).

2.   The obligations of the transferor under the recourse arrangement must be capable of reasonable estimation.

3.   The transferee can not require the transferor to reacquire the receivables except under the recourse provision.   The recourse provision can only require payment by the transferor to the transferee as a result of (a) failure of the debtor to repay, (b) the effects of prepayment, or (c) adjustments related to defects in the eligibility of the receivables transferred.

The note payable recorded in connection with the assignment of the accounts receivable in this type of an assignment arrangement is reported as a reduction in the amount of the accounts receivable and is not reported in the liability section of the balance sheet.   If the sale with recourse does not satisfy these requirements, the sale must be reported as a financing of the receivables as described above.

6.   Notes Receivable

The accounting for notes receivable is substantially the same as accounting for accounts receivable.   Notes receivable are more likely to call for stated interest revenue for the holder.   The interest may be in the form of add-on interest (*e.g.,* the note is payable with interest of 8% per annum) or in the form of discount interest (*e.g.,* a note is signed with a principal amount of $100,000 but the borrower only receives $90,000 with the $10,000 difference being the interest element of the borrowing). In the case of a discount note, the discount is amortized and reported as interest expense pursuant to one of the methods described in Chapter 9 on Accounting for Investments.

7. Imputing Interest

If a note or account receivable is received in exchange for property or services and bears no stated interest, it may be necessary to impute an element of interest on the note with a corresponding recharacterization of the underlying transaction. For example, assume that a business sells equipment no longer needed in the business and receives in return a note receivable in the amount of $100,000 bearing no interest and due at the end of the year. The equipment had an original cost of $200,000 and is fully depreciated at the time of sale. If an appropriate rate of interest for this type of note would be 10%, the note would be recorded at a "discounted" amount of $90,909 with a corresponding reduction in the gain on the sale of the equipment. The entry to record the sale would be as follows:

Notes Receivable	$ 90,909	
Accumulated Depreciation—Equipment	$200,000	
Equipment		$200,000
Gain on Sale of Equipment		$ 90,909

The difference between the discounted amount and the face amount of the note ($9,091) would be recognized as interest revenue over the term of the note. Imputing interest on receivables is not required where the receivables arise from transactions in the ordinary course of business and have a term of not more than one year.

8. Receivables From Related Parties

A business may make loans to certain related parties including but not limited to principal owners, management, members of the immediate families of the foregoing, other businesses controlled by or under common control with the business making the loan, or other parties in a position to significantly influence the management or operating policies of the business. Accounts or notes receivable from related parties, if material, must be separately disclosed in the footnotes to the financial statements. The disclosures must include the nature of the relationships between the company and the related parties, descriptions of the transactions with the related parties, the dollar amounts of the related party transactions occurring during the period, and the total amounts due from the related parties.

D. PREPAYMENTS

Another category of current assets are short term prepaid expenses or prepayments. Short term prepaid expenses are amounts paid for goods and services that are not immediately deductible as an expense but that will be deductible through amortization or write-off during the coming year. Examples of such prepaid assets include prepaid rent, prepaid insurance, prepaid subscription services, prepaid taxes, and prepaid interest. Prepaid expenses are also called deferred charges. They are often not capable of direct conversion into cash. They are amounts that have been paid that will be recognized as expense in the future.

To illustrate accounting for prepaid expenses, assume that on July 1, a calendar year business makes a payment on account of property taxes in the amount of $240,000. That payment applies to the property tax year beginning on July 1 of the current year and extending to June 30 of the next calendar year. On the date of payment, the $240,-000 would be recorded as a prepaid expense as follows:

Prepaid Property Taxes	$240,000	
Cash		$240,000

At the end of the calendar year, one-half of this amount would be recognized as expense by the following adjusting entry:

Property Tax Expense	$120,000	
Prepaid Property Taxes		$120,000

The remaining balance of $120,000 in Prepaid Property Taxes would be reported as a current asset in the December 31 balance sheet.

E. ACCOUNTS PAYABLE

Accounts payable generally arise when goods or services are acquired on terms that do not require that payment for such goods or services be made at the time of acquisition. They are generally due within a fairly short time frame, typically thirty to ninety days. Most accounts payable arise out of the purchase of inventory or supplies.

1. Reporting Accounts Payable

Because of their short term nature, accounts payable are normally recorded at the amount that will be paid when due. When the vendor permits a discount to be taken off the purchase price for the goods or services because of early payment (a cash or purchase discount), the account payable may be recorded at the invoice amount net of the discount. If the cash discount is not taken, the amount of the discount would be reported as a form of interest expense. For example, assume that goods are purchased at a price of $50,000. The terms of the sale are $\frac{2}{10}$, net 30, meaning that the purchaser may take a 2% discount for payments within ten days and must pay in full within thirty days. If the purchase is recorded net of the discount, the entry to record the purchase would be:

Inventory/Purchases	$49,000	
Accounts Payable		$49,000

If the account payable is paid within the discount period, the payment would be recorded as follows:

| Accounts Payable | $49,000 | |
| Cash | | $49,000 |

If the discount is not taken, payment would be recorded as follows:

Accounts Payable	$49,000	
Purchase Discounts Not Taken	$ 1,000	
Cash		$50,000

The "purchase discounts not taken" account is a form of interest expense. At the end of the accounting period, an adjusting entry should be made to record purchase discounts not taken on accounts payable still outstanding for which the discount period has expired.

Alternatively, the accounts payable may be recorded at the gross amount. The entry to record the purchase on a gross basis would be:

| Inventory/Purchases | $50,000 | |
| Accounts Payable | | $50,000 |

If the discount is taken, an adjustment should be made to the cost of the goods and services acquired. The entry to record payment within the discount period would be as follows:

Accounts Payable	$50,000	
Cash		$49,000
Adjustment to Inventory		$ 1,000

The adjustment to inventory would be deducted from the purchase price of the inventory.

2. Imputing Interest

Where an account payable is created in connection with an acquisition of goods or services and there is no stated interest on the account, it may be necessary to impute an interest expense component to the account payable and adjust the cost of the goods or services accordingly. Interest is not imputed when the account payable arises in the ordinary course of business and is due within a year from its creation. Where interest must be imputed, the procedure is similar to the imputation of interest on receivables as discussed in section C.7. above. The account payable would initially be recorded net of the required interest discount with a corresponding reduction in the purchase price of the goods or services.

F. SHORT TERM BORROWINGS

Another category of current liabilities is short term notes payable (generally notes dues within the coming year). A note may be given in exchange for goods and services in place of an account payable. Most notes payable arise, however, as the result of loans of cash made to the business in exchange for the notes (*e.g.,* bank loans, commercial paper, etc.).

1. Interest on Notes Payable

Notes payable may be interest bearing with the interest in the form of add-on interest. An interest bearing note will normally be recorded at its principal or face amount. Interest expense is recorded as paid or accrued at the end of an accounting period.

Alternatively, notes payable may be discount notes where the business receives less than the face amount of the note at the time of the loan with the difference between the face amount of the note and the amount received being treated as interest expense. The discount on a discount note would be amortized as interest expense over the term of the note. Thus, assume that a ninety-day bank loan is obtained. The borrower executes a ninety-day note payable with a face amount $100,000. This note is discounted by the bank at a 12% annual rate so that $3,000 ($100,000 x 12% x ¼) is deducted and the borrower only receives $97,000. This loan would be recorded as follows:

Cash	$97,000	
Discount on Notes Payable	$ 3,000	
Notes Payable		$100,000

This "discount on notes payable" is a contra account that is deducted from notes payable on the balance sheet.

While the effective interest method described in Chapter 9 would be the theoretically correct method for amortizing the discount as interest expense, the straight-line method may be used to recognize interest on short term notes payable because the result will not be materially different from the result using the effective interest method.

2. Currently Maturing Amounts of Long Term Debt

Short term borrowings reported as current liabilities include the portion of long term notes payable or other long term obligations that are due within the year following the date of the balance sheet. However, the maturing amounts of long term obligations may remain classified as long term liabilities under certain circumstances. Continuing classification as long term is appropriate where the debtor intends to refinance the maturing obligations on a long term basis and has the ability to consummate the long term refinancing. Ability to refinance can be established by actually refinancing the debt after the balance sheet date but before the date that the balance sheet is issued or where the debtor has actually entered into a refinancing agreement before the balance sheet is issued that permits refinancing of the debt on a long term basis. Such a refinancing agreement must not expire by its terms within one year, must not be in default at the balance sheet date, and the obligor under the agreement must be financially capable of honoring the agreement.

Conversely, debt that would otherwise be treated as long term may be reclassified as a current liability in certain situations. This results where the borrower is in violation of one or more provisions in a long term debt agreement and these violations make the debt callable within one year from the balance sheet date or, if the violations are not cured within a grace period, will make the debt callable within the next year. No reclassification is required if the creditor has waived its right to accelerate the debt or where it is probable that the violation of the terms of the debt will be cured within the applicable grace period.

G. ACCRUED LIABILITIES

Another category of current liabilities is accrued liabilities that arise in the ordinary course of business. These accrued liabilities normally represent expenses that have been incurred and recognized in the computation of net income prior to actual payment of such expenses. They accumulate over time. For example, when the balance sheet date falls in the middle of a pay period, there will be an accrued liability for the wages, salaries, and related payroll taxes and other payroll-related benefits that have been earned as of the balance sheet date. Similar accruals of expense with corresponding recognition of current liabilities will exist for such items as interest expense accrued between interest payment dates, rent expense that is paid in arrears, property taxes, income taxes, and vacation pay.

To illustrate an accrued liability, assume that a $100,000 face amount note payable is outstanding bearing interest at the rate of 9% per annum, payable semi-annually. On December 31, 199x, the balance sheet date, there are three months of accrued interest on the note since the last interest payment date (October 1). On December 31, $2,250 of interest expense would be recognized and recorded in an entry as follows:

Interest Expense	$2,250	
Accrued Interest Payable		$2,250

The accrued interest payable is an accrued liability representing the amount of interest expense that has been incurred and recognized in the computation of net income but for which payment has not yet been made.

H. DEFERRED REVENUES AND DEPOSITS

Deferred (or unearned) revenues arise when payments for goods and services are received by a business prior to the point in time of the delivery of the goods and services or such other point in time at which the revenue for the goods or services is recognizable under the applicable revenue recognition principles. Classifying the deferred revenues as current liabilities does not necessarily mean that the customers have the right to receive cash from the business (although that right may exist at least under certain circumstances). Rather, recognition of the liability is simply the means of deferring the recognition of the revenue until the appropriate time.

To illustrate the accounting for deferred revenues, assume that a lessor receives a semi-annual rent payment in the amount of $15,000 on December 31, 199x. That rent payment relates to the first six months of the following year. None of the rent received is earned as of December 31 so that no rental revenue may be recognized. The appropriate entry for the receipt of this rent would be to credit the prepaid rent to a deferred revenue account called "Deferred Rental Income." The entry would be:

Cash	$15,000	
Deferred Rental Income		$15,000

During the first six months of the following year, the deferred rental income would be recognized as revenue. If all of the revenue were recorded on June 30 of the following year, the entry would be:

Deferred Rental Income	$15,000	
Rental Revenue		$15,000

Similar entries would be made for any deferred revenue related to services, interest, sales of goods, etc.

Another type of liability similar in some respects to deferred revenues arises where customers or others make some type of deposit with a business. An example of such a deposit would be a security deposit made by a lessee to provide the lessor with security against the possibility of the lessee failing to make a rental payment or the possibility of the lessee returning the property in a damaged condition at the end of the lease term. Deposits differ from deferred revenues in that it is expected that deposits will in fact be returned to the customers in the form of cash. The deposit is initially recorded as a liability. If the party making the deposit breaches the underlying agreement or otherwise forfeits the right to the return of the deposit, the liability for the deposit would be eliminated and the amount of the deposit would be transferred to an appropriate revenue account.

To illustrate, assume the a renter makes a security deposit with the lessor in the amount of $20,000. The receipt of the deposit would be recorded as follows:

Cash	$20,000	
Security Deposits		$20,000

At the end of the lease term, it is determined that the rental property has been damaged and the lessor is entitled to retain $15,000 of the security deposit. The lessor would then pay the lessee $5,000 and would make the following entry:

Security Deposits	$20,000	
Cash		$ 5,000
Compensation for Damages to Leased		
Property		$15,000

I. ESTIMATED LIABILITIES

Estimated liabilities arise when the current revenue-producing activity of a business is generating future costs that clearly will be incurred even though the exact amount of the costs cannot be determined at the present time. In order to properly match these future costs with the current revenues, the estimated costs are recognized as expenses currently and are recorded in a liability account. When the actual costs are incurred in the future, they are debited to the estimated liability account.

One example of an estimated liability is the cost associated with warranties given in connection with the sale of goods. The future costs under the warranty program are estimated and deducted as expenses at the time of sale of the products subject to the warranties. Thus, assume that in 199x, a business sells 1,500,000 units of product x. Product x is sold with a warranty. Based on experience, it can be determined that $\frac{1}{6}$ of the units of product x sold will require warranty work with an average cost of $15 per unit. In 199x, the business would record estimated warranty costs associated with 199x sales in the amount of $3,750,000 (1,500,000 x $\frac{1}{6}$ x $15). The entry would be as follows:

Warranty Expense	$3,750,000	
Liability for Future Warranty Costs		$3,750,000

Assume now that early in the following year, some of the units of product x sold in prior years are brought in for warranty repairs that actually cost $150,000. These costs would not be recorded as an expense. They would be debited to the warranty liability account as follows:

Liability for Future Warranty Costs	$150,000	
Cash and Payables		$150,000

As an alternative approach to dealing with future warranty costs, a business may choose to defer a portion of the sales revenue that would otherwise be recognized at the time of sale and then recognize that deferred sales revenue over the warranty period.

Other examples of estimated liabilities include property taxes in cases where the amount of the assessment is not known at the beginning of the tax period, the cost of future environmental-type clean-up expenses of businesses that are under obligation to restore the environment following economic activity (*i.e.*, reclamation costs of surface mining operations), and the cost of providing future free travel under frequent flyer programs of airlines.

J. CONTINGENT LIABILITIES

Estimated liabilities involve uncertainty about the exact amount of costs that will be incurred. "Contingent liabilities" involve a further element of uncertainty in that it is not known for sure whether a cost has been or will be incurred. Contingent liabilities arise out of litigation and other claims against the company and tax audits (loss contingencies). They also arise in situations where a company has undertaken a guarantee of another entity's obligations. If the items giving rise to these contingencies are frequent for the business, they may be treated as estimated liabilities rather than loss contingencies.

In the case of asserted claims (*i.e.*, litigation that is already pending or has been overtly threatened), the accounting treatment of the contingent items is based on the assessment of the probability that the business will incur a loss and the ability to estimate the amount of the loss. If it is probable ("likely") that a liability will be incurred and it is possible to estimate reasonably the amount of the liability, the contingent liability is treated like an estimated liability. The estimated loss is accrued as an expense and is credited to a liability account pending final resolution of the matter. Thus, if a company has a lawsuit arising out of an injury on the business premises and it is determined that the company will likely be required to pay $150,000 to the claimant, the company would record an expense and liability as follows:

General Liability Expense	$150,000	
Liability for Future Claims Resolution		$150,000

If the case is later settled for $200,000, only the additional $50,000 would be recorded as an expense, as follows:

General Liability Expense	$50,000	
Liability for Future Claims Resolution	$150,000	
Cash		$200,000

If the contingent liability is probable but it is not possible to estimate reasonably the amount of the probable loss, information about the contingent liability would be disclosed in the footnotes to the financial statements, but no expense would be accrued and no liability would be recorded.

Where the likelihood of loss from the contingency is remote ("slight"), there is no entry in the financial records and there is no disclosure of the contingency in the footnotes to the financial statements. (Certain types of guarantee arrangements under which the business has a potential obligation to perform are disclosed categorically in the footnotes even if the likelihood of performing under the guarantee is remote.) Where the likelihood of realizing a loss associated with a loss contingency is "reasonably possible" *(i.e.,* more than remote but less than probable), no entry is made in the financial records but there is disclosure about the contingencies in the footnotes to the financial statements.

The foregoing discussion regarding contingent liabilities is subject to the qualification of materiality. If the contingencies, even if incurred, would not be material, no disclosure or accrual of liabilities will be made except for a general reference in the footnotes to the fact that the company is exposed to various future items that, even if incurred, will not be material.

An additional inquiry is necessary in the case of an unasserted claim or assessment where the potential claimant has not indicated any awareness of the possible claim. This might be the case, for example, when the business has identified internally a possible exposure on a previously filed tax return but the taxing authority has not indicated any awareness of the issue and it is not clear that the issue will be identified. In this type of situation, no disclosure or accrual of a loss contingency is necessary unless it is probable that a claim will be asserted and it is reasonably possible that there will be an unfavorable outcome on the claim.

A business may also have "gain contingencies," representing potential increases in the value of a business if certain events transpire (*e.g.*, a lawsuit in which the business is the plaintiff). Gain contingencies are never accrued and reflected in the accounts prior to resolution of the contingencies but may be disclosed in the footnotes under certain circumstances. This different treatment for gain as opposed to loss contingencies represents an application of the accounting convention of conservatism.

CHAPTER 6

ACCOUNTING FOR INVENTORIES

For many businesses, inventory is one of the most significant current assets on the balance sheet. For businesses engaged in retail or wholesale trade, merchandise inventory is composed of items that are held by the business for the purpose of sale in the ordinary course of business. This is also true of the finished goods inventory held by manufacturing companies. In addition to the completed goods ready for sale by the manufacturer, the manufacturer's inventory also includes raw materials that have not yet been entered into the manufacturing process and "work in process" inventory, which represents the products of the manufacturer that have been started in the manufacturing process but that are not yet ready for sale or delivery. Finally, businesses of all types typically have miscellaneous supplies of items that are not held for resale but that are used in the business. Where these supplies are material in amount, they may be subjected to the inventory accounting process that will be discussed in this chapter.

Accounting for inventory involves three primary steps. First, there must be a procedure for determining the physical quantities of goods actually included in the inventory at the balance sheet dates and typically at certain interim points during the accounting year. Second, items that are included in inventory are acquired from time to time at different prices or costs. In addition to determining the number of items on hand, it becomes necessary to determine the appropriate unit cost to be assigned to the items that are still on hand from time to time. Third, generally accepted accounting principles require that inventory be periodically evaluated to determine if its "value" is less that its cost. Where that is the case, the lower of cost or market rule requires that the carrying amount or book value of the inventory be adjusted to its lower value.

As in the case of many balance sheet accounts, the determination of the correct amount of inventory to report in the balance sheet is closely related to the amount to be reported as "cost of goods sold" in the income statement. This chapter will therefore also review the determination of cost of goods sold.

A. DETERMINING PHYSICAL QUANTITIES ON HAND

One of the key determinations in accounting for inventory is the actual quantities of items on hand from time to time. A number of celebrated cases of fraudulent or misleading financial statements have involved the overstatement of inventory quantities on hand. Overstating inventory normally translates into a corresponding overstatement of income.

In determining the amount of inventory on hand, consideration must be given to the legal ownership of inventory as compared to its physical location. For example, goods in transit may be included in inventory when title has been transferred to the purchaser even though the goods have not arrived. Goods that have been shipped to a consignee under a consignment arrangement should be included in the inventory of the consignor.

There are two primary techniques for determining physical inventory quantities. These are the periodic inventory system and the perpetual inventory system.

1. Periodic Inventory System

The periodic inventory system employs a periodic physical count of the inventory on hand from time to time. This count will usually be performed at the end of the accounting period although some businesses may conduct more frequent counts particularly where inventory is highly valuable. A separate count is made of each type, size, or other component of the inventory.

To illustrate how the periodic inventory system works and how cost of goods sold (*i.e.*, the amount to be deducted from the sales revenue recognized for the goods sold) is determined under this system, assume that a business started the year with 75,000 units on hand and that each unit costs $1. At the end of the year, the business conducts an inventory count and determines that there are now 80,000 units on hand at a cost of $1 per unit. The ending inventory that should be included in the balance sheet for the current year will be $80,000.

To determine cost of goods sold under this system, one more item of information is necessary. The business will have maintained a temporary account during the year called "Purchases" (assuming that we are dealing with a retail or wholesale operation) and all the purchases of inventory items during the year will have been recorded in that account. Let us assume that the balance in the Purchases account for the year is $400,000 (*i.e.,* 400,000 units were purchased during the year at a cost of $1 per unit). A summary journal entry for all of the inventory purchase transactions for the year would be as follows:

Purchases	$400,000	
Accounts Payable (or Cash)		$400,000

In order to determine the cost of goods sold for the year under the periodic inventory system, you first determine the total inventory that was available for sale during the year (the beginning inventory plus the purchases for the year). You then subtract from the goods available for sale the amount of the ending inventory. The difference is the amount of the inventory that was sold (or otherwise lost) during the year. For the example discussed above, the calculation would be as follows:

Beginning Inventory	$ 75,000
Purchases	400,000
Goods Available for Sale	475,000
Less Ending Inventory	(80,000)
Cost of Goods Sold	$395,000

An accounting entry is made at the end of the year to update the inventory account, close out the purchases account, and enter the appropriate amount in the cost of goods sold account. That entry would be as follows:

Inventory (Ending)	$ 80,000	
Cost of Goods Sold	$395,000	
Inventory (Beginning)		$ 75,000
Purchases		$400,000

This entry returns the purchases account to a zero balance, corrects the inventory to be reported in the balance sheet to the appropriate end of the year amount, and records cost of goods sold for the year.

One disadvantage of the periodic inventory system is that there is no way to determine the cost of goods sold at interim points during the accounting period since the inventory currently on hand is not known until the end of the year. Businesses that rely solely on the periodic inventory system use various estimating techniques to estimate ending inventory and cost of goods sold for interim periods and other purposes.

2. The Perpetual Inventory System

As noted above, one problem with the periodic inventory system is that it does not provide information about the inventory on hand until completion of the periodic inventory count. This system also does not permit interim determination of the cost of goods sold. The perpetual inventory system addresses these problems. Under the perpetual system, the business maintains a continuous record of the goods on hand during the year. The accounting records show not only the purchases that occur during the year but they also record the number and cost of the items sold each time a sale occurs. Conceptually, the entries to record the purchase and sale of inventory items are made directly to the inventory account. Thus, a purchase of inventory at a cost of $30,000 would be recorded as follows:

Inventory	$30,000	
Accounts Payable (or Cash)		$30,000

The sale of inventory with a cost of $25,000 for $30,000 would be recorded as follows:

Accounts Receivable	$30,000	
Sales Revenue		$30,000
Cost of Goods Sold	$25,000	
Inventory		$25,000

The gross profit on this sale is immediately determinable as $5,000 ($30,000 minus $25,000). Similar entries are made for all purchases of, and sales from, inventory throughout the year.

Under this system, at any time during the year, the business knows its cost of goods sold and its current inventory balance. As compared to the periodic system, this provides much more timely information not only for purposes of financial reporting but also for operational purposes such as inventory control, reordering procedures, and other operational needs. Particularly with the expanding use of such technology as point of sale terminals, scanning equipment, and high speed computers, many businesses are able to update their inventory records on an immediate and continuous basis.

For companies that use the perpetual inventory system, it is still necessary to conduct periodic inventory counts to confirm the accuracy of the perpetual inventory records. These counts may be conducted at the end of the year or they may occur on a test basis with respect to different parts of the inventory throughout the year. Any corrections necessitated by the results of the count are recorded in the inventory and cost of goods sold account before the books are closed for the year.

B. DETERMINING INVENTORY VALUES

In the examples used in Section A above, it was assumed that the cost or value of the inventory did not change during the year. A major complicating factor in accounting for inventory is the reality that inventory items are acquired at varying costs throughout the year. A procedure is necessary to determine the costs to be assigned to the goods still in inventory at the end of the year and the costs to be assigned to the goods that were sold during the year.

1. Specific Identification

In some situations, it is possible to identify the exact inventory items that are purchased and sold and to determine the actual original cost of each specific item as it is sold. This approach is generally limited to items with a very high unit cost. The classic example is the automobile dealer. The dealer can keep track by registration number of the actual units bought and sold and the cost of those actual units. In this situation, the perpetual inventory system is always used and no special procedures or assumptions are needed to determine the cost of items sold and the cost of items still in inventory.

2. Cost Flow Assumptions

Most businesses cannot practically employ the specific identification method for determining the appropriate costs to assign to inventory sold and inventory on hand. These businesses employ some type of "cost flow assumption" to determine the costs to assign to inventory. Note that these are cost flow assumptions, not physical flow assumptions. If a business uses the first in, first out method described below, in which the cost of the oldest items on hand is assumed to be the cost of the items sold, that does not necessarily mean that the oldest physical units are actually the ones that are sold.

There are three primary cost flow assumptions is use. These are the first in, first out ("FIFO") method, the last in, first out ("LIFO") method, and the average cost method. These methods will be illustrated using the periodic inventory system. The application of these methods to the perpetual system will be discussed briefly at the end of this section. A common example will be used for illustration purposes. Assume that for the current accounting period, the following inventory items are available:

Initial Inventory	10 units at $5 per unit:	$ 50
Purchase One	15 units at $6 per unit:	90
Purchase Two	12 units at $7 per unit:	84
Purchase Three	10 units at $6 per unit:	60
Goods Available for Sale	47 units	$284

Assume also that during the current period, the business sold 32 units leaving 15 in inventory at the end of the period. The problem is to determine how to assign the $284 total cost of goods available for sale to the units sold and to the units still in inventory.

a. First In, First Out Method

Under the FIFO method, it is assumed that the goods sold during the current period are the oldest goods on hand. The cost of the goods sold under FIFO (listed in order of oldest to most recent) would be:

Units	Unit Price	Total Price
10	$5	$ 50
15	6	90
7	7	49
32		$189

This means that the cost of goods still in inventory is $95, which can be computed directly or by subtracting the cost of goods sold as computed above from the cost of goods available ($284).

b. *Last In, First Out*

The LIFO method assumes that the goods sold during the period are the most recently acquired goods that are available for sale. The LIFO method is usually applied by determining the cost of the goods still in inventory and then subtracting that cost from the goods available for sale to determine the cost of goods sold for the period. In the example that we are using, the cost of the ending inventory (15 units) would be composed of two parts, the ten units in beginning inventory and five units from the first purchase during the year, Purchase One. Thus, the ending inventory would be:

Units	Unit Price	Total Price
10	$5	$50
5	6	30
15		$80

The ending inventory is $80 and the cost of goods sold is the cost of goods available for sale of $284 less the $80 ending inventory, or $204.

Note that in a period of rising prices as illustrated in this example, the LIFO method, as compared to FIFO, produces a lower ending inventory and a higher cost of goods sold. The higher cost of goods sold will produce a lower net income for the year. Because of that benefit, many businesses have elected LIFO for purposes of computing their federal taxable income. When LIFO is used for tax purposes, the treasury regulations under the Internal Revenue Code require that the business also use LIFO in preparing its general purpose financial statements (the "conformity requirement"). The business can not, therefore, use LIFO to reduce taxable income and use FIFO to report a higher income in the financial statements.

A potential problem with the LIFO method involves the need to avoid liquidating old layers of inventory. (Each addition to the inventory balance under the LIFO method is sometimes referred to as a layer. The oldest layer is the initial inventory balance at the time of the adoption of LIFO. As the number of units in the inventory increases, each addition represents an additional layer.) Over time, the use of LIFO can result in inventory being carried at book values significantly lower that the current prices. If a business with old LIFO layers were to reduce its ending inventory from one year to the next and be deemed to have sold some of the old inventory layers, there would be a substantial increase in book income and, because of the conformity requirement, in the taxable income as well. Therefore, businesses using the LIFO method carefully monitor their year-end inventories to avoid ending the year in a position of being deemed to have sold old inventory layers.

Many businesses that use LIFO actually use a variation of LIFO called dollar value LIFO. Under dollar value LIFO, inventory carrying amounts are determined on an aggregate basis for a number of related items called inventory pools. Inventory records are actually maintained on the basis of the current costs of the inventory items. Cost indices that measure the change in the price levels applicable to the inventory pools are used to convert the inventory from its current cost value to its value under the LIFO method. Thus, detailed information about the original purchase price of old inventory items need not be maintained under the dollar value LIFO method.

Dollar value LIFO provides two primary benefits to a business, particularly a business with inventories composed of a number of different items. Dollar value LIFO simplifies the procedural aspects of using the LIFO method. It also helps avoid the problem of liquidating old LIFO layers because it is applied on an aggregate basis to large groups of items called inventory pools. Under the pool approach, liquidation of a layer of one item in the pool can be offset by an increase in the inventory of another item in the same pool. The details of the dollar value LIFO procedure are beyond the scope of this work.

c. *Average Cost*

The third cost flow assumption is a compromise between FIFO and LIFO. Under the average cost method, the business determines the average cost of all of the units available for sale in the reporting period. That average cost is then used in computing the ending inventory and the cost of goods sold.

Returning to the example, the average cost of the goods available for sale is $284 divided by 47 units, or $6.04255 per unit (rounded). The cost of goods sold would therefore be $193.36 (32 x $6.04255) and the ending inventory would be $90.64 (15 x $6.04255). Note that both the cost of goods sold and the ending inventory value fall between the corresponding amounts computed under FIFO and LIFO.

d. Application to Perpetual Inventory Systems

The three primary cost flow assumptions have been illustrated using a periodic inventory approach where cost of goods sold is not determined until the end of the period. If FIFO were applied to determine inventory cost under a perpetual inventory system, it would produce exactly the same result as FIFO using a periodic inventory system. Since it is always assumed that the oldest items are sold first, it does not matter how frequently you make that determination is made.

While as a technical matter you could apply LIFO to determine cost in a perpetual inventory system each time a sale occurs, as a practical matter this is not normally done. The frequency at which you would be deemed to be selling units from old layers would rise significantly and the benefits of LIFO would be lost. Therefore, even when a perpetual system is used with the LIFO cost flow assumption, the year-end inventory values are computed based on the activity for the whole year as if the perpetual system were employed.

When average cost is applied to a perpetual system, it is called the moving average system. A new average cost for the available goods is determined immediately after each purchase of additional goods and thus the average price changes periodically throughout the year.

e. Retail Inventory Methods

Retail businesses frequently find it easier to maintain their detailed inventory records on the basis of the selling (retail) price of the inventory. The retail inventory method allows businesses to maintain their inventory records at retail and then convert the retail value of the inventory to a cost basis for financial reporting purposes based on the relationship of retail value to cost. The details of the retail inventory method will not be discussed in this book. It should be noted, however, that the retail method can also be combined with dollar value LIFO concepts to produce an inventory method called dollar value LIFO retail.

C. APPLYING LOWER OF COST OR MARKET

GAAP requires that inventory values based on cost be compared to a market value measure for the inventory. If the "value" of the inventory is less than its cost, the inventory is written down to its lower value. This section will review how lower of cost or market ("LCM") is applied and the effect that LCM has on the financial statements.

1. Determining Market

For this purpose, the market value of the inventory is its replacement value—the cost at which the inventory would be replaced by the business under current conditions—not its retail value. Thus, if inventory that originally cost $100 can now be purchased for $85, the lower market value of $85 would be used to determine the book value of the inventory. If the replacement value were $105, no adjustment would be made and the inventory would remain at its original cost of $100.

Resale value of the inventory can become relevant because the resale value is used as a limit on the replacement value. If the replacement cost of the inventory is greater than the "net realizable value" of the inventory (its expected selling price less costs of disposal), the market value for purposes of LCM would be limited to the net realizable value. Thus, if the inventory item described above could only be resold for $80, then $80, not the $85 replacement cost, would become the "market value" of the inventory and the inventory would be written down to $80. On the other hand, the market value of inventory for purposes of LCM cannot be less than the net realizable value of the inventory reduced by a normal profit margin for the type of inventory involved. This floor on the market value precludes the possibility of taking excessive inventory write-downs in the current period with a corresponding increase in profit in subsequent periods.

Once inventory is written down to market under this approach, it is not subsequently written back up even if market values subsequently increase. In effect, the lower market value of the inventory is treated as the new "cost" of the inventory in applying the lower of cost or market rule at the end of the next period.

2. Effect on Inventory and Cost of Goods Sold

To illustrate the effect of lower of cost or market, assume that a business has beginning inventory of $50, purchases of $500, and an ending inventory at cost of $60. The replacement cost of the inventory at the end of the year is $45. The computation of cost of goods sold under the cost method and the lower of cost or market method would be as follows:

	Cost	LCM
Beginning Inventory	$ 50	$ 50
Purchases	500	500
Less: Ending Inventory	(60)	(45)
Cost of Goods Sold	$490	$505

Under the periodic system, by reducing the ending inventory value from cost to its lower market value, the $15 reduction in value is effectively removed from the inventory and added to cost of goods sold for the year of the decrease in value, which will also reduce income before tax by $15.

Under the perpetual inventory system, cost of goods sold would have been recorded throughout the year and would be $490. Inventory would be carried at $60. To apply the lower of cost or market rule, an adjusting entry would be made at the end of the period as follows:

Cost of Goods Sold	$ 15	
Inventory		$ 15

This entry reduces the inventory to it lower market value and increases expenses by the loss in value of the inventory.

D. MANUFACTURING COMPANIES

Inventory accounting by manufacturers follows the same basic principles as discussed above. The application is more complex because of the need to accumulate all of the manufacturing costs related to products in the inventory computations. Inventory costs of manufacturers include not only the cost of purchased raw materials and components but also a variety of conversion costs including labor costs and depreciation on manufacturing facilities and equipment.

The procedures related to accounting for raw materials inventory are essentially the same as those illustrated above for retail or wholesale business. Instead of determining the costs of goods sold, the inventory procedures for raw materials are used to determine the cost of raw materials entered into the production process.

During the manufacturing process, costs of raw materials and conversion costs are accumulated in a separate category of inventory called work-in-process inventory. The cost of raw materials added during the current period and the conversion costs (labor and overhead) incurred during the period are

added to the amount of work-in-process at the beginning of the period. The ending work-in-process
inventory is subtracted to determine the cost of
goods manufactured during the period. At the end
of the accounting period, cost of goods manufactured would thus be computed as follows:

Work in Process—Beginning		$ 50,000
Production Costs Incurred		
Raw Materials	$100,000	
Labor	300,000	
Other	150,000	550,000
Work in Process—Ending		<40,000>
Cost of Goods Manufactured		$560,000

The costs of the units completed during the period are removed from work in process and transferred to the finished goods category. The following entry would be made to transfer the cost of
completed foods to the finished goods inventory:

Finished Goods Inventory	$560,000	
Work-in-Process Inventory		$560,000

The accounting for finished goods inventory is
substantially the same as that described earlier for
the retail/wholesale operations. For the manufacturers, the "cost of goods manufactured" replaces
the "purchases" of merchandise operations.

CHAPTER 7

PROPERTY, PLANT, AND EQUIPMENT AND DEPRECIATION

In the noncurrent asset section of the balance sheet, the principal component for most businesses is the property, plant, and equipment account, also called the fixed asset account. The property, plant, and equipment account is generally composed of the tangible property other than inventory that is used in the operations of the business and expected to be used for more than one year. It includes land used in the business (but not land held for investment), machinery and equipment, furniture and fixtures, and buildings and other structures. There are four principal issues in accounting for property, plant, and equipment. These issues relate to recording the initial acquisition, allocating the cost of the property to expense over the life of the property through a process called depreciation accounting, reporting post-acquisition costs incurred to keep the property operational, and accounting for the disposal of the property.

A. ACCOUNTING AT ACQUISITION

1. General Rule

The general rule is that the total amount paid to acquire property, plant, and equipment (fixed assets) and to get such assets ready for use in the business is recorded as the initial cost of the fixed assets. Cost thus includes not only the purchase price of the fixed assets but also legal costs and other closing costs, sales taxes, delivery charges, costs of assembly and installation, costs of testing, and other incidental charges. If part of the cost of the fixed assets is payable over time through a credit arrangement, the cost of the fixed assets includes only the present value of the future payments, not the interest portion of the payments.

As will be seen below, historical cost accounting is used to account for fixed assets. There is no attempt to revalue the assets and maintain them at their fair market values. The only exception applies when an asset has experienced a reduction in value to an amount below the current book value of the asset and that loss of value is not temporary. Such a reduction in value would be recorded as a loss in the financial statements.

To illustrate accounting for acquisition of fixed assets, assume that a business acquires a new computer system for use in the business. The company pays $20,000 cash and issues its note payable (bearing reasonable interest) in the principal amount of $80,000. A $5,000 sales tax is incurred. The company pays $6,000 to install the computer and test it. This acquisition would be recorded as follows:

Computer Equipment	$111,000	
Cash		$31,000
Notes Payable		$80,000

2. Exchanges for Other Property

Fixed assets are sometimes acquired in exchange for other property rather than cash or future cash payments. For example, a corporation might issue some of its own stock or give stock of other companies held as an investment in exchange for the fixed assets. When an exchange of this type occurs, the recorded acquisition cost of the fixed assets should generally be based on the market values of the properties being exchanged. If possible, the company acquiring the fixed assets should determine the fair market value of the properties being given in exchange for the fixed assets and record that value as the cost of the new fixed assets. If the market value of the properties given can not be determined, then an attempt should be made to determine the fair market value of the fixed assets being acquired. If that value cannot be readily determined, then the board of directors of the company must determine the value at which the exchange transaction should be recorded.

Assume that a business is acquiring new land on which it will construct a factory building. The land is acquired in exchange for stock of a publicly traded company that is currently reported at $60,-000 in the investments account. At the time of the exchange, the value of this stock is $150,000. As a result of this exchange, the previously unrecognized gain on the investment will be recognized and the land will be recorded at a cost of $150,000. The entry would be as follows:

Land	$150,000	
Investments		$60,000
Gain on Investments		$90,000

A special situation arises where the exchange of properties involves an exchange of "similar properties" (that is, properties of the same general type, that perform the same general function, and that are employed in the same line of business). An example would be the exchange of a manufacturing facility in one city for a manufacturing facility in another city. For this type of exchange involving similar properties, the cost of the new facility is recorded at the book value, not the fair market value, of the property being given in exchange for the new property. This general rule is subject to the qualification that the new fixed asset cannot be recorded at an amount greater than its fair market value at the time of the exchange.

To illustrate an exchange of similar properties, assume that an old facility is reported in the fixed assets account at an original cost of $100,000 and that there is accumulated depreciation on this facility of $60,000. (Depreciation accounting is discussed in section B below. At this point, it is sufficient to know that the book value of the old facility is its original cost of $100,000 less the accumulated depreciation of $60,000.)   This asset is exchanged for a new facility with a current fair market value of $70,000.   Because the facilities are similar in nature, the new facility will be recorded at the book value of the old facility, $40,000, rather than at the $70,000 fair market value.   The entry to record this transaction would be as follows:

Buildings (new facility)	$ 40,000	
Accumulated Depreciation (old facility)	$ 60,000	
Buildings (old facility)		$100,000

This entry removes both the original cost and the accumulated depreciation of the old facility and records the new facility.

If the value of the new facility were only $30,000, the new facility would be recorded at the value of $30,000.   Since the value of the new facility is less than the book value of the old facility, a loss on disposition of the old facility would be recorded. The entry would be as follows:

Buildings (new facility)	$ 30,000	
Loss on Disposal of Facilities	$ 10,000	
Accumulated Depreciation (old)	$ 60,000	
Buildings (old facility)		$100,000

The accounting for exchanges of similar assets becomes more complicated when there is also other dissimilar property ("boot") involved in the exchange.   If the boot is equal to or greater than 25% of the total exchange value, the exchange is record-ed as if no similar property were involved (all assets are recorded based on fair market values at the time of the exchange with full recognition of gain or loss). If the boot is less than 25% of the exchange, then the receipt of boot involves a partial recognition of the gain on old property given up based on the boot received as a portion of the overall exchange.

3. Acquisitions of Multiple Assets

When multiple assets are acquired in a single transaction (sometimes called a basket purchase), it is necessary to allocate the lump sum purchase price paid for the group of assets to the various assets acquired (or at least to the major categories). It will frequently be the case that the sum of the appraised values for the individual assets will not equal the aggregate purchase price. The allocation of the lump sum price is usually made on the basis of the relative fair market values of the assets acquired. Fair market value may be determined by a formal appraisal or by other reliable means of estimating the values.

For example, assume that a business acquires land, building, and machinery for a total cost of $150,000. The appraised fair market values of the assets are $60,000 for the land, $90,000 for the buildings, and $30,000 for the equipment. The total purchase price would be allocated as follows:

Land—$60,000 / $180,000 x $150,000 $ 50,000
Buildings—$90,000 / $180,000 x $150,000 $ 75,000
Machinery—$30,000 / $180,000 x $150,000 $ 25,000

In the case of an acquisition of an entire business (a "business combination"), special rules apply in determining the costs to be assigned to the acquired assets. The accounting for such business combinations is discussed in Chapter 15.

4. Self–Constructed Assets

A business may construct assets for its own use. The cost of such self-constructed assets includes several components. The direct costs are clearly included in the cost of the asset. The direct costs would include the cost of materials used in the construction and the compensation for the labor that works directly on the construction. In addition, some elements of overhead-type costs that cannot be directly traced to the construction would typically be allocated to the cost of construction. An example would be the allocation of a portion of the depreciation on equipment used in the construction process. In addition, portions of certain supervisory costs would typically be allocated to the construction.

Special accounting rules are provided for capitalizing interest expense incurred during the construction of assets. Interest expense deemed incurred on the amount of money invested in the construction process during the construction period is capitalized—that is, included as part of the cost of the assets being constructed instead of being deducted as normal interest expense. This requirement applies whether the company is doing its own construction or when it has hired an outside contractor but is required to make periodic progress payments to the contractor during the construction.

If the company incurs debt specifically to finance the construction, the interest on this debt is capitalized. Where no specific debt is incurred or where the construction expenditures exceed the amount of any specific debt, the capitalized interest is a portion of the interest incurred on the company's general borrowings.

In order to compute the amount of non-specific interest to be capitalized, the business must determine the average interest rate on the company's debt outstanding during the period for which interest is being capitalized. The company also must determine the weighted average amount of expenditures that it has made on the construction for the period. The average interest rate is multiplied times the weighted average expenditures to determine the amount of capitalized interest. The capitalized interest cannot exceed the actual interest incurred for the year.

As an example, assume that a business determines that its average interest rate on its debt for the year is 11%. The business makes the following payments to a contractor on account of construction during the year and computes its weighted average expenditures as follows:

January 31	$100,000 x 11/12	$ 91,667
April 1	$ 75,000 x 9/12	$ 56,250
September 1	$ 60,000 x 4/12	$ 20,000
		$167,917

Thus, on an annualized basis, the business has invested $167,917 for the current year. There is no debt specifically incurred to finance the construction. The interest allocable to these funds invested in the construction process is $167,917 x 11%, or $18,471. This amount would be transferred from the interest expense account for the year to the account in which the construction costs are being accumulated. The entry would be as follows:

Construction in Progress Account $18,471
    Interest Expense $18,471

The construction in progress account is an asset account used to accumulate the cost of the construction until the asset is ready for use in the business. The effect of the foregoing entry capitalizing interest is to increase income for the year by the amount of the interest transferred to the construction account. This interest will eventually be deducted as part of the depreciation expense when the asset is completed and put in service.

B. ACCOUNTING FOR DEPRECIATION

After fixed assets are acquired and recorded in the financial records, it becomes necessary to allocate and deduct as an expense the cost of the asset over the period of time that the asset is expected to be used in the business. The process of cost allocation and recognition of expense with respect to tangible assets is called depreciation accounting. Depreciation accounting is not an attempt to revalue the fixed assets to an amount representing fair market value. It is a systematic and rational approach for allocating the cost of the assets over the period that they are used in the business.

As depreciation is recognized, the general form of the entry to record the depreciation is as follows:

Depreciation Expense	xxxxxxx
Accumulated Depreciation	xxxxxxx

The depreciation expense is deducted in computing net income for the period. In some cases, depreciation for the year is not recorded as an expense. It is recorded as an addition to some other asset account. For example, in the case of a manufacturer, the depreciation on the manufacturing facilities and equipment is initially recorded as part of the cost of the manufactured goods and is included in inventory cost. This depreciation will be recorded as an expense as part of the cost of goods sold when the inventory is sold. Depreciation is also transferred to another asset account when the depreciation is incurred in connection with the self-construction of assets.

Accumulated depreciation is a contra asset account. That means that the accumulated depreciation is an offset to (reduction in) the related asset account in the balance sheet. Maintaining a separate accumulated depreciation account permits the business to retain a record of, and report, the original cost of the fixed assets separately from the amount of depreciation that has been recognized, which gives some indication of the relative age of the assets. This also permits reporting information about assets in the balance sheet even when those assets have become fully depreciated.

To determine depreciation expense, three items of information are necessary. The useful life of the asset must be determined, the salvage value of the asset must be determined, and a method of computing depreciation must be selected.

1. Useful Life

The useful life of the asset is the period of time over which the asset is expected to be used in the business. Determining useful life involves both physical issues and economic issues. An asset may be expected to last physically for fifty years. If that asset will only be economically useful to the business for twenty-five years, then the useful life for depreciation purposes will be twenty-five years. The determination of useful life is a very subjective process and can have a significant effect of the amount of depreciation expense recognized.

A special situation arises with leasehold improvements, which are capital expenditures made by a lessee on the leased property. The useful life for leasehold improvements is the lesser of the expected useful life of the improvements or the remaining term of the underlying lease at the time that the improvements are placed in service.

2. Salvage Value

The salvage value of an asset is the amount that the business expects to be able to realize from a disposition of the asset at the end of its useful life as determined for depreciation purposes. If an asset costs $200,000 and the business believes that the asset will be used for ten years and then sold at that time for $40,000, then the salvage value is $40,000. The significance of the salvage value is that the total depreciation expense recognized on the asset will be $160,000 ($200,000 less $40,000). The asset is not depreciated to an amount less than the expected salvage value.

3. Method of Depreciation

The final determinant of depreciation is the method of depreciation selected. Various methods of depreciation are used and each method produces a different pattern of depreciation expense over the useful life of the asset. Each method will result in the same total depreciation expense, the only difference being how that depreciation expense is allocated over the useful life. The principal methods of depreciation will be discussed below.

a. *Straight Line Method*

The straight line method results in an equal amount of depreciation expense being recognized during each year of the useful life of the asset. The general formula is as follows:

$$\text{Depreciation Expense per year} = \frac{\text{Original Cost} - \text{Salvage Value}}{\text{Estimated Useful Life in Years}}$$

For example, if a machine is acquired at a cost of $150,000, has an expected useful life of eight years, and has an expected salvage value of $30,000 at the end of eight years, the annual depreciation expense would be $15,000, computed as follows:

$$\frac{\$150,000 - \$30,000}{8}$$

Each year, depreciation expense of $15,000 will be recognized. If the asset is originally put in service eight months into the current year, then a prorated amount of the annual depreciation (one-third of $15,000, or $5,000, in this case) would be recognized in the year of acquisition with a similar adjustment at the end of the useful life.

b. Sum-of-the-Years'-Digits Method

The sum-of-the-years'-digits (SYD) method of depreciation is a form of accelerated depreciation. It results in the recognition of greater depreciation expense in the early years and less depreciation expense in the later years. An accelerated method is sometimes deemed to be appropriate where the earnings potential of an asset is consumed more rapidly in the early years of the asset's use. Accelerated methods are frequently used for income tax purposes because of the deferral of tax liability that results from the higher depreciation in the early years. There is no requirement, however, that a business use the same depreciation methods for financial accounting purposes that it uses for tax purposes.

To compute depreciation using the SYD method, you first add up the digits for each year in the useful life of the asset. For an asset with an eight year useful life, that would produce the sum of 36 $(1+2+3+4+5+6+7+8)$. To determine depreciation expense for the year, you multiply the original cost of the asset less its salvage value by a fraction the numerator of which is the number of years remaining in the useful life and the denominator of which is the sum computed above.

For the same machine that was used to illustrate the straight line method, the depreciation expense for the first two years under the SYD method would be computed as follows:

$$\$120,000 \times \frac{8}{36} = \$26,667$$

$$\$120,000 \times \frac{7}{36} = \$23,333$$

The full depreciation expense schedule for this asset using the SYD method would be as follows:

Year	Fraction	Depreciation
1	8/36	$26,667
2	7/36	$23,333
3	6/36	$20,000
4	5/36	$16,667
5	4/36	$13,333
6	3/36	$10,000
7	2/36	$ 6,667
8	1/36	$ 3,333

Where an asset is put in service in the middle of the year and the SYD method is used, a special proration formula is applied. If this asset were placed in service eight months into the year (four months remaining), the depreciation expense in the first two years would be as follows:

Year 1	$26,667 × 4/12	=	$ 8,889
Year 2	$26,667 × 8/12	=	$17,778
	$23,333 × 4/12	=	$ 5,833
			$23,611

A similar proration would be applied through out the life of the asset.

c. *Declining Balance Method*

The other primary accelerated method of depreciation in use is the declining balance method. In the declining balance method, a percentage is first selected. A frequently used percentage is 200% of the percentage determined by dividing 1 by the asset's useful life. For an asset with a ten year life, the appropriate percentage would be 20% (200% of $\frac{1}{10}$). When the 200% factor is used, this method is called the double-declining balance (DDB) method and the DDB method will be used here for illustration of the declining balance method of depreciation. The constant percentage is multiplied by the remaining book value of the asset at the beginning of each year (original cost less previously recognized depreciation) to compute the depreciation expense for that year. No additional depreciation expense is recognized once this method has reduced the remaining book value of the asset to its expected salvage value. When using the declining balance method, businesses frequently shift to the straight line method of depreciation in the year in which changing to straight line would result in greater depreciation than would be computed under the declining balance method. To compute the alternative straight line depreciation, the calculation uses the remaining book value at the beginning of the year and the remaining useful life as of that time.

To illustrate the declining balance method, I will use again the asset used in the straight-line and SYD examples. One divided by the useful life of eight years produces a percentage of 12.5%. This percentage multiplied by 200% is 25%. Therefore, 25% will be the constant percentage applied to the remaining book value each year under the DDB method. The depreciation for the first year would be computed as follows:

$$\$150,000 \times 25\% = \$37,500$$

Note that the percentage is applied to the beginning book value, not the book value less the salvage value. To compute the depreciation for the second year, the beginning book value of the asset is first determined. The beginning book value for year 2 is $112,500 ($150,000 less $37,500). Depreciation for the second year is computed as follows:

$$\$112,500 \times 25\% = \$28,125$$

This process is continued until the book value of the asset has been reduced to its estimated salvage value, at which point, no further depreciation is taken on the asset. Alternatively, the business may shift to the straight-line method when that would produce greater depreciation.

The full depreciation schedule for this asset using the DDB method is as follows:

Year	Beginning Book Value	Depreciation
1	$150,000	$37,500
2	$112,500	$28,125
3	$ 84,375	$21,094
4	$ 63,281	$15,820
5	$ 47,461	$11,865
6	$ 35,596	$ 5,596

Note that in this case, depreciation stopped in year six because the remaining book value is reduced to its salvage value of $30,000 in that year.

d. Units of Production Method

Another depreciation method that is used with some types of equipment and other assets is the units of production method. This depreciation method is similar to the straight line method except that some measure of the number of expected units of output from the asset is used to compute a depreciation rate per unit of output. Thus, the formula would be as follows:

$$\frac{\text{Original Cost} - \text{Estimated Salvage Value}}{\text{Expected Total Units of Production}} = \begin{array}{c}\text{Depreciation} \\ \text{per Unit}\end{array}$$

Depreciation for each year under this method is the actual units of production for the year multiplied by the depreciation per unit. The depreciation per unit would be recalculated as necessary to reflect changes in the estimated total units of production expected from the asset.

To illustrate, assume that the asset that we have been using in the prior sections is estimated to produce 600,000 units of output over its useful life. The depreciation rate for this asset would be computed as follows:

$$\frac{\$150,000 - \$30,000}{600,000} = \$.20$$

If 40,000 units of output are produced in the first year of use of the asset, the depreciation for that year would be $20,000 (40,000 x $.20). Similar calculations would be made in each year based on the units produced in that year.

e. Depletion of Natural Resources

When natural resources are mined, extracted, or otherwise consumed, depletion occurs. Natural resources include such items as hydrocarbons (oil, gas, coal), hard minerals (copper, gold, silver, iron ore), and trees. Depletion is the term used for the consumption of natural resources. It is analogous to the depreciation of buildings, equipment, and other similar assets.

Depletion is generally computed using the units of production approach. The total cost of the natural resources is determined and the estimated salvage value, if any, is deducted to determine the net amount that will be deducted as depletion over the life of the asset. Some measure of the total quantity of the resource that will be recovered over its life is then determined. By dividing the quantity into the cost net of salvage value, an appropriate deple-tion rate per quantity produced is computed and this is multiplied by the actual production for the accounting period to determine total depletion for that period.

To illustrate, assume that a business has acquired the rights to mine coal from a particular piece of land for a total cost of $20,000,000. Since only the right to mine coal is acquired, there is no expected salvage value for these rights. It is estimated that there are 1,000,000 tons of coal that can be extract-ed. The depletion per ton of coal would be:

$$\frac{\$20,000,000}{1,000,000} = \$20$$

If 60,000 tons of coal are extracted during the year, the depletion for that year would be $1,200,-000 (60,000 x $20). The entry to record the deple-tion would be:

Depletion Expense	$1,200,000	
Accumulated Depletion		$1,200,000

f. *Other Methods*

Other methods of computing depreciation are sometimes found in practice. One group of depreci-ation methods are called sinking fund methods. These methods actually produce an increasing amount of depreciation over the life of the asset. These methods are beyond the scope of this discus-sion and are rarely seen as a practical matter.

C. REPAIRS AND IMPROVEMENTS

The third principal accounting issue related to fixed assets is the accounting treatment for expenditures made on fixed assets after they are acquired and placed in service. When a post-acquisition expenditure is made in connection with a fixed asset, two possible accounting treatments are available. The expenditure could be immediately expensed (such an expenditure is sometimes referred to as a revenue expenditure). To expense an item means to recognize it as an expense in full in computing net income at the time the expenditure is made. Revenue expenditures in connection with fixed assets are generally expenditures for normal maintenance of the assets and for minor repairs.

The alternative treatment is to capitalize the expenditure (a capital expenditure). Capitalizing an item means that the expenditure is recorded as an asset (either as a separate new asset or as an adjustment to the book value of the asset to which the expenditure relates). Capital expenditures are expenditures that increase the life of the asset beyond the original estimated life or expenditures that otherwise improve the quality or the productivity of the asset. Extraordinary or unusual repair costs are also often treated as capital expenditures.

Distinguishing between revenue expenditures and capital expenditures is a highly subjective process and can have a significant effect on net income for the year. Companies frequently adopt capitalization policies to simplify the characterization of these items. For example, a company may adopt a policy that all items under a certain cost will be treated as revenue expenditures and items over this threshold will be reviewed on a case by case basis to determine the appropriate accounting.

To illustrate the accounting for post-acquisition expenditures, assume first that a company incurs $5,000 to repair a broken part on a piece of factory machinery. This repair neither extends the life nor otherwise materially affects the productivity of the asset. This amount would be recorded as a repair expense when incurred as follows:

Repair Expense	$5,000	
Cash		$5,000

Assume now that the business installs a new roof on its factory building at a cost $100,000. This new roof extends the useful life of the building beyond its originally estimated useful life. Such an expenditure is often called a replacement or a betterment and is treated as a capital expenditure. One method frequently used to record such an item is to debit the amount of the expenditure to the accumulated depreciation account and adjust the depreciation expense going forward. This entry would be recorded as follows:

Accumulated Depreciation–Buildings	$100,000	
Cash		$100,000

Alternatively, the amount of the capital expenditure could be recorded in the building account.

This is most frequently done when the capital expenditure represents an addition to an existing asset. In either case, the entry has the effect of increasing the book value of the fixed assets, which will cause an increase in depreciation expense in the future.

D. DISPOSAL OF FIXED ASSETS

When a fixed asset is sold or otherwise disposed of, the following steps are taken. First, the depreciation on the asset is brought current to the date of sale by recognizing depreciation for any portion of the current year that has not yet been recorded. Second, the original cost and the accumulated depreciation related to the asset are determined as of the date of sale. Both of these amounts will be removed from the financial records. If the asset is simply being abandoned, any remaining book value (original cost less accumulated depreciation) is simply recorded as a loss. If the asset is being sold, the proceeds are recorded along with the disposal of the asset and any difference between the proceeds and the book value at the time of sale is recognized as a gain or loss as appropriate.

Assume that an asset (a machine) with an original cost of $100,000 and accumulated depreciation of $90,000 is being retired. If the asset is simply abandoned, the entry would be:

Loss on Disposal of Machinery	$ 10,000	
Accumulated Depreciation—Machinery	$ 90,000	
Machinery		$100,000

If the asset is sold for $15,000, the entry would be as follows:

Cash	$ 15,000	
Accumulated Depreciation—Machinery	$ 90,000	
Machinery		$100,000
Gain on Disposal of Machinery		$ 5,000

The treatment of disposals of assets by exchanges for new assets was discussed above in Section A.2. of this chapter.

CHAPTER 8

INTANGIBLE ASSETS

Intangible assets are valuable rights and property interests of a business that are not embodied in tangible pieces of property. They would include such items as patents, trademarks, franchises, and goodwill. Intangible assets fall into two categories called identifiable intangible assets and unidentifiable intangible assets.

A. IDENTIFIABLE INTANGIBLE ASSETS

Identifiable intangible assets are intangible assets that exist separately from the other assets of a business and can be sold separately from such other assets.

1. Types of Identifiable Intangible Assets

Examples of identifiable intangible assets are indicated below.

a. *Patents*

Patents are the exclusive right granted by the federal government to the manufacture, sale, or other use of an invention. A patent generally has a legal life of 17 years. During the life of the patent, the owner essentially has a monopoly in the use of the patented invention.

b. Copyright

A copyright is the legally protected right to the publication, sales, or performance, of such works as books, music, films, and recordings.

c. Trademarks, Service Marks, and Trade Names

Trademarks, service marks, and trade names are distinctive names, symbols, or designs that identify a particular product or service.

d. Franchises

Franchises are agreements giving the franchisee the right to sell products or services under the name of the franchisor. The franchise generally also gives the franchisee the right to use trade secrets and other protected rights belonging to the franchisor. Franchises may also be exclusive rights to provide certain services in designated areas granted to the franchisee by a government.

e. Deferred Charges

A miscellaneous group of intangible assets includes various types of costs that are capitalized and not expensed because the costs are expected to benefit a business over a period of time in excess of one year. Examples include organization costs (the costs incurred to create a new corporation), certain computer software development costs, and long term prepayments.

2. Accounting for Purchased Identifiable Intangible Assets

If identifiable intangible assets are purchased, all the costs of acquiring the intangible assets are generally capitalized. These costs include the purchase price paid to a third party as well as legal costs that may be incurred in perfecting the legal title to the intangible asset. In some cases, it may be necessary to incur post-acquisition costs to defend the right to an intangible asset (*e.g.*, legal costs to establish the validity of a patent). Such costs of successfully defending the title to an intangible asset should be capitalized to the extent that there is a significant remaining life associated with the asset.

These capitalized costs are amortized to expense over the economic life of the assets. The economic life must be determined based on all the facts and circumstances. While the legal life of certain intangible assets is one of the relevant facts, it is not controlling in determining the economic life of the intangible asset since the intangible asset may become obsolete prior to the end of its legal life. In no event may the economic life of an intangible asset exceed 40 years.

The amortization of an intangible asset is generally similar to the depreciation of tangible property. The straight line method is normally used for amortizing intangible assets unless there is convincing evidence that some other method of amortization would provide a better matching of expense with revenues.

When amortization is recognized for intangible assets, there are two ways for recording the credit entry to reduce the book value of the intangible asset. The credit entry could be to an accumulated amortization account similar to the accumulated depreciation account used for tangible property. For intangible assets, however, the amortization is frequently credited directly to the asset account. Under this approach, the entry to record $100,000 of amortization expense related to a patent would be as follows:

Amortization Expense	$100,000	
Patents		$100,000

3. Accounting for Internally Created Identifiable Intangible Assets

Identifiable intangible assets are frequently created internally as opposed to being purchased. Some of the costs associated with the creation and perfection of an intangible asset will be capitalized as part of the cost of the assets and amortized in the same manner as for purchased intangible assets. Examples of capitalized costs would include the legal costs associated with processing a patent application or registering a trademark.

Many of the costs associated with internally created intangible assets are not capitalized. This often results because, at the time that the costs are incurred, it is not known whether a valuable asset will result from the efforts. For example, a valuable trademark is frequently developed over time in part through extensive advertising and promotional efforts related to a product. The advertising and promotional costs are generally expensed as incurred because it is not possible to determine that an asset will result from these efforts. Thus, a valuable trademark (and many other valuable intangible assets) created through internal efforts will frequently not have any significant costs reported in the balance sheet.

a. Research and Development

The accounting treatment for some of the costs related to the internal development of intangible assets is the subject of specific guidance from the FASB. Research and development expenses are expensed as incurred even though the research and development efforts may lead to a valuable patent, trade secret, or other valuable right. This accounting is mandated by FASB Statement No. 2. All of the costs related to research and development must be accumulated and separately classified as research and development expenses since the financial statements must disclose the amount of research and development costs for each period for which an income statement is reported.

b. Computer Software Costs

Computer software development costs are also the subject of specific guidance. The costs of designing, coding, testing, documenting, and preparing training materials for software to be sold or leased are called software production costs. These types of costs incurred up to the date on which technological feasibility of the software is established are treated as research and development costs and are expensed as incurred. Software production costs incurred after technological feasibility but before general release of the software are capitalized. These capitalized costs are amortized over the expected life of the software. Amortization each year is the greater of the (i) the book value of the capitalized costs multiplied by a percentage equal to the current year's gross revenues divided by the expected gross revenues for the current and future years, or (ii) an amount computed using a straight-line method. Software production costs incurred after general release are expensed as incurred.

B. UNIDENTIFIABLE INTANGIBLE ASSETS

Unidentifiable intangible assets do not exist separately from the other assets of a business. The primary example of an unidentifiable intangible asset is goodwill, which is generally defined conceptually as the ability to earn income in excess of the income that would be expected from the business viewed as a mere collection of assets. Goodwill may exist because of a particularly valuable group of employees, the benefit from an attractive geographical location, or other factors that give a business some type of competitive advantage.

The only time that unidentifiable intangible assets such as goodwill are recorded in the financial statements is when they are purchased. A purchase of such an asset occurs when a business is acquired for a purchase price in excess of the fair market value of all of the identifiable assets acquired, less any liabilities. Chapter 15 discusses the recognition of goodwill in connection with a business combination. When goodwill is recognized and recorded as an asset, it must be amortized and expensed over its expected life, which may not be in excess of 40 years.

The cost of goodwill created internally is not recorded as an asset but is expensed as incurred. Goodwill created internally is generally the by-product of a number of activities and costs that are incurred in pursuing those other activities. There is generally little or no direct connection between the expenditures that contribute to the creation of goodwill and goodwill as a separate asset.

CHAPTER 9

ACCOUNTING FOR INVESTMENTS

This chapter will address issues related to accounting for investments. Accounting for short-term investments in securities that are reported as current assets was discussed briefly in Chapter 5. Section A will discuss the appropriate accounting for investments in bonds. Section B will discuss the methods for accounting for investments in the stock of other companies. Section C will address the accounting for certain other investments.

This chapter will discuss in detail the rules for reporting investments including the rules requiring that certain investments be reported at market value. These rules apply to current assets and noncurrent assets. The accounting described in this chapter represents the general rules for accounting for investments for most businesses. Certain specialized industries, particularly finance and investment companies, have special rules for accounting for investments.

A. INVESTMENTS IN BONDS

When bonds are acquired as an investment, there are several steps in the accounting process. The bonds are initially recorded at there cost. The business that invests in the bonds must then account for the receipt of interest revenue and the accrual of interest revenue when interest is not paid currently through the date of the financial statements. Finally, bonds are often acquired at a price that differs from the face amount of the bonds. When this occurs, the business must account for the resulting discount or premium on the bonds. This section will review first the accounting for bonds acquired at face value and then will discuss the accounting treatment when bonds are acquired at a discount or premium. There will then be a discussion of the accounting for changes in market value of the bonds.

1. Acquisition of Bonds at Face Value

When bonds are first acquired, the cost of the bonds is recorded in an appropriate investment account. Assume, for example, that a business invests in a $1,000,000 bond issue. The bonds are acquired on July 1, 199x, and the business pays $1,000,000 (face) for the bonds. The bonds pay interest semi-annually at an annual rate of 9% with interest payable on June 30 and December 31 of each year during their term.

The initial investment in the bonds would be recorded as follows:

Investment in Bonds	$1,000,000	
Cash		$1,000,000

At each interest payment date, the business would record interest revenue. For example, on December 31, 199x, the business would record the receipt of its first interest check as follows:

Cash	$45,000	
Interest Revenue		$45,000

Similar entries would occur at each interest payment date.

Assume now that the bonds described above pay interest semi-annually on March 31 and September 30 of each year. They are acquired by the business on June 30 at a yield equal to the stated rate of 9% so that they are still acquired at face value. When bonds are acquired at a date other than the interest payment date, it is typical that the purchaser pays in addition to the cost of the bonds an amount equal to the interest that has accrued on the bonds from the last interest payment date to the date of purchase. For the bonds in this example, the accrued interest on the date of purchase (June 30) would be approximately $22,500 ($1,000,000 x 9% x ¼). Therefore, the amount paid to the seller of the bonds would be $1,022,500. This amount would not all be recorded as cost of the bonds. The $22,500 amount representing accrued interest would be recorded separately as accrued interest receivable. Thus, the entry at the date of purchase would be:

Investment in Bonds	$1,000,000	
Accrued Interest Receivable	$ 22,500	
Cash		$1,022,500

When the first interest payment following purchase of the bonds occurs, the investor will receive the full interest payment due on that date, not just the interest for the period that the bonds were held. In this case, the investor will receive $45,000 in interest. Of this amount, $22,500 is actually income from holding the bonds. The other $22,500 is repayment of the amount that the buyer was required to pay on account of the interest receivable at the date of purchase. Accordingly, the receipt of the first interest payment would be recorded as follows:

Cash	$45,000	
Interest Revenue		$22,500
Accrued Interest Receivable		$22,500

Assuming that the investor in the bonds is using the calendar year for accounting purposes, it is also necessary to account for the fact that additional interest revenue will have been earned at the end of the year even though this interest will not be received until the next interest payment date, which will be March 31 of the following year. An adjusting entry will be made at the end of the year to accrue interest income earned but not yet received. At December 31, approximately $22,500 will have been earned on the bond investment since the last interest payment date on September 30. The entry to record this additional interest revenue would be as follows:

Accrued Interest Receivable	$22,500	
Interest Revenue		$22,500

The receipt of interest on the following March 31 would be recorded as follows:

Cash	$45,000	
Accrued Interest Receivable		$22,500
Interest Revenue		$22,500

2. Acquisition of Bonds at a Discount or Premium

Bonds are often acquired at a discount from, or premium over, their face value. Discount bonds are bonds acquired at an amount less than their face value and premium bonds are acquired at an amount greater than their face value. Discount or premium results when the bonds are purchased at an effective yield (market interest rate) that differs from the stated coupon rate on the bonds. If the effective yield is greater than the coupon rate, the bonds will be acquired at a discount. If the effective yield is less than the coupon rate on the bonds, the bonds will be purchased at a premium. The discount or premium on the bonds is an adjustment to the stated or coupon rate of interest on the bonds and must be amortized as an adjustment to interest revenue over the remaining term of the bonds. There are two methods of amortizing bond premium or discount. They are the straight line method and the effective interest method.

a. Straight Line Amortization of Bond Discount or Premium

For purposes of illustrating the treatment of bond discount or premium, assume that a $1,000,000 bond issue is acquired on July 1, 199x, with a 9% stated interest rate payable semi-annually on June 30 and December 31. The bonds are ten-year bonds and mature on June 30, 200x. The bonds are acquired at a discount from face value of $119,-500. That means that the bonds are acquired at a price of $880,500. This price reflects an actual yield on the bonds over their term to maturity of 11% rather than the stated or coupon rate of 9%. (The price of the bonds is the discounted present value of the scheduled payments of interest and principal on the bonds using the market rate as the discount rate. See Appendix A for a review of present value calculations.)

The acquisition of the bonds would be recorded as follows:

Investment in Bonds	$1,000,000	
Bond Discount		$119,500
Cash		$880,500

The bonds are recorded at their face value and the discount is recorded in a separate account in order to assist in keeping track of the remaining discount on the bonds. If a balance sheet were prepared immediately after the acquisition of these bonds, they would be reported in the balance sheet at $880,500, the net of the face amount minus the bond discount.

The $119,500 of bond discount will be amortized and recognized as additional interest income over the term of the bonds. As the discount is amortized, the bond discount account will be reduced until the maturity date of the bonds, at which point the bond discount will be zero and the carrying amount of the bonds will be their face value of $1,000,000. Under the straight line method of amortization, the bond discount is amortized in equal amounts over the term of the bonds. For each six-month interest period during the term of the bonds, ½oth of the total discount, or $5,975, will be amortized.

On December 31, 199x, the receipt of the first interest payment and the amortization of bond discount would be recorded as follows:

Cash	$45,000	
Bond Discount	$ 5,975	
Interest Income		$50,975

The total interest income of $50,975 includes the cash interest of $45,000 plus the amortized bond discount of $5,975. The interest income attributable to bond discount will not actually be received in the form of cash until the bonds are repaid at their full face amount on the date of maturity.

If the bonds are acquired at a premium, a similar amortization process is followed. The premium on the bonds represents a reduction in the effective interest rate on the bonds since the purchaser is paying more for the bonds than will be received at the maturity date of the bonds. To illustrate, assume that the 9% bond issue described above is acquired at a premium over the face value of the bonds of $142,120, or a total price of $1,142,120.

The effective yield on these bonds would be 7% rather than the coupon rate of 9%. The entry to record the acquisition of the bonds would be:

Investment in Bonds	$1,000,000	
Bond Premium	$ 142,120	
Cash		$1,142,120

Using the straight line method of amortization, the interest income on December 31, 199x, would be recorded as follows:

Cash	$45,000	
Bond Premium		$ 7,106
Interest Income		$37,894

In effect, a portion of the stated interest payment represents a return of the bond premium paid at the time of acquisition since the holder of the bonds will only receive the face value of $1,000,000 at the maturity date. The same entry would be made for each of the twenty semi-annual interest payments over the life of the bonds. At the end of the term of the bonds, the entire bond premium will have been amortized and the carrying value of the bonds will be their face value of $1,000,000.

b. *Effective Interest Method of Amortizing Bond Discount and Premium*

If the effective interest method is used for amortizing bond discount or premium, the format of all the entries remains the same as illustrated above but the method of computing each period's amortization of bond discount or premium is different. The effective interest method of computing the amortization results in the same effective yield (rate of return) being reported on the bonds for each interest payment period. The amount of amortization in each period is computing by multiplying the carrying value of the bonds (face value of the bonds less any discount or plus any premium) at the beginning of the period by the effective interest rate or yield to maturity implied by the initial purchase price of the bonds. This produces the interest income to be reported for the period. The difference between the interest income computed in this manner and the stated or coupon interest payment for the period is the amount of bond discount or premium to be recognized for that period.

In the illustration above in Section A.2.a., the bonds purchased at a discount provide a yield to maturity of 11% compounded semi-annually. To compute the bond discount for the first interest period under the effective interest method, the carrying value of $880,500 is multiplied by the effective yield for half a year of 5.5%. The resulting amount of $48,427.50 is the total interest income for the period. Since the actual interest payment on the bonds is only $45,000, the bond discount to be amortized is the difference between these two amounts, or $3,427.50. The entry to record interest revenue would be:

Cash	$45,000.00	
Bond Discount	$ 3,427.50	
Interest Income		$48,427.50

At the time of the second interest payment, the new carrying value of the bonds is $883,927.50 (the initial carrying value of $880,500 plus the bond discount amortized in the first period of $3,427.50). For the second interest period ending on June 30 of the following year, the interest income will be $48,-616.01 ($883,927.50 x 5.5%). The bond discount amortized in the second period would be $3,616.01. Note that the bond discount amortized using the effective interest method increases each period because the carrying value of the bonds increases each period. While the semi-annual amortization is initially less than that under the straight line method ($5,975), the semi-annual bond discount amortization will eventually be greater under the effective interest method as the bonds approach maturity.

The procedure for amortization under the effective interest method is the same in the case of bond premium. In the bond premium example above, bonds were purchased at a premium of $142,124 to yield 7% effective interest, compounded semi-annually. To compute the bond premium for the first interest period, the initial carrying value of $1,142,-124 would be multiplied by 3.5% to calculate the total interest income for the first semi-annual period of $39,974.34. Since the stated interest is $45,-000, the amount of bond premium to be amortized would be $5,025.66. In the second interest period ending June 30 of the following year, the carrying value at the beginning of the period would be $1,137,098.34 ($1,142,124 minus $5,025.66). The interest income for the second period using the effective interest method would be $39,798.44 (3.5% of $1,137,098.34). The bond premium amortized in the second period would therefore be $5,201.56 ($45,000 minus $39,798.44). The amount of bond premium amortized in each period will continue to decrease as the bonds approach maturity and the carrying value approaches the face amount of $1,000,000.

3. Changes in Value After Acquisition

If an investor in bonds has the positive intent *and* ability to hold an investment in bonds to maturity, there is no recognition in the financial statements for changes in the market value of the bonds. The bonds are classified as "debt securities held to maturity." The amortized cost method of accounting as described above is used. Under the amortized cost method, the debt securities are reported at their original cost adjusted for amortization of bond discount or premium. If, however, bonds that are intended to be held to maturity suffer a loss in value that is determined to be other than temporary, then the carrying value of the bonds would be written down to their lower fair value.

Under a new FASB Statement (No. 115), changes in market value would be recognized in the financial statements if the bonds are held as "trading securities" or are regarded as "available for sale" prior to maturity. Trading securities are bonds purchased and held principally for the purpose of selling them in the short term. Securities available for sale are bonds that are not trading securities and are not classified as held to maturity. For bonds treated as trading securities, the gain or loss associated with the change in value is included in the determination of net income or loss for the year. For bonds treated as available for sale, the gain or loss is not included in the determination of net income or loss but is recorded in a separate stockholders' equity account until the bonds are sold or are reclassified as bonds held for sale.

Thus, assume that bonds held for sale (trading securities) are initially purchased for $100,000. At the end of the year, the bonds have increased in value to $110,000. The gain of $10,000 would be recorded as follows:

Investment in Bonds	$10,000	
Unrecognized Gain on Bonds Held		
for Sale		$10,000

The $10,000 of unrecognized gain would be included in computing income for the year. If these bonds were held as available for sale, the year-end entry would be:

Investment in Bonds	$10,000	
Changes in Market Value of Bonds		
Held for Sale		$10,000

In the latter case, the bonds would be reported in the balance sheet at their fair market value but there would be no effect on the net income or loss for the year. The account in which the changes in market value are recorded would be included as a separate component of stockholders' equity. For bonds held as trading securities or as available for sale, interest revenue is only reported based on actual stated interest without regard to amortization of discount or premium.

B. ACCOUNTING FOR STOCK INVESTMENTS

Accounting for investments in stock is more complicated than accounting for investments in bonds because the appropriate accounting treatment depends in part on the amount of stock that is owned in the investor company. There are three basic methods for accounting for investments in stock, the cost method, the equity method, and consolidation.

1. The Cost Method

The cost method of accounting for stock investments in generally used when the investor in the stock owns less then 20% of the voting stock of the issuing company. The theory is that at this level of ownership, the investor does not own enough stock to have any significant influence on the dividend and other policies of the issuing company so that the investor is in the position of being a relatively passive investor.

Under the cost method, the investment in stock is initially recorded at its cost of acquisition. Assuming that stock in another company is acquired for cash of $100,000, the entry to record the acquisition of the stock would be as follows:

Investment in Stock	$100,000	
Cash		$100,000

a. Dividend Income

Income would be recognized in connection with this investment at the time of the payment of dividends. If the investor received a $5,000 cash dividend on this stock, the entry to record the income would be:

Cash	$5,000	
Dividend Income		$5,000

Dividends are normally reported in income as received. Technically, dividend income is recognized when the dividends are declared. If material in amount, declared dividends not yet received should be included in income with a corresponding receivable being debited.

If the cumulative dividends received on the stock by the investor exceed the investor's share of the income of the issuing company from the date of acquisition, this excess would be treated as a liquidating dividend and would reduce the carrying amount of the stock instead of being reported as income. Thus, in the above example, if the investor's share of the issuer's earnings since the date of acquisition of the stock were only $4,000, the receipt of the $5,000 dividend would be recorded as follows:

Cash	$5,000	
Dividend Income		$4,000
Investment in Stock		$1,000

b.   Changes in Value After Acquisition

With respect to post-acquisition changes in the value of stock for which the cost method is being used and for which there is a fairly determinable fair value, the approach is similar to that described for marketable debt securities.   Changes in value, both gains and losses, will be recognized as they occur for these equity securities.   If the stock is held as a "trading security" (i.e., held for sale), the gains and losses will be recognized in computing net income or loss.   If the stock is treated as "available for sale," the unrecognized gains and losses will be reflected in the balance sheet but the gains and losses will be reported as an adjustment to stockholders' equity and will not be included in determining net income or loss until the stock is actually sold (or if the stock is subsequently reclassified as a trading security).   In order for these rules to apply, stock must have a readily determinable fair market value.   Prior to the adoption of FASB Statement No. 115, a lower of cost or market approach was used in valuing marketable equity securities so that only net decreases in the value of marketable equity securities were recognized in the financial statements prior to actual realization.

To illustrate accounting for a change in value, assume that stock is initially acquired at a cost of $50,000 and it is classified as available for sale. The initial purchase would be recorded as follows:

Investment in Stock	$50,000	
Cash		$50,000

At the end of the year in which the stock was acquired, its value has dropped to $45,000. The decrease in value would be recorded as follows:

Unrealized Change in Value of Stock	$5,000	
Allowance for Change in Value of		
Investment in Stock		$5,000

The unrealized change account does not affect net income for the year. It is a separate component of stockholders' equity. The allowance account is deducted (in this case) or added to the investment in stock account to determine the amount to be reported as investment in stock ($45,000 in this case) in the balance sheet.

Assume now that the stock is sold early in the following year for $60,000. The *recognized* gain of $10,000 will be included in net income or loss for the year and the unrecognized loss recognized from the prior year will be reversed. The entry would be:

Cash	$60,000	
Allowance for Change in Value of In-		
vestment in Stock	$ 5,000	
Investment in Stock		$50,000
Unrealized Change in Value of In-		
vestment in Stock		$ 5,000
Gain on Stock Available for Sale		$10,000

c. *Stock Splits and Stock Dividends*

An investor in stock may receive additional shares of stock as a result of a stock split or a stock dividend declared by the issuing company. No income is recorded and no change is made to the carrying value of the investment at the time of the stock split or stock dividend. The existing book value of the investment will now be spread over a greater number of shares, which will have an effect on the amount of gain or loss as a result of a subsequent sale or exchange of a portion of the investment.

2. The Equity Method

When an investor acquires stock representing 20% or more but less than a majority of the voting stock of the issuing company, the equity method of accounting for the stock investment applies. (The 20% ownership level actually creates a presumption of significant influence over operating and financial policies sufficient to warrant application of the equity method. This presumption may, however, be overcome by evidence to the contrary.) Under the equity method, because of the presumed ability of the investor to exercise significant influence over such matters as dividend policy, the investor reports its share of the issuing (investee) company's income or loss as income or loss on the investor's financial statements. Since no cash or other property is received, the income (loss) recognized under the equity method increases (decreases) the carrying amount of the stock on the balance sheet. Dividends received are not treated as income but are treated as a return of investment and reduce the carrying amount of the stock investment.

When the amount paid by the investor for the stock of the investee corporation differs from the investor's share of the book value of the net assets of the investee corporation, certain additional adjustments to income must be made. The difference between the purchase price and the book value of the investor's share of net assets of the investee corporation is allocated to the various assets and liabilities of the investee, including goodwill. These amounts will result in additional depreciation or amortization. The process is similar to the application of the purchase method for accounting for business combinations discussed in Chapter 15.

Assume that the $100,000 stock investment described above is made on January 1, 199x, and represents 25% of the voting stock of the issuing company (Company G). The entry to record the investment in the stock is the same as the entry under the cost method. Assume now that Company G has income for calendar year 199x of $60,000. The investor in the stock would report 25% of this amount, or $15,000, as income from investments reported under the equity method and would increase the book value of the investment by the same amount. The entry would be as follows:

| Investment in Company G | $15,000 | |
| Income—Company G | | $15,000 |

Assume that the $5,000 dividend from Company G was received on November 30, 199x. The receipt of this dividend would not result in the recognition of any additional income but would be treated as a return of part of the investment in the stock. The entry would be as follows:

Cash	$5,000	
Investment in Stock		$5,000

Assume also that the book value of the net assets of Company G at the time of the acquisition of stock in Company G was $200,000. The investor's share of this book value (25%) is $50,000. An examination determines that the difference between the purchase price of $60,000 and the book value of the net assets of $50,000 is attributable to a patent owned by Company G that is not reflected on Company G's financial statements. At the time of the purchase of Company G stock, this patent has a remaining life of 5 years. The investor would amortize the $10,000 difference over the five-year life of the patent. This additional deduction reduces the investor's income from its investment in Company G and the amount shown as investment in Company G. The entry would be:

Income—Company G	$2,000	
Investment—Company G		$2,000

There is no corresponding entry related to this patent on Company G's books.

Similar entries would be made in future years to reflect the investor's share of income and the receipt of any dividends. When stock is accounted for under the equity method, changes in market value of that stock are not recognized under new FASB Statement No. 115. A permanent impairment in value of stock accounted for under the equity method would, however, be recognized.

3. Consolidated Financial Statements

When one corporation acquires stock representing a majority voting interest in the issuing company, a fundamentally different approach is taken with respect to accounting for the investment. The acquiring company will consolidate the separate financial statements of the acquired company into the investor's financial statements. Consolidation essentially results in an accounting for the investor and investee (parent and subsidiary) as a single economic entity and not as the two distinct legal entities.

Consolidation is accomplished through a worksheet process. The parent and subsidiary each maintain their own set of financial records as separate legal entities. On its own records, the parent company would account for the subsidiary using the cost method or the equity method (the method used is not critical because the accounting for the investment will be converted to the consolidated method as described below). At year end, the separate financial statements of the parent and subsidiary are consolidated through a worksheet process that combines the asset, liability, and equity accounts of the two entities and eliminates certain "reciprocal" accounts on the books of the two companies to avoid double counting of certain items. Similarly, the income statements and statements of cash flows for the two entities will be combined in the consolidation process.

To illustrate the basics of consolidation, assume that P forms a new subsidiary (S) on January 1,

199x, by transferring $10,000 to S in exchange for all of the stock of S. For the year 199x, the separate income statements of the two companies are as follows:

	P	S
Sales	$200,000	$100,000
Cost of Goods Sold	(100,000)	(60,000)
Depreciation Expense	(20,000)	(10,000)
Compensation Expense	(30,000)	(20,000)
Income Tax Expense	(20,000)	(4,000)
Net Income	$30,000	$6,000

At December 31, 199x, the balance sheets (in summary format) of the two companies are as follows:

	P	S
Current Assets	$ 20,000	$ 5,000
Fixed Assets	60,000	15,000
Investment in Sub.	16,000	
Current Liabilities	(10,000)	(3,000)
Long Term Debt	(20,000)	(1,000)
Contributed Capital	(20,000)	(10,000)
Retained Earnings	(46,000)	(6,000)

The preparation of the consolidated income statement in this situation would be quite simple. The various line items from the two income statements would be added together to produce the income statement of the consolidated P/S entity. The consolidated income statement would thus appear as follows:

Sales	$300,000
Cost of Goods Sold	(160,000)
Depreciation Expense	(30,000)
Compensation Expense	(50,000)
Income Tax Expense	(24,000)
Net Income	$36,000

The preparation of the consolidated balance sheet is more complicated because certain items would be double counted if the two balance sheets were simply added together and these duplications must be eliminated. To understand the necessary eliminations, it is helpful to review the entries that were made by P and S in connection with the formation of S and P's accounting for its investment in S on its own financial records for the year. At the time of formation of S, P would have made the following entry:

Investment in S	$10,000	
Cash		$10,000

S would have made the following entry on its separate books:

Cash	$10,000	
Contributed Capital		$10,000

At the end of 199x, P, using the equity method, would have made the following entry to record its share (100%) of S's income for 199x:

Investment in S	$ 6,000	
Income from Investment in S		$ 6,000

Viewed as a single economic entity, the balance in the Investment in S account of $16,000 is really a duplication of the net assets (assets minus liabilities) of S. Also, since the stock of S is owned by P and not by outside shareholders, the stockholders' equity accounts of S should really be ignored (remembering that the retained earnings of S is actually already included in the retained earnings of P as a result of applying the equity method of accounting for the investment in S on P's separate accounting records). Thus, in order to prepare appropriate consolidated financial statements and avoid double-counting, the following elimination entry would be recorded on a worksheet used to prepare the consolidated financial statements:

Contributed Capital—S	$10,000	
Retained Earnings—S	$ 6,000	
Investment in S		$16,000

If this entry is taken into account when combining the two balance sheets of P and S presented above, the consolidated balance sheet would appear as follows:

Current Assets	$25,000	Current Liabilities	$13,000
Fixed Assets	75,000	Long Term Debt	21,000
Investment in		Contributed Capital	20,000
Subsidiary	0	Retained Earnings	46,000
	$100,000		$100,000

It should be noted that the net assets of P and P's net income for the year will be the same whether the equity method or consolidation is used for reporting P's investment in S. The difference between the two methods is in the amount of detail shown in the income statement and balance sheet.

The foregoing is a very simplified example of the consolidation method of accounting for investments. In actual practice, the consolidation process is complicated by a number of factors. First, if the parent company owns less than 100% of the subsidiary, there is a recognition of the minority interest in the subsidiary in the consolidated financial statements. The minority interest's share of the subsidiary's net assets is reported as a single amount in the balance sheet as a separate component of stockholders' equity or as a separate amount between long term debt and stockholders' equity. The minority interest's share of net income for the year is deducted in computing consolidated net income.

Consolidation is also complicated by various intercompany transactions between the parent and subsidiary (or between multiple subsidiaries). Certain effects of these intercompany transactions must be eliminated. For example, intercompany sales between the parent and subsidiary must be eliminated so that only sales to entities outside of the group preparing consolidated financial statements are reported in the consolidated income statement.

C. OTHER INVESTMENTS

A business may have a number of other amounts reported as investments in the noncurrent assets. Some of the common examples are described below.

1. Land

Where land is held for investment and is not currently being used in the business of the owner, the land is reported as an investment. The land is generally carried at its acquisition cost unless there is an indication of a permanent loss of value in the land.

2. Cash Value of Life Insurance

A company may purchase life insurance for various purposes (*e.g.,* to compensate the company for the loss of a key executive). Certain types of life insurance accumulate a cash surrender value as premiums are paid on the insurance. If the insurance policy is surrendered prior to the death of the insured, the company would receive the cash surrender value.

The premiums paid on life insurance with a cash surrender value are not treated entirely as expense. Rather, the cash surrender value increase is recorded as an asset. Assume, for example, that a business pays a $10,000 premium on a life insurance policy. Because premiums are typically paid in advance, this premium might initially be recorded as prepaid insurance as follows:

Prepaid Insurance	$10,000	
Cash		$10,000

At the end of the first life insurance policy year, it is reported by the insurance company that the cash surrender value has increased for that year by $7,000. The prepaid insurance would now be allocated to expense and to an investment account as follows:

Insurance Expense	$3,000	
Cash Surrender Value of Life Insurance	$7,000	
Prepaid Insurance		$10,000

The cash surrender value of life insurance is carried in the investments section of the noncurrent assets.

3. Sinking Funds and Other Permanent Funds

A business may be required to (or may voluntarily elect to) set aside certain amounts in separate funds for specific purposes. Examples are sinking funds required to be set aside for the retirement of bonds and amounts set aside for a specific plant expansion project. When such a fund is created, the balance in the fund is typically reported in the noncurrent asset section of the balance sheet along with other long term investments. Contributions to the fund are debited to the appropriate fund balance. The revenues, expenses, gains, and losses associated with the funds are still reported in the income statement but the resulting changes in the cash and securities making up the fund are recorded in the long term investment accounts.

These types of internally maintained funds should be distinguished from funds that the business is required to set aside with a third party, such as a pension fund. In the case of these types of funds, the income, expense, gains, and losses are reported by the trustee or other custodian of the funds. The sponsoring company will record the contribution to these funds as an expense or in some other appropriate asset or liability account depending on the nature of the funds.

CHAPTER 10

ACCOUNTING FOR LONG TERM DEBT

Accounting by the debtor for long term debt such as bonds payable and mortgages payable is very similar to the accounting by investors in debt securities that are intended to be held to maturity. This Chapter will review the principal accounting rules applicable to long term debt. In appropriate places, reference will be made to the discussion of investments in debt securities in Chapter 9 for more detail regarding certain computations.

A. FORMS OF LONG TERM DEBT

Long term debt is generally debt with a term to maturity in excess of one year from the date of the balance sheet. If a portion of the otherwise long term debt is due within the coming year, that portion of the debt is reclassified and reported as part of current liabilities.

Long term debt is issued in a variety of forms. The debt may be in the form of a note payable, particularly where the loan is negotiated with a single lender such as a bank. Frequently, however, long term debt is issued in the form of bonds that

divide an aggregate debt into smaller pieces that
may be sold to different investors. Notes or bonds,
in turn, may take different forms. The notes or
bonds may be unsecured obligations of the debtor,
in which case they are frequently referred to as
debentures. Mortgage notes or bonds are secured
by a mortgage on the debtor's real property. Long
term debt may also be secured by personal property
such as equipment, in which case they may be in
the form of equipment trust certificates. These are
the basic forms. The financial markets have developed numerous additional specialized forms of debt.
For accounting purposes, the form of the debt is not
important. The accounting treatment will be based
on the substantive terms of the debt and the market conditions at the time of issuance. In this
nutshell, bonds will be used to illustrate the accounting for long term debt because bonds generally
present all of the significant issues related to accounting for most long term debt.

B. ACCOUNTING FOR LONG TERM DEBT ISSUED AT PAR VALUE

1. Issuance on an Interest Payment Date

When bonds are issued at an interest rate equal
to the current market interest rate at the time of
issuance, the bonds will initially be recorded at the
principal amount of the debt (face amount of the
bonds). Assume for purposes of illustration that a
company issues bonds on January 1, 199x, with a
face amount of $1,000,000 payable at the end of

twenty years. The debt has a stated interest or coupon rate of 12% payable semi-annually on July 1 and January 1 during the term of the bonds. If the market interest rate at the time of issuance is 12%, the issuer of the bonds should receive the principal or face amount of the bonds (ignoring bond issue costs, discussed below). The entry to record the issuance of the bonds would be:

Cash	$1,000,000	
Bonds Payable		$1,000,000

Assuming that the bonds remain outstanding until maturity, no further entries would be made to the bonds payable account until the bonds are repaid.

On July 1, 199x, the first interest payment on the bonds would be made. The payment of interest would be recorded as follows:

Interest Expense	$60,000	
Cash		$60,000

On December 31, 199x, the borrower has incurred the interest expense for the period from July 1 through December 31 even though the interest is not actually payable until the following year. Accordingly, an adjusting entry would be made to record the accrued but unpaid interest expense on the bonds as of the balance sheet date. The entry for recording accrued interest is as follows:

Interest Expense	$60,000	
Accrued Interest Payable		$60,000

Accrued interest payable would be reported in the current liabilities section of the balance sheet. On January 1 of the following year, the second interest payment is made. No additional expense is recognized as the result of this payment. The payment would be recorded as a discharge of the liability as follows:

Accrued Interest Payable	$60,000	
Cash		$60,000

2. Issuance of Bonds Between Interest Payment Dates

If bonds are issued between interest payment dates, the issuer will receive, in addition to the principal amount of the bonds, the interest due for the period from the last interest payment date to the date of issuance. This is done to simplify the servicing of the debt by avoiding the need to calculate the interest due separately for each bond depending on the date of issuance. On the next interest payment date, the full, semi-annual coupon interest payment will be made. The net amount of the interest collected at the time of issue deducted from the full interest payment will be the appropriate amount of interest for the period from the date of issuance to the first interest payment date.

To illustrate issuance between interest payment dates, assume that the bonds described above were issued on April 1, 199x. The bonds are issued at par value. The entry to record the issuance would be as follows:

Cash	$1,030,000	
Accrued Interest Payable		$ 30,000
Bonds Payable		$1,000,000

The $30,000 credited to Accrued Interest Payable represents interest from January 1, 199x, to the date of issue, April 1, 199x. When the first interest payment is made on July 1, 199x, the full coupon payment of $60,000 would be made and the entry to record this payment would be as follows:

Interest Expense	$30,000	
Accrued Interest Payable	$30,000	
Cash		$60,000

C. ACCOUNTING FOR THE ISSUANCE OF BONDS AT OTHER THAN PAR VALUE

When the market interest rate for bonds on the date of issuance differs from the stated or coupon interest rate, the bonds will be issued at a discount from their par value (if the market rate exceeds the coupon rate) or at a premium over the par value (if the market rate of interest is less than the coupon rate). Thus, if the bonds discussed in Section B. are issued at a market yield different from the stated rate of 12%, there will be a discount or premium associated with the issuance of the bonds. As in the case of investments in bonds, this discount or premium must be amortized over the life of the bonds and will affect the amount of interest expense reported each period.

1. Bonds Issued at a Discount

To illustrate the accounting for bonds issued at a discount, assume that the 12% bond issue is issued on January 1, 199x, at a yield of 13.5%. The issuer would receive less than the par value of the bonds and the difference would be recorded as bond discount. The actual proceeds would be approximately $897,040 and the entry to record the issuance would be as follows:

Cash	$897,040	
Discount On Bonds Payable	$102,960	
Bonds Payable		$1,000,000

If the effective interest method is used to amortize the bond discount, the total interest expense on the first interest payment date (July 1) would be $60,550 ($897,040 x 13.5% x ½). Since the actual interest payment on July 1 is only $60,000, the amount of bond discount amortized at this time would be $550 ($60,550–$60,000). The entry to record the interest payment and the amortization of the bond discount would be:

Interest Expense	$60,550	
Discount on Bonds Payable		$ 550
Cash		$60,000

The remaining bond discount would be $102,410. If a balance sheet were prepared on July 1, 199x, immediately after recording this entry, the bonds would be reported in the long term debt portion of the balance sheet as follows:

Bonds Payable	$1,000,000
Less: Discount	(102,410)
	$ 897,590

Frequently, the bonds payable will be shown in the balance sheet at the net amount of $897,590 without separate disclosure of the bond discount.

2. Bonds Issued at a Premium

Bonds may be issued at a premium. This would occur if the coupon rate on the bonds exceeds the market interest rate at the time of issuance of the bonds. Assume, for example, that the 12% bonds are issued at an effective yield of 11%. The proceeds from the sale of the bonds would then be $1,080,230. The premium of $80,230 would be amortized over the term of the bonds and will reduce the amount of the interest expense on the bonds to an amount less than the stated interest. Using the effective interest method of amortization, the total interest expense on the first interest payment date of July 1, 199x, would be $59,413 ($1,080,230 x 11% x ½). The difference between the interest expense so calculated and the $60,000 interest payment, or $587, would be the premium amortized on July 1, 199x. The entry on July 1, 199x, to record interest expense and amortization of the bond premium would therefore be:

Interest Expense	$59,413	
Premium on Bonds Payable	$ 587	
Cash		$60,000

If a balance sheet were prepared on July 1, 199x, the long term debt would be reported as follows:

Bonds Payable	$1,000,000
Plus: Premium	79,643
	$1,079,643

Bond discount or premium may in some cases be amortized using the straight line method of amortization discussed in Chapter 9 in connection with investments in bonds. The straight line method of amortization may only be used if the difference between the amortization computed using that method and the amortization computed under the effective interest method would not be material.

D. BOND ISSUANCE COSTS

When bonds are issued, the issuer normally incurs certain costs referred to as bond issuance or issue costs. These costs include underwriters' fees, attorneys' fees, printing costs, and other similar items. These bond issue costs are not recognized as expenses at the time that they are incurred since these costs generally relate to the entire term of the bonds. These costs are capitalized in as asset account called Bond Issue Costs. The bond issue costs are then amortized and deducted as expenses over the term of the bonds. Amortization of these amounts is normally computed using a straight line method of amortization. The unamortized amount in the bond issue costs account is reported as an asset in the noncurrent asset section of the balance sheet, usually as part of the miscellaneous deferred charges or other asset categories.

To illustrate, assume that $150,000 of costs are incurred in connection with the issuance of 20–year bonds. Each year, $7,500 ($150,000 divided by 20) would be recognized as expense through amortization. The annual entry for amortizing the bond issue costs would be:

Bond Issue Expense (expense)	$7,500	
Bond Issue Costs (asset)		$7,500

E. RETIREMENT OF BONDS PRIOR TO MATURITY

1. Actual Retirements

Bonds may be retired by the issuer prior to the maturity date of the bonds. This may occur pursuant to a provision in the bond indenture allowing the issuer to call the bonds at a date prior to their maturity or it may occur by the issuer repurchasing the bonds on the market. When the bonds are retired pursuant to a call provision in the bond indenture, the issuer typically is required to pay in addition to the face amount of the bonds a premium to the holders of the bonds to compensate them for the early retirement of the bonds since the issuer will normally exercise the right to call the bonds only when the market interest rates have fallen to a level below the market rate at the time of issuance. If the bonds are purchased in the market, the amount paid to retire the bonds will depend on the market price of the bonds at that time, which may be greater or less than the face amount of the bonds.

When bonds are retired prior to their maturity, the first step in accounting for the retirement is for the issuer to record any accrued but unpaid interest on the bonds as of the date of retirement and to record amortization of any bond discount or premium for the period through the date of retirement. Similarly, the amortization of bond issue costs should be brought current to the date of retirement. The difference between (1) the amount paid to retire the bonds (including any premium paid pursuant to a call provision) and (2) the carrying amount of the bonds, including unamortized bond discount or premium and bond issue costs, as of the date of retirement is the gain or loss that is recognized as the result of the retirement of the bonds.

Assume, for example, that a $10,000,000 bond issue is retired prior to its scheduled maturity date. At the time of retirement, there is unamortized bond premium of $300,000 on the bonds and unamortized bond issue costs of $100,000. The issuer pays a call premium of 5% of the face value of the bonds in order to retire the bonds. The carrying amount of the bonds at the date of retirement is $10,200,000 (the $10,000,000 face value of the bonds plus the $300,000 premium and less the $100,000 of bond issue costs). The amount paid to retire the bonds is $10,500,000, the face value of the bonds plus the 5% call premium. The issuer has thus realized a loss on retirement of the bonds in the amount of $300,000. The gain or loss on early retirement of debt is reported as an extraordinary item (net of any tax effect) in the income statement. The journal entry to record this transaction would be as follows:

Bonds Payable	$10,000,000	
Premium on Bonds Payable	$ 300,000	
Loss on Retirement of Bonds	$ 300,000	
Bond Issue Costs		$ 100,000
Cash		$10,500,000

The same accounting treatment applies to the retirement of the old bonds even if a new issue of bonds presumably bearing a lower coupon interest rate than the old bonds is used to generate the funds necessary to retire the old bonds (often referred to as a refunding). Arguments have been made that the loss on retirement should be deferred and amortized over the remaining term of the old bonds or the term of the new bonds. These arguments have been rejected and the loss (or gain) on the retirement is not deferred and amortized over the life of the new bond issue (or the remaining life of the old bond issue) but is reported in full at the time of retirement.

2. In–Substance Defeasance

A retirement of debt may result for accounting purposes from an in-substance defeasance. An in-substance defeasance results when assets that will generate sufficient cash flow to make all future payments on the outstanding debt are placed in a trust for the purpose of making future payments on the debt. In order for the in-substance defeasance to be treated as a retirement of the debt for accounting purposes, several requirements must be met:

1. The trust must be irrevocable.

2. The trust must be restricted to owning monetary assets that are essentially risk-free with respect to the amount timing, and collection of interest and principal (*e.g.,* U.S. government securities).

3. The assets in the trust must provide cash flows that are similar in timing and amount to the interest and principal payments scheduled on the debt.

If these requirements are satisfied, then the accounts related to the debt are removed from the balance sheet and the assets placed in the trust are also removed from the balance sheet. Any difference between the cost of the assets placed in the trust and the net liability attributable to the debt is reported as an extraordinary gain or loss in the same manner as an actual retirement of debt. Footnote disclosures regarding the debt and the in-substance defeasance arrangement would be made as long as the debt actually remains outstanding.

F. RESTRUCTURING OF LONG TERM DEBT

In some situations, an issuer of bonds or other long term debt will negotiate a restructuring of one or more of the terms of the outstanding debt. The restructuring may include a reduction in the interest rate on the debt, a deferral of the maturity date, a forgiveness of a portion of the principal amount or accrued interest on the debt, or a combination of these and other changes in the terms. Such a renegotiation or restructuring is referred to as a "troubled debt restructuring." Where a troubled debt restructuring occurs, the debtor must first determine the carrying amount of the debt and all related items at the date of the restructuring. This includes the face amount of the debt, any accrued interest on the debt, and any discount or premium associated with the debt. The debtor next determines the *total* amount of cash that will be paid out under the terms of the restructured debt regardless of whether those amounts are designated as principal or interest and regardless of the time of payment. If the total cash to be paid out exceeds the carrying amount of the debt, then no gain or loss is recognized by the debtor as the result of the restructuring. The excess of the total cash to be paid out for the remaining term of the debt over the current carrying amount of the debt would be recognized as interest expense pursuant to an effective interest type of calculation. If the total cash to be paid out under the restructured debt is less than the current carrying amount of the debt, the difference is a gain to be recognized on the date of the restructuring. In this case, all future payments on the restructured debt would then be treated as principal payments regardless of how they are characterized by the parties.

1. Restructuring With No Gain or Loss

To illustrate a restructuring where no gain or loss is recognized, assume that a debtor currently has a debt recorded on its books in the amount of $250,-000 of principal plus $50,000 of accrued interest. The creditor agrees to forgive the accrued interest of $50,000. The $250,000 is to be paid at the end of five years and the debtor will pay interest on the principal balance at the rate of 5% per annum payable annually. The total interest to be paid over the five year term of the restructured debt would be $62,500 (5% of $250,000 for five years). Since the total cash to be paid out ($312,500) exceeds the current carrying amount of the debt ($300,000), no gain or loss is recognized. Further, the "forgiveness" of the accrued interest does not result in any reversal of prior interest expense. The accounting effects will occur in the period going forward from the date of restructuring. The interest expense to be recognized over the five year period beginning on the date of the restructuring is the $12,500 excess of the total cash payments to be made over the pre-restructuring carrying amount of the debt, not the $62,500 of stated interest. Using appropriate present value calculations, it can be determined that the restructured debt has an effective interest rate for accounting purposes of .89229%. That rate would be used to compute the interest expense to be reported each year by treating the restructured debt as a discount loan with an initial issue price of $300,000, a maturity amount of $262,500, and annual payments of $12,500 for each of the first four years. The amortization of the $12,500 as interest expense for each of the five years would be as follows:

Year	Carry Amount At Beginning Of Period	Interest Expense	Cash Payment	Carrying Amount At End of Period
1	$300,000.00	$2,676.87	$ 12,500	$290,176,87
2	$290,176.87	$2,589.22	$ 12,500	$280,266.09
3	$280,266.09	$2,500.79	$ 12,500	$270,266.88
4	$270,266.88	$2,411.56	$ 12,500	$260,178.44
5	$260,178.44	$2,321.56	$262,500	$ 0.00

The entry to record the interest expense and the cash payment for year one would be :

Interest Expense	$2,676.87	
Restructured Debt	$9,823.13	
Cash		$12,500

The debit entry to restructured debt reduces the amount of the debt reported in the balance sheet.

2. Restructuring With Recognition of Gain

If the debt were restructured as described above except that the new interest rate for the five years following the restructuring were 3% per annum rather than 5%, the total cash to be paid out would be $287,500 (the $250,000 principal balance plus nominal interest of $37,500). Since the aggregate cash payments are now less than the current carrying amount of the debt, a gain on the restructuring would be recognized in the amount of $12,500 ($287,500—$300,000). The entry to record the restructuring would be as follows:

Old Debt	$250,000	
Accrued Interest Payable	$ 50,000	
Restructured Debt		$287,500
Gain on Debt Restructuring		$ 12,500

All payments on the restructured debt over the five year term would be treated as repayment of principal regardless of the characterization of the payments by the parties. No further interest expense would be recognized on this debt.

G. CONVERTIBLE DEBT

Companies may issue bonds or other debt instruments that are convertible at the option of the holder into stock of the issuing corporation. Financial theory indicates that the amount paid by the purchaser of convertible debt consists of two components, (1) the value of the debt exclusive of the conversion feature and (2) the value of the conversion option. In accounting for the issuance of convertible debt, however, the convertibility feature is ignored. The proceeds are all recorded in the convertible debt account, which is reported as a liability in the balance sheet. Any discount or premium from face value is accounted for in the normal manner.

1. Conversion—Book Value Method

If the holder elects to convert the debt into stock, the book value method of recording the conversion is normally applied. Under the book value method, all of the accounts related to the converted debt are eliminated and the carrying amount or book value of the convertible debt is treated as the amount received upon issuance of the stock pursuant to the conversion.

To illustrate, assume that convertible debt is issued for its par value of $500,000. This debt is convertible into 25,000 shares of the issuer's $1 par value common stock. On the date of issuance, the entire proceeds are recorded as a liability as follows:

Cash	$500,000	
Convertible Debt		$500,000

One year later, the holder elects to convert at a time when the market value of the stock is $30 per share. To record the conversion under the book value method, the amount of the debt and not the market value of the stock is recorded as the proceeds from issuance of the stock. The entry to record conversion would be:

Convertible Debt	$500,000	
Common Stock		$ 25,000
Additional Paid-in-Capital		$475,000

2. Conversion—Market Value Method

Alternatively, conversion of the debt can be recorded under the market value method. Under the market value method, the shares issued as a result of the conversion are recorded at their market price at the time of the conversion. The difference between the market value of the shares and the carrying amount of the debt at the time of conversion would be recorded as a gain or loss.

Under the market value method, the 25,000 shares issued on conversion of the debt described above would be recorded at their market value of $750,000 (25,000 shares x $30). The difference between the market value of the stock and the carrying amount of the bonds ($750,000—$500,000 = $250,000) would be reported as a loss. The entry would be:

Bonds Payable	$500,000	
Loss on Conversion	$250,000	
Common Stock		$ 25,000
Additional Paid-in-Capital		$725,000

3. Induced Conversions

Where an issuer modifies the terms of convertible debt to induce a conversion of the bonds, a different accounting approach is followed. To the extent that additional shares or other consideration is issued as the result of the change in the terms, this additional consideration is recorded as an expense associated with the conversion.

For example, assume that the issuer of the convertible bonds described above modifies the conversion ratio so that 30,000, rather than 25,000, shares are issuable upon conversion. As a result, the bonds are converted. The book value method is utilized to account for the conversion. The expense associated with the inducement to convert would be the additional shares issuable on conversion (5,000) multiplied by the market price of the stock of $30. The expense is $150,000. The entry to record the conversion would be:

Bonds Payable	$500,000	
Bond Conversion Expense	$150,000	
Common Stock		$ 30,000
Additional Paid-in-Capital		$620,000

4. Debt Issued With Stock Warrants

A variation on convertible stock is the issuance of debt together with warrants. The warrants are like stock options that permit the holder to purchase stock of the issuer at a fixed price set forth in the warrants. If the warrants are "detachable," that is, the holder may separate the warrants and sell them separately from the debt, the total proceeds from the issuance of the debt with warrants must be allocated between the debt and the warrants based on their relative fair market values. The debt and the warrants are then accounted for separately under the normal rules applicable to each separate instrument.

To illustrate, assume that bonds with detachable warrants are issued for total proceeds of $525,000. The debt has a face amount of $500,000. The warrants permit the holder to acquire up to 25,000 shares of common stock at a price of $20 per share. At the time of issuance an analysis indicates that the fair market value of the warrants is $50,000 and the fair market value of the debt is $475,000. The issuance of the debt with warrants would be recorded as follows:

Cash	$525,000	
Discount on Bonds Payable	$ 25,000	
Bonds Payable		$500,000
Stock Warrants		$ 50,000

The bonds payable less the bond discount would be reported in the long term debt section of the balance sheet. The stock warrants account would be reported in stockholders' equity.

After initial issuance, the accounting for the debt would follow the normal rules. With respect to the warrants, if they are exercised, the amount in the stock warrants account would be added to the cash received and recorded in the common stock and additional paid-in-capital accounts. If stock warrants lapse unexercised, the amount in the stock warrants account would be reclassified as additional paid-in-capital through an account called stock warrants lapsed. For example, assume that one-half of the warrants described above are exercised. The company would receive $250,000 in cash (12,500 shares x $20). The entry to record the exercise of the warrants would be:

Cash	$250,000	
Stock Warrants	$ 25,000	
Common Stock		$ 12,500
Additional Paid-in-Capital		$262,500

For the warrants that lapse, the entry to reclassify the remaining amount in paid-in-capital would be:

Stock Warrants	$25,000	
Stock Warrants Lapsed		$25,000

CHAPTER 11

ACCOUNTING FOR LEASES

Closely related to the topic of accounting for long term debt is the accounting treatment of leases. Long term leases, sometimes called finance leases or capital leases, are an alternative to the use of debt financing for the acquisition of assets. If the acquisition of an asset is accomplished by the means of a lease rather than through debt, the financial accounting consequences can be quite different. In addition, the income tax consequences of the two forms of financing are different as are the legal rights of the parties under commercial law including bankruptcy.

A. INTRODUCTION

In order to understand why the issue of accounting for leases is so significant, it is helpful to illustrate the difference in the accounting that results if the lease is treated as a "true" lease for accounting purposes as compared to the accounting that would apply if the asset were acquired with borrowed funds. Assume that a piece of equipment with a cost of $100,000 is being acquired. The seller offers two alternatives for financing the acquisition of the asset. The "buyer" could sign a lease giving the buyer the right to use the asset for twenty years in return for the payment of a monthly rental in the amount of $1,101.09. Alternatively, the buyer could sign a twenty-year note payable with an interest rate of 12% per annum payable in 240 equal monthly payments. The monthly payment on this note would be $1,101.09.

If the proposed lease of the equipment is treated as a "true lease" for accounting purposes, no accounting entry is made at the time of the delivery of the equipment. The lease is an executory contract under which the monthly rental payments are the cost of using the equipment over the life of the lease. Each month, the rental payment would be reported as an expense. No asset or liability would be shown on the balance sheet with respect to this lease.

If the debt financing alternative is used, the purchase of the asset and the execution of the note are both recorded on the accounting records. The entry would be:

Equipment	$100,000	
Notes Payable		$100,000

The primary significance of the different accounting treatment relates to the effect that recording the asset and the liability has on the balance sheet. The asset and liability exactly offset each other so that there is no change in the net assets or equity of the business as of the date of execution of the lease. However, the debt-equity ratio of the business may be substantially affected by the purchase of the asset. Assume that immediately before the acquisition of this asset, the business has assets of $300,-000, liabilities of $150,000 and equity of $150,000. The debt-equity rate is 1:1 ($150,000 / $150,000). If the asset is leased, the debt-equity ratio is unchanged since there is no change in the assets or the liabilities. If the asset is purchased, the debt-equity ratio rises to 1.67:1 ($250,000 / $150,000). This change in the debt-equity ratio may have adverse effects on the value of the company's debt and stock and may cause a violation of negative covenants in loan documents, which frequently require that the borrower maintain a debt-equity ratio below a specified amount.

B. CHARACTERIZING AND ACCOUNTING FOR LEASES

Given the motivation of borrowers to structure loans in the form of leases to accomplish financial accounting and other objectives, GAAP has a set of rules that are used to determine when a transaction structured as a lease will be treated as a lease for accounting purposes and when such leases will instead be recharacterized and accounted for as purchases of assets financed with debt. The basic guidance on this issue is found in FASB Statement No. 13 and several amendments to, and interpretations of, that document. Under FASB Statement No. 13, if a lease is not recharacterized, it is referred to as an "operating lease." If the lease is recharacterized as a purchase of an asset with debt, the lease is referred to as a "capital lease."

1. Accounting by the Lessee

From the standpoint of the lessee, a lease transaction will be recharacterized as a capital lease if the lease meets any of the following four tests:

    a. Under the terms of the lease, the title to the leased property passes to the lessee by the end of the lease term.

    b. The lease contains a "bargain purchase option" under which the lessee has the right to acquire the leased property for an amount expected to be substantially less than the fair market value of the leased property at the time of the exercise of the option.

    c. The present value of the minimum rent payments that the lessee is obligated to make under the lease (including any guarantees by the lessee of the residual value of the leased property) is 90% or more of the fair market value of the leased property at the inception of the lease. The minimum lease payments do not include any executory costs (*e.g.*, property taxes and insurance) that the lessee agrees to pay during the term of the lease. If the lessee has not agreed to pay these amounts, they are deducted from the rent payments to compute the minimum lease payments. If there is a bargain purchase option, the option price is treated as a minimum lease payment. For purposes of determining present value of the minimum lease payments, the lessee uses as a discount rate its incremental borrowing rate (the rate of interest the lessee would have to pay to borrow funds for the purchase of the asset for a term similar to the lease term) unless the lessee knows the lessor's implicit interest rate in the lease *and* that rate is less than the lessee's incremental borrowing rate. The lessor's interest rate implicit in the lease is the discount rate that would cause the present value of the minimum lease payments and any expected residual value not guaranteed by the lessee to equal the fair value of the leased property at the time of the lease.

d. The noncancellable term of the lease is 75% or more of the expected useful life of the leased property at the time of the inception of the lease. In determining the term of the lease, there is included any periods for which the lessee has the right to renew at a below market rental rate (a bargain renewal option).

If none of these tests are met, the lease will be treated as an "operating lease" under FASB Statement No. 13. Where the lease commences within the last 25% of the estimated economic life of the property, neither test c nor test d is used in classifying the lease.

If the lease is treated as an operating lease, the accounting treatment is as follows. No entry is made at the time that the lease is executed. At the time of each rent payment, the following entry would be made:

Rent Expense	XXXXXX	
Cash (or Rent Payable)		XXXXXX

No amount would appear in the balance sheet related to the operating lease except any prepaid rent (a current asset) or accrued rental expense (a current liability) depending on the timing of rent payments under the lease.

If the lease is treated as a capital lease for accounting purposes, the transaction is treated as in substance the purchase of the leased asset for an amount equal to the present value of the minimum rent payments to be made under the lease. The present value of the minimum lease payments is computed using the same interest rate that is used to test whether the lease is treated as a capital lease under the third test described above. The present value of the minimum lease payments is recorded as both an asset and as a liability. The rent payments that are made are treated as payments on account of an installment debt and each payment is allocated between an interest portion and a principal portion such that after all the minimum lease payments are made, the liability will have been reduced to zero.

The capitalized cost of the asset is depreciated using the same depreciation method that would be used on similar purchased assets of the business. If the lease is determined to be a capital lease because it provides for transfer of title by the end of the lease term or because of a bargain purchase option in the lease, the asset is depreciated over the expected useful life of the asset. If the asset is determined to be a capital lease because of the length of the lease term or because the present value of the lease payments exceeds 90% of the fair market value of the property, then the asset is depreciated over the shorter of the useful life of the asset or the term of the lease.

To illustrate the accounting for a capital lease, assume that an item of equipment is leased for a ten year period commencing on January 1, 199x, at a monthly rental amount (payable in advance) of $10,000. The equipment has a fair market value of $800,000. The expected useful life of the equipment is twelve years. The lessee's increment borrowing rate is 10%. The lease term of ten years is 83.33% of the useful life of the equipment. Accordingly, the lease is a capital lease since the lease term is 75% or more of the useful life of the equipment. In addition, the present value of the minimum lease payments is $763,000 (approximately) using the incremental borrowing rate of 10% as the discount rate. Since the present value of the minimum lease payments ($763,000) is 90% or more of the fair market value of the equipment, the lease is also a capital lease under this test.

The entry to record the capital lease would be as follows:

Equipment Under Capital Lease	$763,000	
Capital Lease Liability		$763,000

The initial lease payment is made on January 1, 199x, the lease commencement date, so there is no interest accrued at the time of the first payment. The first lease payment would therefore be recorded as a reduction in the principal amount of the debt as follows:

Capital Lease Liability	$10,000	
Cash		$10,000

On February 1, 199x, there would be $6,275 of accrued interest ($753,000 x 10% / 12). Thus, the second lease payment would be recorded as follows:

Capital Lease Liability	$3,725	
Interest Expense	$6,275	
Cash		$10,000

Subsequent lease payments would be recorded in the same manner except that the interest portion of each payment would decrease over time and the principal portion would increase.

At the end of 199x, depreciation expense would be recorded on the leased asset. Since the lease term is less than the useful life of the asset, the asset would be depreciated over ten years. If the straight line method is used for computing depreciation, the entry to record the depreciation expense for 199x would be as follows:

Depreciation Expense	$76,300	
Accumulated Depreciation—		
Equipment Under Capital Lease		$76,300

Similar entries for depreciation expense would be recorded over the ten year lease term. The leased asset is not depreciated down to a point below any guaranteed residual value.

2. Accounting by the Lessor

From the perspective of the lessor, the determination of whether a lease is a capital lease or an operating lease is a two step process. In order for the lease to be a capital lease, it must meet one of the four steps described above for classifying leases from the perspective of the lessee. In addition, the lease must meet *both* of the following requirements for it to be a capital lease:

a. The collectibility by the lessor of the minimum lease payments must be reasonably predictable.

b. No important uncertainties may exist surrounding the amount of unreimbursable costs yet to be incurred by the lessor under the lease.

If the lease does not meet both of these requirements and one of the four basic tests, the lease will be treated as an operating lease.

If the lease is an operating lease, the lessor keeps the leased property in its balance sheet as an asset and no entry is made to record the execution of the lease. The lessor would record depreciation expense on the leased property in accordance with its normal depreciation policy. As lease payments are received by the lessor, they would be recorded as rental income in an entry as follows:

Cash (or Rent Receivable)	XXXXXXX	
Rental Revenue		XXXXXXX

If the lease is treated as a capital lease by the lessor, it will be reported as a direct financing lease or as a sales-type lease. The difference between the two is that in the sales-type lease, the fair market value of the leased property exceeds the lessor's carrying amount (book value) of the property at the time of execution of the lease. This would occur typically where the lessor is a manufacturer of the leased property or is otherwise in the business of merchandising the leased property. The direct financing lease is more often found where the lessor is a financial institution and the leased property is acquired simultaneously with the execution of the lease.

To illustrate accounting for a sales-type lease, assume that the lessor of the property described above is a manufacturer and that the lessor's carrying amount of the leased property at the time of the lease is $600,000. The implicit interest rate used by the lessor in its lease calculations is 10% so that the present value of the lease payments to the lessor is $763,000. At the time of the execution of the lease, the lessor would make an entry as follows:

Lease Receivable—Gross	$1,200,000	
Cost of Goods Sold	$ 600,000	
Inventory		$600,000
Unearned Interest on Lease Receivable		$437,000
Sales Revenue		$763,000

The amount of the Lease Receivable—Gross is the undiscounted sum of the minimum lease payments under the lease and any unguaranteed residual value estimated for the property (a guaranteed residual value would already be included in the minimum lease payments). The unearned interest on lease receivable would be a contra account to the lease receivable account (similar to the bond discount account discussed in Chapter 10) and in the balance sheet, the unearned interest would be deducted from the gross lease receivable so that the lease receivable would be included in the balance sheet at its net amount of $763,000. Each payment by the lessee would be reported as a combination of interest income and return of principal to the lessor. The first payment would be recorded as follows (since this payment occurs on the first day of the lease, none of the interest is as yet earned):

Cash	$10,000	
Lease Receivable—Gross		$10,000

The next monthly lease payment would be recorded as follows:

Cash	$10,000	
Unearned Interest on Lease Receivable	$ 6,275	
Lease Receivable—Gross		$10,000
Interest Revenue		$ 6,275

If a balance sheet were to be prepared by the lessor immediately following this payment, the lease receivable would be reported as follows:

Lease Receivable—Gross	$1,180,000
Less: Unearned Interest on Lease Receivable	(430,725)
	$749,275

A direct financing lease would be accounted for by the lessor in a similar fashion except that there would be no gross profit recognized at the time of the execution of the lease. The accounting for the lease payments would be the same as illustrated above for the sales-type lease.

C. SPECIAL RULES

The foregoing rules for classifying and accounting for operating and capital leases are the generally applicable rules. There are situations where special rules are applied to accounting for lease transactions.

1. Leveraged Leases

One of the special situations is where a leveraged lease is involved. For accounting purposes, the definition of a leveraged lease is quite technical. A leveraged lease exists where (a) the lease would meet the test of a direct financing lease as described above, (b) there is a creditor providing nonrecourse financing to the lessor and that nonrecourse financing gives the lessor substantial leverage in the property, and (c) the lessor's net investment in the lease (which excludes the nonrecourse financing) declines during the early years and increases in subsequent years. Although the details are beyond the scope of this nutshell, the lessor essentially accounts for the leveraged lease based on its investment in the leased property net of the nonrecourse financing.

2. Leases Involving Real Estate

Special rules are also necessary in the case of lease involving land or buildings since the tests for determining whether a lease is capital or operating must be adjusted. The unlimited life of land makes certain of the lease classification rules inapplicable. Only test 1 (transfer of title at the end of the lease term) or test 2 (bargain purchase option) is used to test a lease involving only land for classification as operating or capital. Where land and buildings are both included in a lease, the various payments under the lease must be allocated between the land and buildings for purposes of classifying a lease as operating or capital and in determining the accounting for a lease treated as a capital lease. However, in classifying leases involving land and buildings, the normal rules apply where the value of the land is less than 25% of the value of the land and buildings.

3. Sale/Leasebacks

Frequently, an owner of property will refinance the property by selling the property to a lessor at the property's current fair market value and leasing the property back from the buyer/lessor. This type of transaction is called a sale/leaseback transaction. In many cases, the property that is sold and leased back has been depreciated by the lessee and the sale transaction results in a gain measured by the excess of the sales price over the lessee's carrying amount in the property at the time of the sale.

In general, GAAP precludes full recognition of the gain on the sale part of the sale/leaseback transaction at the time of the sale. The gain realized by the lessee is deferred and recognized over the term of the leaseback. The portion of the gain recognized each period depends on the classification of the lease. If the lease is an operating lease, the gain is recognized in proportion to the rental payments under the lease. If the lease is a capital lease so that the lessee treats the property as having been repurchased, the deferred gain is recognized in proportion to the lessee's amortization (depreciation) of the capitalized value of the lease property. If the sale results in a loss, the loss is not deferred but is recognized in full at the time of the sale.

To illustrate, assume that the seller/lessee has an asset with a carrying amount of $600,000 (original cost of $1,000,000 and accumulated depreciation of $400,000) and sells that property for $750,000. It then leases the property back agreeing to make monthly payments of $10,000 per month for five years under a lease that qualifies as an operating lease. The sale of the property would be recorded as follows:

Cash	$750,000	
Accumulated Depreciation	$400,000	
Equipment		$1,000,000
Deferred Gain on Sale/Leaseback		$150,000

No entry would be made to record the leaseback since this is an operating lease. Lease payments would be recorded as rent expense. Assume that in the first year six rental payments are made. These rental payments would represent 10% (‰) of the total lease payments and 10% of the deferred gain would be recognized. The entry to record the recognition of deferred gain would be as follows:

Deferred Gain on Sale/Leaseback	$15,000	
Gain on Sale/Leaseback		$15,000

Similar entries would be made throughout the term of the lease.

The rules for reporting deferred gains on sale/leasebacks are modified in certain situations. If the leaseback period is relatively short, the requirement to defer recognition of the gain does not apply and the full gain is recognized at the time of the sale. This rule applies where the present value of the lease payments to be made under the leaseback arrangement is 10% or less of the fair market value of the property at the time of the leaseback. In cases where the seller's gain exceeds the value of the interest in the property retained in the leaseback arrangement, the excess gain will be recognized immediately. Special rules also apply to the recognition of the gain in the case of sale/leasebacks involving real estate.

D. DISCLOSURES REGARDING LEASES

In addition to the rules regarding the proper accounting for lease transactions, GAAP has established certain requirements for disclosures about leases in the footnotes to the financial statements. The principal disclosure requirements for the lessee are the rental expense for the current year included in determining net income or loss, the future rental obligations of the lessee for each of the next five years and in five-year increments thereafter, the gross amount of assets held under capital lease arrangements, and a general description of the lessee's leasing arrangements. Lessors must disclose the components of their lease receivable assets in the case of capital leases (*e.g.,* the gross rentals receivable under the leases and the unearned income related to those rentals) the cost and carrying amount of property held under operating lease arrangements, the rental amounts to be received by the lessor for each of the next five years, and a general description of the leasing arrangements of the lessor.

CHAPTER 12

ACCOUNTING FOR OTHER LONG TERM LIABILITIES

In the financial statements of many companies, there are certain additional amounts shown in the long term debt section of the balance sheet that are different in nature from the amounts owed on bonds, mortgages, notes, and even capital leases. This chapter will review the principal issues related to three of these other liabilities: deferred income taxes, pension liabilities, and liabilities for other post-retirement benefits. Actually, either of these types of items can result in the creation of assets, particularly deferred taxes. It is typical, however, to discuss these items in the context of liabilities.

A. ACCOUNTING FOR INCOME TAXES

The principal accounting issues related to income taxes arise from the fact that the rules for determining income for income tax purposes are different from the rules of GAAP used in determining income tax for financial reporting. There are two types of differences. "Temporary differences" arise when a particular item of income or expense is taken into account in determining financial or book income in a different period from the period in which the item is taken into account in determining taxable income. Permanent differences arise because some items that are income for one purpose are never treated as income for the other purpose and similarly some items that are deducted as expenses for one purpose are never deducted as expenses for the other purpose.

1. Temporary Differences

Temporary differences cause book income and taxable income to be different temporarily. This difference will reverse at some future time. Temporary differences create a need to recognize deferred tax liabilities or deferred tax assets. To illustrate the concept of deferred tax liabilities or assets, assume a tax rate of 40% applies to a business. This business lasts for two years. Because of temporary differences (unspecified for now), its book income and taxable income for the two years are as follows:

Year	Book Income	Taxable Income
1	$200	$150
2	$150	$200

If this business were to report its actual tax liability each year as its income tax expense for book purposes, its tax expense for year 1 would be $60 ($150 x 40%). Its income tax expense as a percentage of book income for year 1 would be 30% ($60 divided by $200). In year 2, the actual tax liability will be $80 $200 x 40%). If this amount is reported as income tax expense on the books, the tax expense as a percentage of book income would be 53.3%.

In this situation, GAAP requires the creation of a deferred tax liability in year one. Essentially, the business identifies the $50 difference between book income and taxable income as a temporary difference. The business therefore computes the tax that will be paid in the future when the temporary difference reverses. This will be $20 if the 40% tax rate will still apply. In year 1, this future tax of $20 is included in determining income tax expense. The entry to record income tax expense would be:

Income Tax Expense	$80	
Income Tax Payable		$60
Deferred Income Taxes		$20

The difference between the two tax liability accounts is that the income taxes payable is an amount actually due to the taxing authority based on taxable income for year 1. The deferred income tax liability is an additional liability recognized for financial reporting purposes only to reflect the effect of the $50 temporary difference.

In the following year, the temporary difference reverses. The actual tax liability to the taxing authority at the end of year 2 is $80. Of this amount $20 was already recognized as expense on the books in year 1. The entry to record tax expense in year 2 will be:

Deferred Income Taxes	$20	
Income Tax Expense	$60	
Income Taxes Payable		$80

In effect, the accounting for deferred taxes permits the business to allocate its tax liability as expense to each accounting period in a manner that reflects the book income from a timing perspective. If the relationship between book and taxable income had been reversed with taxable income greater than book income in year 1, the same procedure would have recognized a deferred tax asset in year 1 that would then be reversed in year 2.

a. Types of Temporary Differences

There are four basic categories of temporary differences in determining the accounting for deferred income taxes.

- Some items of revenue are included in book income in a period prior to the period that they are included in determining taxable income. An example would be a sale that is eligible for installment reporting for tax purposes. The entire gain from the same sale may be included in book income at the time of the sale even though the gain is reported in installments for tax purposes.

- Some items are included in determining taxable income in a period prior to the period that they are included in determining book income. An example would be prepaid rent. Prepaid rent is normally reported as income for tax purposes at the time of receipt by the lessor. For book purposes, however, the lessor would normally report the prepaid rent as deferred revenue and would not include it in book income until the period to which the rent relates.

- Some expense items are deducted in determining taxable income in an earlier period that they are deducted in determining book income. The primary example of this type of item is depreciation. Companies normally elect statutorily approved short lives and use accelerated methods in computing their depreciation for tax purposes. For book purposes, they use longer useful lives and more frequently use straight line methods in computing their depreciation expense. The result is that depreciation is deducted faster for tax purposes than for book purposes.

- Some expense items are deducted for book purposes before they are deducted for tax purposes. Businesses that sell products subject to warranties will normally accrue an expense for expected warranty costs at the time of the sale. For tax purposes, however, no deduction is allowed until the warranty costs are actually incurred. The result is that the warranty expenses are deducted earlier for book purposes than they are for tax purposes.

b. *Deferred Tax Liabilities*

When a business has taxable income that is less than its book income, the government is in effect allowing the business to defer a portion of its income tax expense to a later period. For example, assume that a business has book income of $500 but has taxable income of $400. The $100 difference is attributable to the fact that depreciation for tax purposes is $100 greater than depreciation for book purposes. If the income tax rate is 30%, the actual tax liability for the year will be $120 (30% of $400). If the business were required to pay tax on its book income, its tax liability would be $150 (30% of $500). In some future period or periods, the company's book income will be $100 less than its taxable income because the tax depreciation will be less than the book depreciation. Thus, the company is deferring $30 of income tax to some future period.

In the foregoing example, the business would have two components to its income tax expense on its financial statements. One component would be the actual liability of $120 that is currently owed to the government. The other component would be the liability related to deferring $30 of tax that will be due when the depreciation for tax purposes is less than the depreciation for book purposes. If the tax rate is expected to be 30% when the reversal related to depreciation occurs, the deferred portion of the income tax expense for the year would be $30. Therefore, the entry to record the income tax expense for the current year would be:

Income Tax Expense	$150	
Income Taxes Payable		$120
Deferred Income Tax Liability		$ 30

In a subsequent year when the depreciation reverses, the company will reverse the deferred income tax liability, which will have the effect of reporting income tax expense less than the actual tax liability for the year. If the actual tax liability for the year in which the reversal occurs is $100, the entry for income tax expense would be:

Income Tax Expense	$70	
Deferred Income Tax Liability	$30	
Income Taxes Payable		$100

c. *Deferred Tax Assets*

When taxable income is greater than book income because of a temporary difference, the company is in effect prepaying to the government a portion of its tax. Assume for example that a business has $800 of taxable income but only $750 of book income. The reason for this difference is that the business has prepaid rental income at the end of the year of $50. This prepaid rent must be included in taxable income in the year received but will not be included in book income until the subsequent year in which it is earned. The actual tax liability of the business for the year will be $240 (30% of $800). In the subsequent year, the taxable income of the business will be $50 less than book income because the $50 of prepaid rent will be reported in book income but will already have been included in taxable income. Accordingly, of the total current tax liability of $240, $15 is treated as a prepayment of taxes on income of the next year. To record the income tax expense in this situation, the following entry would be made:

Income Tax Expense	$225	
Deferred Tax Asset	$ 15	
Income Taxes Payable		$240

Thus, $15 of the $240 actual tax liability for the year is not treated as an expense of the current period but is treated as a prepayment of tax liability related to a future period. If the actual tax liability for the following year is $200, the income tax expense will be this amount plus the reversal of the deferred tax asset reported in the prior year. The income tax expense would be recorded as follows:

Income Tax Expense	$215	
Deferred Tax Asset		$ 15
Income Taxes Payable		$200

Generally, as illustrated in the foregoing examples, the income tax expense for the year is the actual taxes payable for the year plus or minus the change in deferred tax liabilities and deferred tax assets for the year.

d. Analysis of Deferred Taxes

The deferred tax liabilities and deferred tax assets are merely accounting deferral techniques used to match income tax expense with the related book income. A deferred tax liability does not represent a present obligation to make a future payment to any governmental agency. Whether any liability to the government will exist in the future depends on the future taxable income of the business. Similarly, a deferred tax asset does not represent a present right to receive a future tax refund from any government. Further, deferred tax assets and deferred tax liabilities can become very substantial in amount as they accumulate over time. Take, for example, a growing capital-intensive business. Each year, the business adds new equipment and other depreciable property eligible for the accelerated tax depreciation that causes deferred tax liabilities to arise. While the book depreciation on older assets may exceed the tax depreciation on those assets and such reversals would lead to a reduction in the deferred tax liabilities, the addition of new assets requires additional amounts in the deferred tax liability account thus causing that account to grow larger and larger every year.

Because of this tendency for cumulative deferred taxes to grow from year to year, some users of financial statements may be more interested in the actual cash tax liabilities of the business. Financial analysts will often "adjust" the financial statements to remove the effects of the deferred taxes before they perform their analysis of the financial statements. General users of financial statements should simply keep in mind the fact that the deferred tax amounts are different in nature from actual tax liabilities.

e. Multiple Period Effects

The actual computations and accounting for deferred taxes becomes quite complex. Even in the simple situation described above with only the depreciation and prepaid rent, additional analysis is necessary before the amount to be recorded as deferred tax assets and liabilities can be determined. Technically, the pattern of reversal of temporary differences must be examined to determine how much of a deferred tax liability or deferred tax asset should be created. Continuing the example from above, assume that the book and tax depreciation will be as follows over the life of the asset:

	Year 1	Year 2	Year 3	Year 4
Book Depreciation	$100	$100	$100	$100
Tax Depreciation	$200	$100	$ 50	$ 50
Difference	($100)	$ 0	$ 50	$ 50

The prepaid rent of $50 in year 1 will reverse in year 2. Book income for year 1 is $500 and taxable income for year 1 is $450.

Because the tax depreciation in year 1 exceeds the book depreciation by $100, there is a future "taxable amount" of $100, that is, in future periods, the reversal of the depreciation effect will result in taxable income in excess of book income of $100. In this case, the reversal will occur in two increments of $50 each in years 3 and 4. If the tax rate is expected to remain at 30% in future years, the deferred tax liability associated with the depreciation would be $30. Assume, however, that there is an enacted change in the applicable tax rate to 40% that will become effective in Year 4. In that case, the deferred tax liability would be $35 (30% of the $50 reversal in year 3 and 40% of the $50 reversal in year 4).

With respect to the deferred tax asset, the $50 of prepaid rent included in taxable income in year 1 creates a future "deductible amount" in year 2. As a result of the reversal of the prepaid rent, taxable income will be $50 less than book income in year 2.

If there were a taxable amount in year 2 attributable to temporary differences and if that amount were at least $50, then the $50 reversal of the prepaid rent would be treated as an amount that would be deducted in year 2 and the deferred tax asset would be measured at the tax rate expected to be in effect in year 2. In this case, there is no taxable amount from temporary differences expected in year 2. The accounting rules would then say that the $50 deductible amount in year 2 would be available as a carryback to year 1 (assuming that the tax law allows carrybacks of net operating losses, as is the case in the U.S.) and the deferred tax asset would be measured using the year 1 tax rate of 30%. Thus, the deferred tax asset would be $15.

If the deferred tax liability is $35, the deferred tax asset is $15, and the current year actual tax liability is $135 ($450 x 30%), the tax expense for the year for financial reporting purposes would be $155 and would be recorded as follows:

Income Tax Expense	$155	
Deferred Tax Asset	$ 15	
Deferred Tax Liability		$ 35
Income Taxes Payable		$135

If the prepaid rent included in determining taxable income in year 1 were $500, only $450 (the taxable income in year 1) of the deductible amount in year 2 could be carried back to year 1. In this case, the other $50 would be carried forward to year 3. The amount of the deferred tax asset would be $150 ($450 x 30% plus $50 x 30%) assuming that the tax rate is still expected to be 30% in year 3.

2. Net Operating Losses

A net operating loss for a corporation arises when the expenses deductible for tax purposes in the current year exceed the taxable income for the current year. In the United States, a net operating loss can be carried back to the three years preceding the loss year. If the corporation has taxable income in any of those years, the corporation may deduct the net operating loss and recompute its liability. The reduction in tax is refunded to the corporation. Since the refund from a carryback can be determined when the loss arises, the refund associated with a net operating loss carryback is normally recorded immediately. If a corporation has a net operating loss of $100 that can be carried back to produce a refund of $30, the following entry would be made:

Income Tax Refund Receivable	$30	
Tax Benefit From Loss		$30

A net operating loss can also be carried forward for fifteen years. A carryforward results when the net operating loss cannot be fully utilized in the carryback period. A carryforward represents a potential future reduction in tax liability.

Actual net operating loss carryforwards of a corporation are treated in a manner similar to temporary differences that create future deductible amounts (like the prepaid rent in the example above). The corporation determines the future period in which the net operating losses will be utilized and determines the applicable tax rates in those future periods. The amount of the loss to be utilized in a year times the expected tax rate for that year gives the deferred tax asset to be recognized in connection with the net operating loss. As a general rule, a corporation cannot assume the existence of future book or taxable income. In determining when the loss carryforward will be utilized, the corporation can take into account future taxable amounts created by temporary differences such as accelerated depreciation. Thus, at a minimum, the net operating loss carryforwards can be used to offset what would otherwise be deferred tax liabilities. To illustrate, assume that a corporation has a net operating loss for 1 year in the amount of $200. The book loss before tax is also $200. The corporation determines that the loss can be utilized in year 2 when the tax rate will be 35%. The corporation would recognized a tax benefit of $70 (35% of $200) and would record a deferred tax asset in this amount. The entry would be:

Deferred Tax Asset	$70	
Income Tax Benefit from Loss Carry-back		$70

3. Valuation Allowances on Deferred Tax Assets

A further analysis must be made before recording a deferred tax asset related to temporary differences that create future deductible amounts or net operating loss carryforwards. If there is uncertainty about whether the tax benefit associated with a deferred tax asset will actually be realized, a "valuation allowance" must be established in connection with the deferred tax asset. A valuation allowance is a mechanism for reducing the amount of the deferred tax asset to be recognized. In determining whether a valuation allowance may be necessary, a determination is first made about whether there are future taxable amounts created by existing temporary differences that have resulted in the creation of deferred tax liabilities. If these future taxable amounts are equal to or greater than the future deductible amounts resulting from temporary differences or net operating losses that will be available within the applicable carryforward periods, a deferred tax asset may be recorded for the net operating losses and future deductible amounts without any valuation allowance.

If the future taxable amounts used in computing deferred tax liabilities are not sufficient to cover the future deductible amounts, the corporation may consider the availability of "tax planning strategies" that are feasible and could be used to create future taxable amounts as necessary to utilize future deductible amounts. An example of a tax-planning strategy would be the sale and leaseback of an asset that has a tax basis that is lower than the current book value of the asset. By assuming a sale of this asset at its book value, the business would create a future taxable amount that could be used to claim the benefit of a future deductible amount such as a net operating loss carryforward. If these two sources are insufficient to assure full utilization of the future deductible amounts, certain businesses can assess the likelihood of generating future taxable income on the basis of past earnings records. After all of these facts and circumstances have been considered, a determination must be made as to how much of the deferred tax asset will "probably" be realized. Probably for this purpose is measured by a more likely than not standard. A valuation allowance must be established to reduce the deferred tax asset to the amount that will probably be realized. The valuation allowance also effects the amount of tax benefit included in the income statement.

4. Reporting Deferred Tax Liabilities and Assets in the Balance Sheet

Deferred tax liabilities and deferred tax assets are each classified as current or noncurrent. The classification as current or noncurrent is based on the classification of the asset or liability to which the deferred taxes relate. For example, a deferred tax liability resulting from depreciation on fixed assets is treated as a noncurrent deferred tax liability because the fixed assets are noncurrent. A deferred tax asset caused by prepaid rental income would be classified as current because the prepaid rent is most likely current. If the deferred tax asset or liability does not relate to any specific asset or liability, the classification of the deferred tax item is based on when the future taxable amounts, in the case of deferred tax liabilities, and future deductible amounts, in the case of deferred tax assets, will be reversed.

The current deferred tax assets and deferred tax liabilities are netted and the net amount is reported as a current liability or current asset. Similarly, the noncurrent deferred tax assets and deferred tax liabilities are netted and the resulting net amount is reported as a noncurrent deferred tax asset or liability.

To illustrate, assume that a corporation has analyzed its deferred tax assets and liabilities as follows:

When Realized	Deferred Tax Assets	Deferred Tax Liabilities
Within the Next Year (Current)	$200	$150
More Than One Year Out (Noncurrent)	$350	$600

There is a net current deferred tax asset of $50 ($200–$150). The corporation would report a current deferred tax asset of $50. In addition, there is a net noncurrent deferred tax liability of $250 ($600–$350). The corporation would report a noncurrent deferred tax liability of $250.

5. Intraperiod Tax Allocation

Temporary differences and net operating losses result in *inter*period tax allocation issues. In addition, there is a need to make *intra*period allocations of tax in some cases. The need for intraperiod tax allocation exists where a business must disclose certain amounts separately in the income statement such as extraordinary items, effects of changes in accounting principles, or amounts attributable to disposals of business segments (see Chapter 17). This issue also arises where there is a prior period adjustment recorded directly to retained earnings or where gains and losses are recorded directly in stockholders' equity and are not included in income (e.g., unrecognized gains and losses on marketable securities treated as available for sale as discussed in Chapter 9). In each of these cases, the separate component of net income or the direct entry to stockholders' equity must be reported net of any related tax effect and the business must show on the income statement the amount of tax expense attributable to income before any of the separately reported amounts described above. The amount of tax expense for each of the separately stated amounts (including both actual taxes and deferred tax effects) would be computed by determining the amount of tax expense with and without the particular item. The difference between these two calculations would be the tax expense attributable to the separate item.

To illustrate, assume that a company has pre-tax book income before extraordinary items of $500,000 and an extraordinary loss of $100,000. The company's total tax expense for the year is $150,000. If the extraordinary loss did not exist, the company's tax expense for the year would be $175,000. Therefore, the tax benefit attributable to the extraordinary loss is $25,000 (that is, the tax expense for the year has been reduced by $25,000 as a result of the extraordinary loss). The bottom portion of the income statement would appear as follows:

Income Before Income Tax and Extraordinary Items	$500,000
Less: Income Tax Expense	(175,000)
Income Before Extraordinary Items	325,000
Extraordinary Loss (Net of Tax Benefit of $25,-000)	(75,000)
Net Income	$250,000

Thus, the total tax expense for the year has been allocated between the income before extraordinary items and the extraordinary loss. Similar allocations would be made for any other items computed separately from the income before extraordinary items.

6. Permanent Tax Differences

Another issue that arises in the area of income tax accounting is the effect of "permanent differences." Some differences between the calculation of book income and taxable income are not just timing differences but are permanent. For example, municipal bond interest would be included in book income but may be eligible for permanent exclusion from taxable income. With respect to expenses, the federal tax law disallows any tax deduction for 50% of business meals and entertainment even though the full amount of such expenses are deducted in computing book income.

Permanent differences do not present accounting issues but basically raise disclosure issues. No deferred tax assets or deferred tax liabilities arise from permanent differences.

Financial statement users know generally what the corporate tax rate is and are interested in knowing why the tax rate calculated from the income statement differs from that "statutory rate." Information about permanent differences is generally disclosed in the footnotes to the financial statements. Public enterprises are required to include in their footnotes a reconciliation between the statutory tax rate and the effective tax rate actually applicable to the enterprise.

To illustrate, assume that a business has book income of $60,000. Included in this amount are $15,000 of municipal bond interest and an expense that is not deductible for tax purposes in the amount of $5,000. Assuming no temporary differences and a statutory tax rate of 40%, taxable income would be $50,000 and the tax expense for the year would be $20,000. As a percentage of pre-tax book income, this tax expense of $20,000 would be 33-⅓%. The reconciliation of the company's actual tax rate to the statutory tax rate would be as follows:

Income Tax Expense as a Percentage of Pre-Tax Book Income	33-⅓%
Exclusion of Municipal Bond Interest	10%
Nondeductible Business Expense	(3-⅓%)
Statutory Tax Rate	40%

In addition to the foregoing, other disclosures about the components of income tax expense for the year and the significant temporary differences would be included in the footnotes to the financial statements.

B. ACCOUNTING FOR RETIREMENT PLANS

Another significant obligation for many businesses is the obligation associated with retirement plans. As will be discussed below, the obligation of the employer company may result in the recognition of an asset, a liability, or neither depending on the funding policies and the measurement of pension expense. Retirement plans or pensions represent a major obligation in the general sense of many businesses particularly if the businesses have a so-called defined benefit type of retirement plan in which the employees are to receive an amount at retirement that is based on a formula that takes into account such factors as compensation level, years of service, and age at retirement.

1. Defined Contribution Plans

In analyzing the financial accounting for retirement plans, an important distinction exists between defined benefit plans and defined contribution plans. Defined contribution plans are designed so that the employer's undertaking is to make a certain contribution on behalf of the covered employees each year. The amount of the contribution is based on a formula that may involve a simple percentage of the employees' base compensation for the year or may have contingent elements dependent on company performance for the year. The key aspect of a defined contribution plan is that the actual retirement benefits that will be received by the employees are based on the contributions made and on the investment performance realized by the trust or other entity that holds the funds. The employer does not promise that the defined contribution plan will provide any particular level of benefits to the employees at the time of retirement. Frequently, defined contribution plans give the employees the option of determining the types of investments in which their accounts should be invested. The employer does not assume any responsibility for the investment performance or the amount of the ultimate retirement benefits received by the employees.

In the case of the defined contribution plan, the employer's obligation each year is limited to the contractually required contributions for the year. If the employer makes the contributions in a timely manner as required, the basic entry would be as follows (assuming a required contribution for the year of $100,000):

Compensation Expense—Retirement
    Plans $100,000
      Cash $100,000

Note that the assets of the retirement plan are not carried on the books of the employer. The assets are normally held in trusts set up for the benefit of the employees. The only time any amount would appear on the balance sheet in connection with a defined contribution plan is when the employer makes contributions in excess of, or less than, the amount required to be made under the terms of the plan. If the employer has not made all of its required contribution by the end of the year, the employer would record a liability for the amount not contributed and this liability would be included in the current liability section of the balance sheet (assuming that it is due with the following year). Assume, for example, that an employer only makes $50,000 of a $100,000 required contribution by year-end. The entry would be as follows:

```
Compensation Expense—Retirement
      Plans                             $100,000
   Cash                                            $50,000
   Accrued Liability—Retirement Plans             $50,000
```

In some cases, an employer may prepay an amount of contributions not due to a defined contribution plan until a subsequent year, in which case a prepaid asset would be created and reported in the balance sheet. If, for example, the current year's required contribution is $100,000 but the employer decides to make an additional contribution of $25,-000 as an advance against the subsequent year's required contribution, the entry to record the contribution would be:

```
Compensation Expense—Retirement
      Plans                             $100,000
Prepaid Compensation Expense—Re-
      tirement Plan                     $ 25,000
   Cash                                           $125,000
```

2. Defined Benefit Plans

In a defined benefit plan, the employer's obligation is defined in terms of an amount of benefits that will be paid to the employees upon their retirement. The benefits to be paid to each employee will be based on a formula that usually takes into account the years of service rendered by the employee, the employee's pay level, and the employee's age at retirement. Each year an actuary looks at the terms of the defined benefit formula, the make-up of the employer's work force, the likely investment gains and losses, and other factors and makes an "actuarial determination" of how much the employer needs to set aside each year to make available to retirees the defined benefits as they come due under the plan. The determination of the future benefits and the amount that will be necessary to provide their benefits is actuarial in that it reflects a number of facts that cannot be determined in advance. Some of the uncertainties include the characteristics of the employees who will actually be entitled to benefits upon retirement, the years of service that the retiring employees will have, the compensation levels that will be used to determine benefits, and the future investment performance of the trusts holding the assets set aside to pay retirement benefits. In general, the employer's obligation to provide the promised retirement benefits is fixed. If the actuarial assumptions are too "aggressive," the employer will be obligated to contribute the amount necessary to cover the shortfall. If the assumptions are too "conservative" and the contributions turn out to be excessive, there may be ways for the employer to recover these excess contributions.

a. Components of Pension Expense

Measuring the amount of compensation expense associated with defined benefit plans and the amount of liabilities or assets to be recorded in connection with defined benefit plans is much more complicated than the related issues for defined contribution plans. The amount of pension expense related to a defined benefit plan for each year is the sum of six components.

(i) Current Service Cost. The current service cost for the year is the actuarial value of the pension benefits that are earned by the employees as a result of the services rendered by the employees during the current year and based on the benefit formula of the plan. This calculation is based on projections of the future earnings of the employees that will be used in computing the amount of their benefits. Various actuarial methods can be used to determine the amount of future benefits that are deemed earned by employees for their services rendered in the current year.

(ii) Interest Cost. The interest cost represents the increase in the amount of the total projected benefit obligation as of the beginning of the year because of the passage of time. The projected benefit obligation (or PBO) is the present value of the total benefits that have been earned by employees as of the date of the computation taking into account the expected future compensation levels of the employees. Interest cost must be added because the current service cost component and other components of the pension liability are computed using present values. As you get closer to the actual payment of benefits, the future pension liability increases because there is one less year in the present value calculations (one less year to earn a return on the pension funds prior to payout). Interest cost is computed by multiplying the projected benefit obligation as of the beginning of the year by the discount rate that is used by the actuary in computing the projected benefit obligation.

(iii) Amortization of Transition Cost. The next component of pension expense is the result of the initial adoption of the current rules regarding accounting for pension expense (FASB Statement No. 87). When the new rules were first applied by a company, the company measured its projected benefit obligation as of that date as well as the fair value of the plan assets on that date. The excess of the PBO over the plan assets (plus any previously recognized underfunded pension cost) was classified as the transition cost of adopting the new rules. This transition cost must be amortized and recognized as pension expense over the greater of (a) the average service period remaining for the employees expected to receive the transition cost benefits or (b) 15 years.

(iv) Prior Service Cost. Prior service cost is similar in nature to transition cost. It arises whenever an employer initially adopts a defined benefit plan or adopts changes in the benefit formulas under its defined benefit plan and applies those

changes retroactively. The actuarial value of the retroactive benefits is called prior service cost. The prior service cost is amortized and deducted as expense over the expected remaining service periods of the employees who will benefit from the prior service cost.

(v) Actuarial Gains and Losses. Many of the components of pension accounting are based on estimates. Over time, changes are made in these estimates. The estimates relate to the actuarial assumptions used in calculating the projected benefit obligation and also relate to the actual return on the plan assets as compared to the expected return on those assets. These gains and losses are not included in full in the determination of the pension expense for the year in which they occur. Each year the unamortized actuarial gains and losses from the prior period are added to the current actuarial gains and losses (changes in the actuarial assumptions or difference between expected return and actual returns). The resulting amount must be allocated over future periods in determining pension expense. There are alternative methods that can be used to compute the amortization amount including an amortization based on the average remaining service lives of the participants in the plan. No amortization of the unrecognized actuarial gain or loss is required if the amount of such gain or loss is not more than 10% of the greater of (a) the actual projected benefit obligation or (b) the fair value of the plan assets. If the unrecognized gain or loss is within this limit, it is simply carried over to the next period and reevaluated then. If the unrecognized gain or loss exceeds the permissible level, only the excess is subject to amortization.

(vi)   Expected Return on Plan Assets. The final
component of the pension cost calculation is the
expected return on the plan assets. This is the
investment return that is expected to be realized on
the plan's assets. The expected return is a reduction in the pension expense for the year. Note that
the expected return and not the actual return is
used in computing pension expense for the year.
The difference between the expected return and the
actual return on the plan's assets is one of the
components of the actuarial gains and losses that
are amortized as part of step v.

The sum of these six components is the pension
expense that will be recognized each year. A simplified example of the computation of total pension
expense will illustrate these concepts. Assume the
following.

a.   The projected benefit obligation at the begin-
     ning of the year is $5,000,000. The discount
     rate used in computing the PBO is 10%.

b.   The fair value of the plan assets at the begin-
     ning of the year is $4,000,000.

c.   The company's actuary advises that the ser-
     vice cost for the current year is $300,000.

d.   The expected return on the plan's assets for
     the year was $350,000 but the actual return
     was $400,000.

e.   Changes in various actuarial assumptions for
     the year produced a net gain of $50,000.
     There was no unrecognized net gain or loss at
     the beginning of the year.

f. The amortization of unrecognized prior service cost for the current year is $250,000.

The current service cost provided by the actuary is $300,000. The interest cost is the PBO as of the beginning of the year ($5,000,000) multiplied by the discount rate (10%), or $500,000. The amortization of prior service cost is $250,000. There is no unrecognized net gain or loss to be amortized for the current year. The foregoing expense components are reduced by the expected return on the plan assets of $350,000. The pension expense for the year is:

Service Cost	$300,000
Interest Cost	$500,000
Amortization of Prior Service Cost	$250,000
Expected Return	<$350,000>
	$700,000

Note that the difference between the expected return and the actual return and the other actuarial gains for the year are not included in determining pension expense for the year. These amounts may be subject to amortization in subsequent years.

b. Pension Assets and Liabilities

To the extent that the employer's actual funding of its pension obligations through transfers of assets to the trustee is different than the amount of pension expense recognized, an adjustment to a liability or asset will result. If, for example, the total pension expense for the year is $700,000 but the employer transfers $800,000 to the pension plan, the following entry would be made:

Pension Expense	$700,000	
Prepaid Pension Expense	$100,000	
Cash		$800,000

If the company funded only $600,000 for the current year, an accrued liability of $100,000 would be recognized.

As in the case of the defined contribution plan, the assets that have been transferred to the plan trustee are not reported on the employer's balance sheet. Similarly, as a general matter, the projected benefit obligation of the employer under the defined benefit plan is not reported in the liability section of the employer's balance sheet. An asset or a liability will arise only to the extent that the cumulative funding by the employer (contributions to the plan) exceeds or is less than the cumulative amount of pension expense reported by the employer.

c. *Minimum Liability*

In certain circumstances, however, the employer is required to recognize on its balance sheet a "minimum liability." In order to describe the minimum liability, it is necessary to first define an additional concept called the *accumulated benefit obligation*. The accumulated benefit obligation is similar to the projected benefit obligation in that it reflects the actuarial estimate of the benefits that will be paid under the pension that have been earned as of the date of the measurement. Unlike the projected benefit obligation, the accumulated benefit obligation is based on the current salary levels of the participants and not on the expected future salary levels of the participants. Therefore, the accumulated benefit obligation will be less than the projected benefit obligation.

If the accumulated benefit obligation exceeds the sum of the fair market value of the plan assets, plus any amount already recorded as accrued liability on account of the plan, and less any prepaid pension cost reported as a current asset, the employer must recognize an additional liability equal to this excess amount. Normally, the recognition of a liability of this type would also involve the recognition of an expense. However, the recognition of this minimum liability is primarily a method of disclosing the obligation. Accordingly, instead of recognizing an expense, the minimum liability is matched by the recognition of an intangible asset in the same amount.

Assume that as of the end of the year, a company has an ABO of $6,000,000, plan assets valued at $5,000,000, and unamortized prior service cost of $2,000,000. In addition, the company reports prepaid pension cost (a current asset) of $200,000. The minimum liability for the company is the excess of the ABO over the plan assets, or $1,000,000. Since the company has prepaid pension cost of $200,000, the additional liability that must be recorded is $1,200,000. Since this amount does not exceed the unamortized prior service cost, an offsetting intangible asset in the amount of $1,200,000 would also be recorded. The entry to record the minimum liability of $1,200,000 would be as follows:

Deferred Asset—Pension Obligations $1,200,000
  Additional Liability for Pension
    Obligations $1,200,000

In this case, there is no effect on the net assets of the employer since the asset equals the additional liability. If the intangible asset would exceed the amount of the unrecognized prior service cost (including any unrecognized transition cost component), this excess would not be included in the computation of the intangible asset. In that situation, the excess that can not be included in the intangible asset would be recorded as a direct reduction in stockholders' equity and would be reported as a separate component of stockholders' equity. Thus, this amount would still not result in any reduction of net income.

d. Disclosures

In addition to the accounting issues discussed above, GAAP requires that certain information amount retirement plans be included in the footnotes to the financial statements. The information that is required to be disclosed includes information about the plans including benefit formulas, information about the employer's funding policies with respect to the plans, detailed information about the amount of pension expense included in the determination of net income, and information about the plan assets, projected and accumulated benefit obligations, vested benefits, and any liabilities ore assets included in the balance sheet.

FASB Statement No. 88 provides additional information about accounting for retirement plans. That statement deals with settlements and curtailments of pension plans and accounting for the benefits resulting from a termination of a pension plan. The details of these rules are beyond the scope of this nutshell.

C. ACCOUNTING FOR OTHER POST–RETIREMENT BENEFITS

In addition to pension plans, many employers have agreements or plans under which the employers undertake to provide retired employees with other post-retirement benefits such as medical coverage or life insurance. Until recently, these other post-retirement benefits were accounted for solely on the pay-as-you-go method. No recognition of expense associated with the future obligations under these plans occurred until actual payment of benefits and there was no recording or even disclosure of the future liability associated with these plans.

FASB Statement No. 106 has adopted requirements to account for these arrangements on an accrual basis somewhat similar to the accounting for defined benefit pension plans. Accrual of the expense related to these plans will now occur over the service lives of the employees that are entitled to the benefits.

In the accounting for post-retirement benefits, the first step is to develop an estimate of the future

costs that will be associated with the post-retirement benefits. The estimate will be based on certain assumptions and on the use of actuarial procedures. The estimated cost of the post-retirement
benefits is then recognized as an expense over the
remaining service lives of the covered employees.
The cost to be recognized as an expense each year
has several components that are generally similar
but not identical to the components of pension
expense discussed in Section B. above. There is a
current service cost component, an interest component, the actual return on the plan assets, if any,
amortization of any unrecognized prior service cost
as the result of the creation of a plan or amendment
of a plan with retroactive qualification, a recognition of any gains or losses associated with the plan,
and an amortization of the amount of any unrecognized transition obligation or transition asset at the
time of the initial adoption of the accounting requirements of FASB Statement No. 106.

One significant difference between nonpension
post-retirement benefits on the one hand and pension benefits on the other hand is that the nonpension benefits are much less likely to be funded by
the employer prior to the actual payment of benefits. Thus, as the expense for the nonpension benefits is recognized, there is likely to a be a significant
liability reported in the balance sheet since there
are no plan assets to offset the liability.

With respect to the unrecognized transition obligation or asset at the time of the initial adoption of
FASB Statement No. 106, the employer may elect

one of two treatments for this amount. The amount may be amortized over the average remaining service lives of the covered employees, or twenty years if longer. Alternatively, the employer may elect to report the unrecognized transition amount as an expense or an income item immediately. The amount recognized would be treated as an amount attributable to a change in accounting principle and would be reported separately in the income statement (see Chapter 17).

In addition to the accounting issues discussed above, there is certain information that must be disclosed in the footnotes to the financial statements regarding the employer's post-retirement benefit plans. The terms of the plans are disclosed. The components of the amount recognized as expense for the year are disclosed. There is also discussion regarding the amount of any liabilities reported in the financial statements related to these benefit plans.

CHAPTER 13

ACCOUNTING FOR STOCK AND STOCKHOLDERS' EQUITY

For corporations, there are a number of accounting issues related to the owner's equity section of the balance sheet. Owners' equity in corporations is usually referred to as stockholders' equity. This chapter will discuss the principal accounting issues for stockholders' equity.

A. CONTRIBUTIONS TO CAPITAL

The first issue that arises in accounting for stockholders' equity is accounting for contributions to the capital of a corporation. A contribution to capital normally involves the issuance of stock by the corporation and the receipt of assets by the corporation. In order to review the accounting for contributions to capital, the principal accounts that are included in stockholders' equity must be introduced.

1. Contributed Capital Accounts

Historically, contributions to capital have been recorded in two stockholders' equity accounts. The issuance of common stock will be discussed first. When common stock is issued, an amount equal to the par value of the stock being issued is recorded in an account called "Common Stock." If the corporation has stock without par value, the amount of stated capital determined by the board of directors at the time of issuance is recorded in the Common Stock account.

The amount received for the stock being issued frequently exceeds its par or stated value. In that situation, the excess is recorded in an account that might be called "Contributed Capital in Excess of Par or Stated Value" or "Additional Paid-in-Capital." The latter title will be used in this discussion. Segregating the par or stated value is important only to the extent that the amount of par or stated value retains significance under the applicable state corporate law. If the applicable state corporate law has abandoned the distinction between par or stated value and additional capital in excess of par or stated value, all of the proceeds from the issuance of stock could be recorded in an account called "Contributed Capital." In all situations, it is important to distinguish the amount of contributed capital from the retained earnings of the corporation (to be discussed below). In this nutshell, it is assumed that the stock of the corporation has a par value and the separate recording of that amount will be used in the illustrations.

2. Issuing Stock for Cash

To illustrate a contribution to capital of cash, assume that a corporation has common stock with a par value of $1 per share. The corporation issues

100,000 shares of this common stock for cash in the amount of $10 per share. The entry to record this issuance of stock would be:

Cash	$1,000,000	
Common Stock		$100,000
Additional Paid-in-Capital		$900,000

Similar accounting applies to the issuance of preferred stock. The par or stated value of the preferred stock would be recorded in an account called "Preferred Stock." Any additional amount received for the stock would be recorded in an additional paid-in-capital account for the preferred. Thus, if 10,000 shares of $100 par value preferred stock are issued for $105 per share, the entry to record the issuance would be as follows:

Cash	$1,050,000	
Preferred Stock		$1,000,000
Additional Paid-in-Capital—Preferred		$ 50,000

3. Issuing Stock for Noncash Property

Stock may be issued in exchange for property other than cash. In that situation, the fair market value of the property received must be determined from market prices, if available, or by the board of directors with or without the assistance of a formal appraisal. Once the fair market value of the contributed property is determined, the accounting is the same as for cash contributions. Assume that land and a building are contributed to a corporation in exchange for 1,000,000 shares of $1 par value common stock. The land and building are determined to be worth $2,000,000 and $8,000,000, respectively. The entry to record the receipt of the land and building and the issuance of stock would be:

Land	$2,000,000	
Buildings	$8,000,000	
Common Stock		$1,000,000
Additional Paid-in-Capital		$9,000,000

4. Stock Subscriptions

The actual issuance of stock by a corporation is sometimes preceded by the prospective shareholder and the corporation entering into a stock subscription agreement. When a subscription agreement is executed, the corporation may choose to record the subscription agreement, assuming that the subscription represents a valid and enforceable contract between the corporation and the subscriber. To illustrate, assume that an individual has subscribed to the issuance of 50,000 shares of $1 par value common stock at a price of $20 per share. The entry to record the subscription would be as follows:

Stock Subscription Receivable	$1,000,000	
Common Stock—Subscribed		$ 50,000
Additional Paid-in-Capital		$950,000

Because of the potential legal significance of the par value of actually issued and outstanding stock, the par value at the time of the subscription is recorded in a separate account (Common Stock—Subscribed) to distinguish it from the par value of actually issued and outstanding stock. The subscriptions receivable account may be reported in one of two ways on the balance sheet. The subscription receivable may be treated as a contra stockholders' equity account, which would be shown as a deduction from the regular stockholders' equity accounts. This is the approach required by the SEC. Alternatively, the subscriptions receivable may be reported as an asset in the same manner as other receivables.

When the actual proceeds are received from the subscriber and the stock is issued, the following entry would be made:

Cash	$1,000,000	
Common Stock—Subscribed	$ 50,000	
Stock Subscription Receivable		$1,000,000
Common Stock		$ 50,000

This entry recognizes the collection of the receivable and reclassifies the par value from the separate account for subscribed stock to the regular common stock account.

5. Stock Issuance Costs

Corporations frequently incur costs in connection with the issuance of stock. These costs include the cost of printing stock certificates, the cost of legal services related to the issuance of stock, and the costs of registering the stock or complying with requirements for obtaining an exemption from the registration of the stock. Particularly in the case of a public offering of stock, these costs can be quite significant in amount. There are two ways in which stock issuance costs may be handled. One approach treats the costs of issuing stock as part of organization costs. These costs are initially record-ed as an asset (see Chapter 8). The costs are then amortized and reported as expense over a relatively short period, such as five years. This treatment of stock issuance costs is generally appropriate only for the stock issued in connection with the initial formation and organization of the corporation.

To illustrate, if stock issuance costs of $20,000 are incurred, the entry to record these costs as organization costs would be:

Organization Costs	$20,000	
Cash		$20,000

The amortization of these costs for the first year (assuming amortization over a five year period) would be $4,000. The entry to record the amortiza-tion would be:

Amortization Expense	$4,000	
Organization Costs		$4,000

The other approach is to treat the stock issuance costs as a reduction in the proceeds otherwise re-ceived for the stock. The net effect of this approach is usually to reduce the amount that is otherwise credited to additional paid-in-capital. Assume, for example, that a corporation issues 20,000 shares of $1 par value common stock for a price of $40 per share. The corporation incurs $20,000 of stock issuance costs. The $20,000 of costs would be net-

ted against the $800,000 received for the stock and
the entry would be:

Cash	$780,000	
Common Stock		$ 20,000
Additional Paid-in-Capital		$760,000

In comparing the two approaches, treating the
costs as organization costs initially results in greater stockholders' equity. When the organization
costs have been fully amortized, stockholders' equity will be the same in total but the allocation
between contributed capital and retained earnings
will be different.

B. ACCOUNTING FOR RETAINED EARNINGS

The third principal component of the stockholders' equity in a corporation is the account called
"Retained Earnings." This account includes the
accumulated net income of the corporation reduced
by dividends, other distributions to stockholders,
and certain miscellaneous items that are charged or
credited directly to retained earnings. If the balance in the retained earnings account is a negative
or debit balance (because the corporation has experienced losses), the account is usually called "Accumulated Deficit" in the balance sheet.

The entries made in the retained earnings account are quite limited. At the end of each year in
connection with the closing of the books, the net
income or loss for the year is transferred from the

temporary accounts to the retained earnings permanent account. If a corporation has net income for the year of $150,000 and the corporation used an "income summary" account to summarize the net income for the year, the entry to transfer the net income to retained earnings would be:

Income Summary	$150,000	
Retained Earnings		$150,000

Other entries to the retained earnings account will be illustrated in connection with the transactions giving rise to those entries.

C. ACCOUNTING FOR DIVIDENDS AND OTHER DISTRIBUTIONS

Corporations periodically make distributions to the stockholders of the corporations. The distributions are normally in the form of dividends. Dividends may be in the form of cash, property, or stock of the corporation making the distribution. This section will discuss the accounting for dividends and other forms of distributions.

1. Key Dates Related to Dividends

There are three dates that are important in connection with the declaration and payment of dividends. The "declaration date" is the date on which the board of directors authorizes the payment of a dividend. The "date of record" is the date on which the stockholder records are closed and the identities of the stockholders entitled to receive the dividends are determined. If A owns stock on the date of record and sells that stock the next day, A will still receive the dividend on the stock owned on the record date. (Actually, the right to receive dividends is terminated on the "ex dividend date," which occurs several days before the date of record and allows time for the corporation to enter stock transfers in the stock records before the date of record.) The third key date is the date of the actual payment of the dividend.

2. Cash Dividends

In the case of a cash dividend, the company becomes legally obligated to pay the dividend on the date of declaration. Accordingly, on the date of declaration, a liability is recognized by making the following entry (assuming a cash dividend to be paid in the amount of $200,000):

Dividends Declared	$200,000	
Dividends Payable		$200,000

This recognizes the legal obligation to pay the dividend. When the dividend is paid, the entry to record the payment would be:

Dividends Payable	$200,000	
Cash		$200,000

The dividends declared account is a temporary account in which the dividends for the year are recorded. At the end of the year, the amount in the dividends declared account would be transferred to, and deducted from, retained earnings. If the total amount in the dividends declared account at the end of the year were $1,000,000, the following entry would be made:

Retained Earnings	$1,000,000	
Dividends Declared		$1,000,000

This closes out the dividends declared account and reduces the retained earnings by the amount of the dividends for the year.

3. Property Dividends

A property dividend is recorded in the same manner as a cash dividend. On the date of declaration, the corporation will recognize any gain or loss on the property that is being distributed. Further changes in the market value of the property after the date of declaration are for the account of the shareholders who will be receiving the property. To illustrate, assume that a corporation declares a dividend payable in the form of shares of stock in another company. On the date of declaration, the stock to be distributed has a book value of $100,000 and a market value of $150,000. The first entry on the date of declaration would be:

Investment in Stock	$50,000	
Gain on Securities		$50,000

This entry increases the book value of the stock to be distributed to its current market value and recognizes the related gain. The next entry on the date of declaration records the dividend as follows:

| Dividends Declared | $150,000 | |
| Property Dividend Payable | | $150,000 |

On the date of payment, the following entry would be made:

| Property Dividend Payable | $150,000 | |
| Investment in Stock | | $150,000 |

4. Stock Dividends

A stock dividend is a dividend payable in the form of additional shares of stock of the corporation making the distribution. The accounting for a stock dividend depends on the number of shares being issued in relation to the currently outstanding shares. A "small" stock dividend is generally a dividend representing no more than 20–25% of the currently outstanding shares. Stock dividends of more than this amount are treated as large stock dividends.

All stock dividends are recorded by capitalizing a certain amount of retained earnings, *i.e.,* by transferring an amount from retained earnings to the appropriate contributed capital accounts. For a small stock dividend, the amount of retained earnings capitalized is the fair market value of the stock on the date of distribution. For a large stock dividend, the amount of retained earnings capitalized is limited to the par or stated value of the stock distributed. Because there is no legal liability associated with the declaration of a stock dividend, there is normally no entry made in the case of a stock dividend until the actual date of distribution.

To illustrate, assume that a corporation declares a stock dividend of 100,000 shares of $1 par value stock. If this represents a 10% stock dividend (a small stock dividend) and the market value of the stock immediately after distribution of the stock dividend is $100 per share, the following entry would be made:

Retained Earnings	$10,000,000	
Common Stock		$ 100,000
Additional Paid-in-Capital		$9,900,000

This entry transfers the fair market value of the stock distributed from retained earnings to contributed capital.

If, on the other hand, this stock dividend represented 40% of the outstanding stock (a large stock dividend), the entry on the date of issuance would be:

Retained Earnings	$100,000	
Common Stock		$100,000

This entry results in capitalization of the legally required amount (par value) and no more.

5. Distributions of Stock Rights

Corporations may distribute to their shareholders stock rights permitting the shareholders to purchase additional shares of the corporation's stock, typically at a price that is somewhat less than the current market price of the company's stock at the time of the distribution of the stock rights. When these rights are distributed, the issuing corporation does not make any entries in the financial records to assign any cost or other amount to the stock rights. If the rights are exercised and additional stock is issued, the corporation will record the issuance of the stock in the normal manner.

6. Stock Splits

Another form of distribution of stock to stockholders is a stock split. In a stock split, the company causes the existing stock to be divided into a greater number of shares. For example, a 2 for 1 stock split would result in each outstanding share being split into two shares thus doubling the number of shares of stock outstanding. A reverse stock split is similar except that the number of shares is reduced. Thus, a reverse stock split of .25 to 1 would result in a reduction in the outstanding shares and four of the pre-split shares would be necessary to equal one share after the reverse stock split.

Normally, a stock split or reverse stock split is accompanied by a corresponding change in the par or stated value per share so that there is no change in the various components of stockholders' equity as a result of the split. Thus, a 2 for 1 stock split would normally be accompanied by a 50% reduction in the par or stated value per share of the stock and there would be no change in the total par value of the stock. In this situation, the corporate records need to be revised to reflect the changes in the number of shares and the par value per share but the amounts in the various stockholders' equity accounts are unchanged.

If the par or stated value is not changed in proportion to the stock split, an adjustment to the common stock accounts would be necessary. Assume, for example, that a corporation has 300,000 shares of $1 par value common stock outstanding. The stock is split 2 for 1 but there is no change in the par value per share of the stock. This would necessitate a transfer of $300,000 from additional paid-in-capital (or from retained earnings if there is not sufficient additional paid-in-capital) to the common stock account because the aggregate par value of the outstanding stock has been increased by $300,000. The entry would be as follows:

Additional Paid-in-Capital $300,000
    Common Stock $300,000

D. OTHER ADJUSTMENTS TO RETAINED EARNINGS

1. Prior Period Adjustments

Certain items called prior period adjustments are recorded directly in retained earnings and are not included in the determination of net income or loss. These prior period adjustments include the corrections of errors from prior years and the effects of certain changes in accounting principles. Appropriate entries are made to the affected asset and liability accounts and the net effect of the error or other item is debited or credited to retained earnings.

2. Appropriations

In some situations, a corporation may appropriate its retained earnings by transferring an amount from retained earnings to an account called appropriated retained earnings. There appropriations are solely for disclosure purposes. They do not create any legal restrictions on the retained earnings. It is not appropriate to record any expenses or losses directly to the appropriated retained earnings. When the appropriation is no longer necessary, it is transferred back to the general retained earnings.

E. ACCOUNTING FOR TREASURY STOCK

Another type of transaction that affects the stockholders' equity accounts is a corporation repurchasing its own outstanding stock. The stock repurchased is frequently called "treasury stock." The accounting for a corporation's repurchases of its own outstanding stock may be under one of two methods. These methods are the cost method and the par value method.

1. The Cost Method

When the cost method is used to record a purchase of treasury stock, the entire purchase price for the stock is debited to an account called "Treasury Stock." This account is a contra stockholders' equity account. It is shown as a deduction from the other components of stockholders' equity. To illustrate the cost method, assume that a corporation has 100,000 shares of common stock outstanding and that the stockholders' equity accounts are as follows:

Common Stock	$ 100,000
Additional Paid-in-Capital	$ 900,000
Retained Earnings	$1,500,000
	$2,500,000

The corporation repurchases 20,000 shares of its common stock at a price of $30 per share. The entry to record this purchase under the cost method would be:

Treasury Stock	$600,000	
Cash		$600,000

Immediately following this purchase, the stockholders' equity accounts would be reported in the balance sheet as follows:

Common Stock	$ 100,000
Additional Paid-in-Capital	$ 900,000
Retained Earnings	$1,500,000
Less: Treasury Stock	$ (600,000)
	$1,900,000

Once purchased, the treasury stock may be re-sold. Under the cost method, the purchase price of the shares that are now being resold would be removed from the treasury stock account. Any difference between the repurchase price and the subsequent sales price (a form of gain or loss) would not be included in determining net income for the year but would be entered directly in the stockholders' equity accounts. If the difference is a "gain," the excess would be credited to additional paid-in-capital. If the difference is a "loss," the difference would be debited to retained earnings or additional paid-in-capital if the loss exceeds the available retained earnings. To illustrate, if 10,000 of the treasury shares originally purchased for $30 per share are resold at a price of $35 per share, the entry to record the sale would be as follows:

Cash	$350,000	
Treasury Stock		$300,000
Additional Paid-in-Capital		$ 50,000

If the 10,000 shares were resold for $25 per share (less than the purchase price of $30 share) the resale of the treasury stock would be recorded as follows:

Cash	$250,000	
Retained Earnings	$ 50,000	
Treasury Stock		$300,000

2. The Par Value Method

The alternative approach to accounting for treasury stock is the par value method. Under the par value method, the purchase of treasury shares is treated as a "retirement" of those shares. Accordingly, a pro rata portion of the purchase price is debited to each of the stockholders' equity accounts at the time of the purchase. Using the example from section D.1. above, there would be allocated to the 20,000 shares repurchased $20,000 from the common stock account ($1 per share), $180,000 of additional paid-in-capital (20% of $900,000), and $400,000 of retained earnings (the difference between the $600,000 purchase price and amounts allocated from the first two accounts). The entry to record the purchase would be:

Treasury Stock	$ 20,000	
Additional Paid-in-Capital	$180,000	
Retained Earnings	$400,000	
Cash		$600,000

The stockholders' equity accounts would be reported in the balance sheet at their reduced amounts reflecting the repurchase of the shares. The account called "Treasury Stock" used under the par value method is a contra account to the common stock account. This account is used in states where the treasury stock retains its status as legally issued stock and can be resold by the corporation free of some of the legal restrictions normally associated with an initial issuance of stock.

Under the par value method, a subsequent resale of the treasury stock would be recorded just like any other issuance of stock except that the par or stated value of the reissued stock would be credited to "treasury stock" rather than to "common stock."

A redemption of preferred stock pursuant to a call provision in the preferred stock certificate or as the result of an open market purchase would typically be accounted for using the par value method of accounting for purchases of treasury stock.

F. CONVERTIBLE STOCK

Corporations may issue convertible preferred stock. Convertible preferred stock is typically convertible into a fixed number of shares of the common stock of the issuing corporation. Even though the value of the convertible preferred stock could be allocated between the value of the preferred stock without conversion rights and the value of the conversion feature, no such allocation is made when the convertible preferred stock is issued. The entire proceeds of the issuance of the preferred stock are credited to the normal preferred stock accounts (Preferred Stock and Additional Paid-in-Capital, as necessary).

When a conversion occurs, there is no gain or loss recognized by the corporation. The carrying amount or book value of the preferred stock that is converted is transferred to the appropriate common stock accounts in the balance sheet. To illustrate, assume that 50,000 shares of $100 par convertible preferred stock are outstanding. These shares were issued at their par value. Pursuant to their terms, these shares are converted into 400,000 shares of $1 par value common stock when the market value of the common stock is $15 per share. The entry to record the conversion would be as follows:

Preferred Stock	$5,000,000	
Common Stock		$ 400,000
Additional Paid-in-Capital		$4,600,000

No gain or loss is recognized but the contributed capital associated with the preferred stock is now in the common stock accounts. In the unlikely event that the carrying amount of the preferred stock converted is less than the par value of the common stock issued on conversion, the excess par value would be recorded as a debit to (reduction of) the retained earnings of the corporation.

G. COMPENSATORY STOCK OPTIONS AND STOCK APPRECIATION RIGHTS

Corporations often issue stock options and other stock-based compensation rights to key employees of the corporation. This section will discuss the accounting rules for two commonly utilized stock compensation devices—stock options and stock appreciation rights.

1. Stock Options

Stock options issued to employees give the employees the right to acquire shares of stock of the issuing corporation at a fixed price stated in the option agreement for a fixed period of time also set forth in the option agreement. The option agreements may contain a variety of terms and conditions including vesting requirements under which the options only become exercisable after the passage of a stated period of time.

In accounting for stock-based compensation devices such as stock options, it is necessary to identify the "measurement date." The measurement date is the first date on which you know the number of shares awarded to an employee and the exercise price, if any, payable by the employee. The compensation expense, if any, that will be recognized is the excess of the value of the stock on the measurement date over the amount payable upon exercise by the employee. If compensation expense is required to be recognized, it is not necessarily recognized in full on the measurement date. The compensation expense is allocated over the vesting period (sometimes called the service period). If there is no vesting period, then the compensation expense is recognized immediately. If there is a vesting period associated with the stock compensation, the compensation expense is recognized over the vesting period.

To illustrate these accounting rules, we will use the terms of a typical stock option plan. It should be noted, however, that there are many variations possible on these basic illustrations. Assume that an employee is granted an option on January 1, 199x, to purchase 100 shares of the employer's $1 par value common stock. The option is exercisable immediately. The exercise price is $20 per share, which is also the market value of the stock on the date of grant. In this case, the measurement date is January 1, 199x. On that date, we know both the exercise price and the number of shares covered by the option. Since the exercise price is equal to the market value of the stock on the date of grant, there is no compensation expense to be recorded on the date of grant. On the date of exercise, the issuance of stock would be recorded in the normal manner. If this stock option were exercised in full, the entry on the date of exercise would be:

Cash	$2,000	
Common Stock		$ 100
Additional Paid-in-Capital		$1,900

If the option had been issued at an exercise price of $15 per share, compensation expense would have been recognized on the date of grant equal to $500, the difference between the fair market value of the stock on the date of grant and the exercise price ($5) multiplied by the number of shares (100). At the date of grant, the following entry would be recorded:

Stock Compensation Expense	$500	
Stock Options Outstanding		$500

Until exercise, the stock options outstanding account would be included as a component of stockholders' equity. At the date of exercise, the following entry would be made to reflect the receipt of cash, the transfer of the stock options outstanding amount to the regular stock accounts, and the issuance of shares:

Cash	$1,500	
Stock Options Outstanding	$ 500	
Common Stock		$ 100
Additional Paid-in-Capital		$1,900

If an option on which compensation expense has been recognized expires unexercised, there are at least two methods of accounting that can be used. The amount in the stock options outstanding account can be transferred to a permanent stockholders' equity account, such as additional paid-in-capital. If the option used in the example above lapsed unexercised, the entry would be:

Stock Options Outstanding	$500	
Additional Paid-in-Capital		$500

Alternatively, the amount previously recognized as compensation expense could be reversed and recorded as a reduction in compensation expense during the period of the lapse and some reasonable number of future periods. This alternative would result in the following entry on the date of lapse (assuming that all compensation expense is reversed in the year of lapse):

Stock Options Outstanding	$500	
Compensation Expense		$500

2. Stock Appreciation Rights

Stock appreciation rights award additional compensation to employees based on changes in the value of the employer's stock. When a stock appreciation right is granted to an employee, the starting value of the stock is determined. During the term of the stock appreciation right, the employee may elect to exercise the SAR. As in the case of stock options, there may be a vesting period during which the SAR cannot be exercised. Upon exercise, the employee is entitled to receive the difference between the starting value of the stock and the market value of the stock on the date of exercise. This difference may be payable to the employee in the form of cash, stock, or some combination.

The final measurement date for such an SAR is the date of exercise by the employee and that is the date that will finally fix the amount of compensation expense to be recognized. Prior to the exercise date, compensation expense will be recognized on an estimated basis reflecting the changes in the market value of the SAR. If there is a vesting period for the SAR, the compensation expense will be allocated to the entire vesting period.

To illustrate, assume that an employee receives SARs on January 1, 199x. The SARs provide that on the date of exercise, the employee will receive in cash an amount equal to the excess, if any, of the market price of 100 shares of the employer's common stock on the date of exercise over $20 per share. The SARs are not exercisable until December 31 of the following year (a two year vesting period). Compensation expense will be estimated until the actual date of exercise. Because of the vesting period, the compensation expense (based on the estimates) will be allocated over the two-year vesting period.

If the value of the common stock on December 31, 199x, is $26 per share, the value of the SARs on that date would be $600 ($26 minus $20 multiplied by 100 shares). At that date, one-half of the vesting period is completed so that one-half of the value of the SARs will be recognized as current expense and the other half will be deferred. The entry on December 31, 199x would be:

Compensation Expense—SARs	$300	
Deferred Compensation Expense—		
SARs	$300	
Stock Appreciation Rights Liability		$600

The Stock Appreciation Rights Liability is reported as a liability account if it is expected that the holder of the rights will elect to receive cash. If it is expected that the holder will elect to receive stock upon exercise, this account would be reported as part of stockholders' equity.

On December 31 of the following year, the value of the common stock is $28 per share. The total value of the SARs is now $800. Since the vesting period is now complete, the amount of compensation expense recognized will be the increase in the value of the SARs for the current year ($200) plus the compensation expense that was deferred in 199x ($300). The entry on December 31 would be:

Compensation Expense—SARs	$500	
Deferred Compensation Expense—		
SARs		$300
Stock Appreciation Rights Liability		$200

Compensation expense will continue to be recognized until the actual exercise of the SARs. Changes in the market value of the stock will be recognized by adjusting the compensation expense and the liability account for the SARs. Assume that on June 30 of the following year, the SARs are exercised when the stock value is $32 per share.

The total amount to be paid is $1,200. Of this amount, $800 has already been recognized as compensation expense so an additional $400 of expense is now recognized. The entry at the date of exercise would be:

Compensation Expense—SARs	$400	
Stock Appreciation Rights Liability	$800	
Cash		$1,200

3. Disclosures

When a company has stock-based compensation plans such as stock options or SARs, the company is required to disclose information in the footnotes to the financial statements about the plans. The information disclosed includes the number of shares granted under the plans for the current year and the total number of shares or rights outstanding, the exercise price under the plans, vesting requirements, and similar information.

CHAPTER 14

PARTNERSHIP ACCOUNTING

The partnership form of entity presents some unique accounting issues that do no exist with the corporation, which is the form of entity that is typically used to illustrate accounting for owner's equity. These differences are attributable primarily to the fact that a separate account is maintained for the owners' equity of each partner in the case of a partnership and the book value of each partner's interest in the partnership may vary from that of the other partners, even partners that have the same general percentage interest in the partnership. This chapter will review the key issues related to accounting for partnerships that differ from the accounting rules applicable to corporations.

A. CAPITAL ACCOUNTS

In the case of a partnership, a separate capital account is maintained for each partner. Each partner's capital account is used to record that partner's contributions to the partnership, that partner's share of income or loss, and any distributions made to the partner. This differs from the accounting for stockholders' equity of a corporation, which does not maintain a separate account for each shareholder in the corporation.

A partnership may use a single account for each partner's capital. That account may be called, for example, "Partner X, Capital Account." This capital account could be used to record all entries affecting the capital of the partner. Contributions by partners are credited to their capital accounts. Contributions of assets other than cash are recorded at their fair market values at the time of contribution.

To illustrate accounting for a contribution, assume that Partner X contributes $50,000 cash to the partnership. That contribution would be recorded as follows:

Cash	$50,000	
Partner X, Capital Account		$50,000

During the year, distributions could be recorded as reductions in this account and at the end of the year, the partner's share of income or loss would be recorded here. A distribution of $6,000 to the partner could be recorded as follows:

Partner X, Capital Account	$6,000	
Cash		$6,000

The allocation of $12,000 of income for the year to Partner X would be recorded as follows:

Income Summary Account	$12,000	
Partner X, Capital Account		$12,000

Alternatively, separate accounts could be used for each partner during the year to record income and loss and distributions during the year. For example, distributions during the year could be recorded in a "drawing account." At the end of the year, the debit balance in the drawing account would be deducted from the capital account by crediting the drawing account and debiting the capital account for each partner. Similarly, a separate account could be used to record the share of income or loss that accrues to the partner. If such separate accounts are maintained, each partner's capital in the partnership would be the total of the amounts in each of these accounts.

B. DEFINING A PARTNER'S INTEREST IN PROFITS AND LOSSES

Each partner in a partnership will have a defined interest in the profits and losses of the partnership. That interest could be a simple percentage of all profits and losses. It is possible, however, to have profit and loss sharing schemes that are more complicated than a simple percentage.

1. Allocating Individual Items of Income or Loss

Some partnerships provide that each partner has a different percentage interest in different items or components of income and loss. Thus, a partner might have a 20% interest in the net income or loss from the primary operations of the partnership but have a 30% interest in the gain or loss from the sale of certain assets of the partnership. Some partnerships provide that partners will have a different percentage interest in income of the partnership than they will in losses of the partnership.

2. Recognizing Different Forms of Partner Contributions

Partnerships may use more complicated schemes to allocate the income or loss of a partnership than a simple percentage allocation. These more complicated schemes are particularly useful when partners have different roles and make different types of contributions to the partnership. Three factors that are frequently used in determining how to allocate partnership income or loss are the time spent by partners in working on partnership business, the amount of capital contributed to the partnership, and a residual sharing interest.

This concept can best be illustrated with an example. Assume a partnership composed of three partners (A, B, and C). A contributes $10,000 to the partnership and B and C each contribute $45,-000 to the partnership. A will be working fulltime in the partnership but B and C will only be spending a modest amount of time on partnership affairs. The partners have agreed to split the overall profits and losses from the partnership on an equal basis (one-third to each) but they also want to take into account the different contributions of the partners.

a. Salary for Services

The first $30,000 of net income of the year is allocated to A because of A's work on behalf of the partnership. Note that under this arrangement, the partnership must have net income for the year in order for A to get an allocation of income for services. Alternative arrangements are possible if the desire is to guarantee to a service partner like A the receipt of compensation for services. A could be employed by the partnership in a true employee capacity and receive a salary from the partnership similar to that paid to nonpartner employees. Another alternative is to award to A a "guaranteed payment" that would be received by A in his or her capacity as a partner but that would be paid to A regardless of the amount of any net income in the partnership for the year. For partnership accounting purposes, such a guaranteed payment would be treated as an expense of the partnership in computing the residual net income or loss to be allocated to the partners.

b. Interest on Capital

The second allocation of income for the year could be an allocation of income to each partner in an amount equal to 8% of the partner's average capital account balance for the year. This would recognize each partner's differing contribution of capital for use in the partnership. As in the case of the initial allocation to A for services, this allocation would only be made to the extent that there is sufficient partnership income available (after the allocation of the first $30,000 of income to A). If it is desired to make this 8% interest-type allocation to the partners regardless of the income of the partnership for the year, two alternatives are possible. Part or all of the contributions from the partners could be structured as true loans to the partnership bearing 8% interest. Alternatively, a "guaranteed payment" could be made to the partners in their capacity as partners in an amount equal to the 8% desired return on their capital accounts. This guaranteed payment would be made regardless of the existence of income in the partnership.

c. *Residual Income and Loss Sharing Ratios*

Finally, the residual income or loss of the partnership would be allocated one-third each to A, B, and C. While the first two types of income sharing are optional, the partnership must always have a formula for allocating any residual income and loss.

To illustrate the application of this particular income allocation scheme, assume that the partnership has income of $200,000 for the year. In accordance with the allocation scheme set forth in B.2.a., b., and c., this income would be allocated as follows:

	A	B	C
First $30,000 to A	$30,000		
8% of Capital Account	800	$ 3,600	$ 3,600
Residual	54,000	54,000	54,000
Total	$84,800	$57,600	$57,600

The "8% of Capital Account" allocation was computed on the basis of the beginning capital account balances with no additional contributions or distributions occurring during the year. The entry to record the allocation of income for the year would be as follows:

Income Summary	$200,000	
Partner A, Capital		$84,800
Partner B, Capital		$57,600
Partner C, Capital		$57,600

C. ADMISSION OF NEW PARTNERS

The admission of new partners may raise accounting issues for partnerships that do not normally arise in the case of corporations. Admissions of partners may occur through the purchase by a new partner of the interests (part or all) of one or more existing partners or may occur through the new partner contributing new assets to the partnership.

To facilitate the discussion of these issues, the following hypothetical partnership will be used as the basis for illustrating the alternative accounting treatments available for the admission of new partners. The assumed partnership has two existing partners, E and F. Each partner has a capital account balance in the amount of $60,000 and they share in profits and losses in the ratio of 50% to each partner. G will be admitted as a new partner to the partnership.

1. Transfer of Partnership Interests

G could be admitted to the partnership by purchasing an interest from one or more of the current partners. Assume that G will be admitted to the partnership by purchasing one-half of F's interest in the partnership for $50,000. G will share in 25% of the income or loss of the partnership and F's share of income and loss will be reduced to 25%.

a. No Adjustments to Partnership Net Assets

On the partnership books, this transaction could be recorded by simply transferring the appropriate amount from F's capital to a new capital account for G. G's capital account would be 50% of the book value of F's capital account, or $30,000. The transfer would be recorded as follows:

Partner F, Capital	$30,000	
Partner G, Capital		$30,000

A similar approach would be followed if G acquired the interest in part from each of the partners.

b. Adjusting Partnership Net Assets

In the accounting illustrated in 1.a. above, no reference is made to the actual purchase price for the interest acquired by G. The partnership could, however, elect to recognize on its books the implied value of the partnership's net worth by adjusting the values of the partnership's net assets and the partners' capital accounts. G's purchase of a 25% interest in the partnership's net income and loss and capital for $50,000 implies that the total value of the partnership's capital is $200,000 ($50,000 / .25). In this illustration (and the other examples in this chapter) it is assumed that the adjustment to fair market value relates to goodwill. Since the book value of the partnership's net assets is presently $120,000, the implied goodwill is $80,000 ($200,000—$120,000). The partnership would recognize the goodwill by an entry as follows:

Goodwill	$80,000	
Partner E, Capital		$40,000
Partner F, Capital		$40,000

The goodwill is allocated among, and credited to the capital accounts of, the existing partners according to their ratio for sharing in partnership income. The transfer of 50% of F's capital account to G would now be recorded as follows:

Partner F, Capital	$50,000	
Partner G, Capital		$50,000

Note that G's capital account is now recorded on the books in the same amount as the amount paid by G to F for the partnership interest.

2. Contribution to the Partnership

A new partner may also be admitted to the partnership in return for a contribution of additional assets to the partnership. The amount required to be contributed by the new partner will frequently reflect the fair market value of the net assets of the partnership so that the new partner may be required to contribute an amount to the partnership that represents a premium over, or discount from, the amount that would be expected based on the current book values of the capital accounts. In the example involving the EF partnership, assume that G is now to be admitted to the partnership as a 25% partner in return for a contribution to the partnership of cash in the amount of $50,000. If G's contribution were simply combined with the current book value of the capital accounts of E and F, G would have a capital account equal to approximately 29.4% (50,000 / 170,000) of the total partnership capital following G's admission. There are three approaches to accounting for G's admission.

a. No Adjustment to Partnership Capital Accounts

Under one approach, no adjustment is made to the partnership's net assets or the partners' capital accounts. G's contribution is recorded in his or her capital account. Following G's admission, the capital accounts of the partners will not be in the same proportion as their interest in income and loss. Under this approach, the entry to record G's admission would be as follows:

Cash	$50,000	
Partner G, Capital		$50,000

Each partner's share of capital is based on the amount recorded in the capital account. The partnership agreement would provide that in the event of the liquidation of the partnership, distributions would be made to the partners on the basis of the their capital account balances so that G's disproportionately higher capital account would be honored at that time.

b. The Goodwill Method

Under a second approach, called the goodwill method, the partnership would record the goodwill (or revaluation of other partnership assets) implied by the amount that G contributes for an interest in the partnership. The computation of the goodwill proceeds as follows. Assume that when G contributes $50,000, G is to get a 25% interest in the capital of the partnership as well as a 25% interest in profits and losses. That implies that the total value of the partnership capital following G's admission should be $50,000 / .25, or $200,000. The existing capital of the partnership immediately prior to G's admission should be 75% of $200,000, or $150,000. The book value of the present capital accounts is only $120,000. The difference, or $30,-000 is the goodwill that must be recognized. This goodwill would be allocated among the current partners on the basis of the ratio in which they share income. Since E and F presently share income on a $^{50}/_{50}$ basis, each would be credited with 50% of the goodwill, or $15,000. The entry to record the goodwill and increase the existing partners' capital accounts would be as follows:

Goodwill	$30,000	
Partner E, Capital		$15,000
Partner F, Capital		$15,000

The entry to record the contribution of $50,000 by G would be:

Cash	$50,000	
Partner G, Capital		$50,000

The total capital of the partnership is now $200,-000. The foregoing example illustrates the situation where the existing partnership is determined to have unrecorded goodwill. In some cases, it may turn out that the goodwill is determined to be an unidentified additional asset being contributed by the new partner.

c. The Bonus Method

The partners may deal with the discrepancy between the amount of the capital being contributed by a new partner and the existing capital accounts under a third method called the bonus method. Under the bonus method of recording the admission of a new partner, it is assumed that the existing partnership assets are correctly valued on the partnership's books. The incoming partner is allocated his or her share of the total book value of the capital of the partnership including the contribution to be made by the new partner. If the amount so allocated to the new partner is less than the partner's actual contribution, the excess is allocated as a "bonus" to the existing partners. If the amount allocated to the new partner is more than the new partner's actual contribution, the difference is a bonus allocated form the capital accounts of the existing partners to the new partner.

In the example involving the EF partnership, the book value of the capital of the partnership following the contribution by G will be $170,000 ($120,-000 + $50,000). G's 25% share of this capital would be $42,500. Under the bonus method, this is the amount to be allocated to G's capital account. G is actually contributing $50,000 to the partnership. The difference of $7,500 is the bonus amount to be allocated to E and F in the proportion in which they share in income of the partnership. Each will therefore get credited with $3,750. The entry to record the admission of G using the bonus method would be as follows:

Cash	$50,000	
Partner E, Capital		$ 3,750
Partner F, Capital		$ 3,750
Partner G, Capital		$42,500

D. RETIREMENTS OF PARTNERS

Issues similar to those raised by the admission of new partners also may arise in connection with the retirement or withdrawal of a partner. If the retiring partner is entitled to receive the book value of the departing partner's capital account, the accounting for the retirement is simple. The distribution to the retiring partner would be debited to the partner's capital account, which would then have a zero balance.

If the retiring partner is entitled to receive the fair market value of his or her interest at the time of the retirement, accounting for the difference between that amount and the book value of the departing partner's capital account is necessary. The capital account of the retiring partner must be adjusted to the amount that will be distributed to the retiring partner. Once again, the goodwill and bonus methods are two approaches for dealing with this issue.

To illustrate accounting for the retirement of a partner, assume that there is a partnership called the RST partnership with three partners. The partners, the current balances in their capital accounts, and their income and loss sharing ratios are as follows:

R	$50,000	50%
S	$25,000	25%
T	$25,000	25%

T retires from the partnership. It is determined that T is entitled to a distribution from the partnership in the amount of $40,000.

1. Goodwill Method

Under the goodwill method, the partnership would determine the amount of the adjustment that should be made to the net assets of the partnership implied by the amount of the distribution to be made to the retiring partner. For ease of illustration, it will be assumed that all of this adjustment is to made to a single asset called goodwill. In this case, T should have a capital account equal to 25% of the total capital or net assets of the partnership. Since T will receive $40,000 in the distribution, T's capital account must be increased to $40,000. That implies that the total capital of the partnership should be $40,000 / .25, or $160,000. Since the current book value of the net assets is $100,000, the implied amount of goodwill is $60,000 ($160,000—$100,000). This goodwill is allocated to the partners in accordance with their income sharing ratios. The entry to record this goodwill would be:

Goodwill	$60,000	
Partner R, Capital		$30,000
Partner S, Capital		$15,000
Partner T, Capital		$15,000

T's capital account is now on the books in the amount of $40,000. The distribution to T can now be recorded as follows:

Partner T, Capital	$40,000	
Cash		$40,000

T's capital account is now reduced to zero as a result of the distribution. Without the allocation of goodwill, the distribution of $40,000 to T would have reduced T's capital account to a negative $15,-000.

2. Bonus Method

The alternative approach to dealing with the retiring partner is the bonus method. Under the bonus method, amounts in the capital accounts of the partners are reallocated among them in order to adjust the retiring partner's capital account to the amount to be distributed to the retiring partner. In this case, T's capital account must be increased by $15,000. If the book value of the net assets are to remain the same, this capital must come from the capital accounts of the other partners. The $15,000 will be charged against the capital accounts of the continuing partners in the ratio in which they share partnership losses. Since R and S share income and loss in a 2:1 ratio (50% for R and 25% for S), $10,000 will be charged to R's capital account and $5,000 will be charged to S's capital account. The entry would be as follows:

Partner R, Capital	$10,000	
Partner S, Capital	$ 5,000	
Partner T, Capital		$15,000

Under this approach, the net assets of the partnership have not been changed. Partner T's capital account is now $40,000 and the retirement distribution can be recorded:

Partner T, Capital	$40,000	
Cash		$40,000

The capital account for Partner T has now been reduced to zero.

CHAPTER 15

ACCOUNTING FOR BUSINESS COMBINATIONS

This chapter will discuss the financial accounting treatment of certain types of acquisitions referred to as "business combinations" in the relevant accounting literature. The accounting rules for business combinations are primarily set forth in two opinions issued by the Accounting Principles Board in 1970. Opinion No. 16 addressees the accounting rules for business combinations and Opinion No. 17 addresses the closely related issue of accounting for goodwill, an intangible asset that generally arises only in business combinations.

Under paragraph one of APB Opinion No. 16, a business combination occurs when a corporation and one or more incorporated or unincorporated businesses are brought together in one accounting entity. Thus, there generally must be an acquisition of sufficient assets (directly or indirectly by the purchase of stock) to constitute a separate business. An acquisition of a selected group of assets not constituting a separate business would not qualify as a business combination. A business combination may be structured as a purchase of assets, a purchase of stock, or a statutory merger or consolidation.

The rules for accounting for business combinations are not applicable to a transfer by a corporation of its net assets to a newly created corporate entity, nor does it apply to a transfer of assets among corporations under common control (*e.g.,* between a parent and its subsidiary or between two subsidiaries of a common parent corporation). The rules apply to an acquisition of the assets of an unrelated entity or to the acquisition of stock of an unrelated entity. All references to "acquisitions" in this chapter mean acquisitions that meet the definition of a business combination.

A. PURCHASE AND POOLING METHODS

1. Overview

When a business combination occurs, there are two alternative methods that are used to account for the business combination. One method is referred to as the purchase method or purchase accounting and the other method is the pooling of interests method or pooling.

Under purchase accounting, the accounting for the acquisition of a business is similar to any purchase of assets. The assets are recorded on the purchaser's books at their purchase price. To the extent that the purchaser's stock or some other type of noncash property is used as consideration for the acquisition, the purchase price of the assets will be based on the fair market value of the consideration being given or the fair market value of the acquired assets, whichever is more readily determinable. The book values of the assets and liabilities of the target are ignored. There is no carryover of any particular accounting attributes from the seller.

Where the pooling method applies, the accounting for the acquisition is significantly different from purchase accounting. In general, the purchaser carries over the book value of the assets and liabilities of the seller in recording those assets and liabilities on the financial records of the purchaser. As will be seen below, pooling accounting is only applicable where the purchaser's stock is used to acquire the assets. Certain accounting attributes are carried over from the seller to the purchaser. Most notably, the purchaser succeeds to the retained earnings of the seller. Even the target's income for the period prior to the acquisition is carried over and included with the income of the purchaser from its existing businesses.

2. Determining Which Method Applies

Because of the fundamentally different accounting under the purchase and pooling methods, APB Opinion No. 16 established specific criteria for when these accounting methods are to be used. The opinion sets forth the requirements for applying pooling accounting. If those requirements are satisfied, then the pooling method of accounting must be used. If the criteria are not met, the purchase method of accounting must be used. These accounting methods are not elective except to the extent that an acquisition can be structured to meet the requirements for one or the other method of accounting.

The following material will review the principal requirements for using the pooling of interests method of accounting. These requirements will not be discussed in detail but will be covered sufficiently to permit the lawyer to help structure business combinations and understand the significance of certain structuring issues and their effect on the accounting treatment.

a. Autonomy

The first requirement is that each of the parties to the acquisition must be autonomous and must not have been a subsidiary or division of another corporation within two years prior to the acquisition. Thus, if P wishes to acquire T, which is a subsidiary of S, the pooling method of accounting cannot be used because T would not meet the autonomy requirement (since it is a subsidiary of S). Pooling treatment would also not be available if the target T had been a subsidiary of S within the previous two years even if it had been spun off by S prior to the acquisition by P. The autonomy requirement does not preclude pooling accounting for a triangular acquisition in which P uses one of its subsidiaries to acquire T as long as the subsidiary uses stock of P to effect the acquisition.

b. Independence

The second requirement for pooling accounting is that each of the companies must be independent of the other company. The combining companies must not own more than 10% in total of the outstanding voting common stock of any combining company. Thus, if P has a preexisting ownership of 15% of the voting common stock of T at the time of the initiation of the acquisition, pooling treatment would not be available. (Initiation of a business combination occurs when the major terms of a proposed combination are made public or otherwise communicated to the shareholders of a combining company or when the shareholders of a combining company are notified in writing of an exchange offer for their stock in the combining company.)

c. Single Transaction

The acquisition must be completed in a single transaction or it must be completed pursuant to a specific plan within one year after the combination is initiated. The one year period may be extended where delays occur because of governmental agency proceedings or litigation.

d. Voting Common Stock as Consideration

The purchaser must acquire "substantially all" of the common stock of the target in exchange for common stock of the purchaser and the purchaser's common stock must have voting rights that are identical to the voting rights of the majority of the purchaser's outstanding voting stock. Substantially all means 90% or more. Thus, the purchaser could acquire 5% of the target's stock for cash or could leave a minority interest in the target as long as the purchaser holds at least 90% of the target's common stock as a result of issuance by the purchaser of its common stock. It is not permissible, however, to give to all of the target's shareholders on a pro rata basis a package consisting of 95% purchaser common stock and 5% cash. Determining compliance with this requirement is complicated where there are intercorporate investments by the purchaser and the target in each other's stock.

The purchaser may assume the outstanding debt securities of the target. Alternatively, the purchaser may issue substantially identical debt or equity securities (or voting common stock) in exchange for the target's debt and equity other than common stock. Cash may be distributed to holders of target debt and equity securities that are callable or redeemable.

Where the purchaser acquires the net assets of the target rather than its equity and debt, the target must transfer all of its net assets to the purchaser. The target may hold back cash, receivables, or marketable securities to satisfy liabilities, contingencies, or items in dispute as long as any remaining assets are to be transferred to the purchaser upon resolution of the contingencies. Only voting common stock may be issued by the purchaser unless the target has stock other than voting common stock outstanding, in which case the purchaser may issue voting common stock and other stock in the same proportions as the outstanding stock of the target.

e. No Equity Restructuring

Neither the purchaser nor the target may restructure its voting common stock either within two years before the initiation of the acquisition or between the date of initiation and consummation of the acquisition. Prohibited restructurings may, depending on the particular facts, include distributions to stockholders and issuances, exchanges, and retirements of securities. Normal dividend policy may be continued without violating this requirement.

f. Limitation on Treasury Stock

Neither of the parties may acquire shares of treasury stock for purposes of making the acquisition. Acquisitions of treasury stock for purposes of stock option or compensation plans or pursuant to regular repurchase programs may occur pursuant to preexisting systematic plans established at least two years before the initiation of the acquisition or in connection with the adoption of a new stock option or compensation plan.

g. Maintaining Shareholder Ratios

Shareholders of the target corporation must receive voting common stock of the purchaser in the same proportion as their holdings of common stock in the target.

h. Full Voting Rights

There may be no restrictions on the voting rights of the common stock in the combined corporation following the acquisition. Thus, the common stock issued to the shareholders of the target may not be placed in a voting trust or subjected to a voting agreement that deprives them of the free exercise of their voting rights.

i. No Contingencies

The acquisition must be fully resolved at the date of the consummation of the plan. There can be no provision for the future issuance of securities or other consideration to the shareholders. This requirement precludes earnout provisions in which the ultimate consideration to the target shareholders depends on the performance of the company following the acquisition. Nor may any of the shares be placed in an escrow arrangement pending the resolution of contingencies. It is possible, however, to provide for an adjustment in the consideration based on the final resolution of a contingency such as a lawsuit (*e.g.*, at an amount other than the amount recorded by the combining company at the time of the acquisition).

j. Absence of Planned Transactions

Certain types of post-acquisition transactions are prohibited. There can be no agreement to reacquire or retire any of the common stock issued in connection with the acquisition. The combined company may not enter into any financial arrangements that would have the effect of undermining the notion of an exchange of equity securities. An example would be for the combined company to arrange for the guarantee of loans to the target shareholders that are secured by stock received in the acquisition. There can be no plan to dispose of assets acquired in the combination except for dispositions of assets in the ordinary course of business or dispositions representing duplicate facilities or excess capacity.

As noted above, if all of these criteria are satisfied, then pooling treatment is required in accounting for the acquisition. If *any* of these criteria are not satisfied, then purchase accounting must be used.

3. Application of Purchase Accounting

If the purchase method of accounting is to be used, the acquiring company records the acquired net assets on the basis of their fair market values at the date of acquisition. (In illustrating the accounting for business combinations, I will assume an acquisition of assets of the target rather than an acquisition of the target's stock. The rules for acquisitions of stock are essentially the same but an acquisition of stock adds the additional complexity of application of the rules for consolidating a subsidiary, as discussed in Chapter 9.) The following balance sheets of the purchaser and the target will be used to illustrate both purchase accounting and pooling accounting.

Purchaser's Balance Sheet

Assets		Liabilities/Equity	
Current Assets	$ 40,000	Current Liabilities	$ 20,000
Fixed Assets	100,000	Long Term Debt	50,000
		Contributed Capital	30,000
		Retained Earnings	40,000
	$140,000		$140,000

The target's balance sheet and the fair market value of its assets and liabilities are as follows:

Target

	Book Value	Fair Market Value
Current Assets	$15,000	$15,000
Fixed Assets	60,000	80,000
Current Liabilities	10,000	10,000
Long Term Debt	20,000	20,000
Contributed Capital	10,000	
Retained Earnings	35,000	

Assume that the purchaser acquires the net assets of the target by issuing purchaser common stock to the target. The stock issued has a fair market value at the time of the acquisition of $80,-000. The acquisition is to be accounted for as a purchase.

a. Recording the Acquisition

In purchase accounting, the net assets of the target are to be recorded based on their fair market values at the date of acquisition. The first step is to determine the fair market value of the net assets being acquired. Each asset (including any "identifiable intangible assets" such as patents, trademarks, and copyrights) and each liability of the target must be reviewed to determine its fair market value as opposed to its book value on the date of acquisition. In this illustration, all target assets and liabilities are assumed to have a book value equal to fair market value except for the fixed assets, which have a fair market value that is $20,-000 greater than the book value of those assets.

The next step is to determine whether any goodwill results from the acquisition. In this case, the fair market value of the net identifiable assets is $65,000 ($95,000 less $30,000). The fair market value of the net identifiable assets is compared to the purchase price for the net assets. The purchase price in this illustration (the fair market value of the common stock being issued) is $80,000. The difference between these two amounts ($15,000) is "goodwill," or the excess of purchase price over the fair market value of the identifiable net assets. Goodwill is only recognized in an acquisition accounted for under the purchase method of accounting. It is the difference between the purchase price paid for a business and the fair market value of the identifiable net assets. Goodwill must be amortized and deducted as an expense of the business over its expected life, which may not be more than 40 years. The accounting rules for goodwill are set forth in APB Opinion No. 17.

Occasionally, "negative goodwill" may be created in an acquisition. This could occur where the fair market value of the consideration given in the acquisition is less than the fair market value of the identifiable net assets of the acquired business. The excess value of the net assets is treated as follows. The excess is first applied to reduce proportionately the fair values of the *noncurrent assets* of the acquired business. Long term investments in marketable securities are excluded from this write-down procedure. If the noncurrent assets are reduced to zero, any remaining excess is treated as negative goodwill. Negative goodwill is a deferred credit (reported in the liability section of the balance sheet). Following the acquisition, the negative goodwill is amortized over a period not to exceed forty years. This amortization results in an increase in net income (as compared to the amortization of positive goodwill, which reduces income).

Under the purchase method, the entry to record the acquisition on the purchaser's books would be as follows:

Current Assets	$15,000	
Fixed Assets	$80,000	
Goodwill	$15,000	
Current Liabilities		$10,000
Long Term Debt		$20,000
Contributed Capital		$80,000

The balance sheet of the purchaser immediately following this acquisition would appear as follows:

Balance Sheet

Current Assets	$ 55,000	Current Liabilities	$ 30,000
Fixed Assets	$180,000	Long Term Debt	$ 70,000
Goodwill	$ 15,000	Contributed Capital	$110,000
		Retained Earnings	$ 40,000
	$250,000		$250,000

Note that the purchaser's retained earnings are unchanged following the acquisition. Note also that no change was made to the book value of the assets and liabilities owned by the purchaser prior to the acquisition.

b.   Effects of the Purchase Method on the Income Statement

There are two primary consequences of applying the purchase method of accounting.   The first effect results from recording the target's assets and liabilities at their fair market values.   The fixed assets of the target have been written up in value over their book value on the books of the target.   Also, goodwill was recognized and recorded as a result of the acquisition.   The increased value of the fixed assets and the goodwill both must be amortized and will result in additional expense deductions thus reducing what would otherwise be the combined income of the two companies.   The increased value of the fixed assets will be depreciated or amortized over the useful life of those assets and the goodwill will be amortized over a period of up to forty years.   This increased expense on the income statement is one of the reasons that the pooling method is often viewed as the preferable method for accounting for an acquisition.

The second effect on the income statement is that the income of the acquired target will only be included in the purchaser's income statement for the period following the date of the acquisition.   Further, the prior year income statements of the purchaser will not be affected by the acquisition of the target.   As will be seen below, the pooling method of accounting produces significantly different results on income.

c. Accounting for Acquisition Costs

Costs associated with an acquisition accounted for under the purchase method are classified in three ways with the accounting treatment varying for each class of costs. The direct costs associated with the acquisition are capitalized and included in determining the cost of the assets recorded on the books of the purchaser. Costs of registering and issuing any stock used in the acquisition are treated as a reduction in the fair value of the securities being issued in the acquisition. Indirect costs associated with the acquisition are treated as expenses at the time they are incurred.

4. Application of Pooling Accounting

The pooling method of accounting for acquisitions differs from the purchase method primarily in that the acquiring company records the assets and liabilities of the acquired company at the book values shown on the target's financial statements. No adjustment is made to recognize differences between book values and fair market values and no goodwill is recognized when using the pooling method of accounting for an acquisition. In addition, the purchaser succeeds to the target's retained earnings and adds it to the purchaser's retained earnings under the pooling method. The theory underlying this accounting is that following the acquisition the purchaser and the target are treated as if they had always been a combined operation.

a. Recording the Acquisition Using Pooling

Using the same assumptions as set forth above in the purchase example, the entry to record the acquisition of target using the pooling method would be:

Current Assets	$15,000	
Fixed Assets	$60,000	
Current Liabilities		$10,000
Long Term Debt		$20,000
Contributed Capital		$10,000
Retained Earnings		$35,000

The book values of the assets and liabilities of the target are recorded and no goodwill is recognized. The purchaser has also recorded the contributed capital and retained earnings of the target instead of the normal entry to record the issuance of stock by crediting the purchaser's contributed capital accounts only. The balance sheet of the purchaser following the acquisition of target accounted for under the pooling method would be as follow:

Balance Sheet

Current Assets	$ 55,000	Current Liabilities	$ 30,000
Fixed Assets	$160,000	Long Term Debt	$ 70,000
		Contributed Capital	$ 40,000
		Retained Earnings	$ 75,000
	$215,000		$215,000

Note that the assets and liabilities are all carried over at book value and that the retained earnings of the purchaser following the acquisition have been increased by the amount of the target's retained earnings.

b. The Income Statement Under the Pooling Method

With respect to the income statement, post-acquisition expenses will be lower under the pooling method than under the purchase method because of the absence of goodwill and the absence of any increase in the book value of the fixed assets. This will cause the income of the new entity to be increased if the pooling method applies. The other effect on the income statement is that under the pooling method, the purchaser would include in its income statement the income of the target for the entire year in which the acquisition occurs, not just for the period following the date of the acquisition. This consequence of the pooling method results in the ability to create "instant earnings" even if an acquisition occurs late in the year. In addition, the income of the target is retroactively included in the income statements of the purchaser for any prior periods included in the financial statements for comparative purposes.

c. Costs Under the Pooling Method

All costs associated with an acquisition accounted for under the pooling method of accounting are deducted as expenses at the time of the acquisition. None of these costs are capitalized. The costs that are treated as expenses include costs associated with the issuance of stock such as registration fees and the costs of preparing disclosure documents.

5. Application to Acquisitions of Stock

The procedures described above for pooling and purchase accounting are equally applicable to an acquisition of stock in another corporation. In the case of an acquisition of stock, the adjustments to the fair market value of the assets and the liabilities of the acquired business (assuming the purchase method of accounting) are recorded in the process of preparing consolidated financial statements. These adjustments are not generally recorded in the regular books of the target. In certain situations where the acquired subsidiary must issue its own separate financial statements, a procedure called "push down accounting" is employed. Under push down accounting, the assets and liabilities of the acquired subsidiary are adjusted based on the market values at the time of the acquisition in the same manner that those values are adjusted in the preparation of the parent company's consolidated financial statements.

CHAPTER 16

EARNINGS PER SHARE AND FINANCIAL RATIOS

This chapter will discuss two ways in which the information in financial statements is used by securities analysts and other interested parties to evaluate the securities of a particular company and to compare that company with other companies. The two topics are the computation of earnings per share and the use of financial ratios as analytical tools. Financial ratios are analytical tools developed by financial statement users and analysts to assist in summarizing the information in the financial statements.

A. EARNINGS PER SHARE

Earnings per share is a financial measurement for a corporation that is commonly used by securities analysts and others in their review of different companies. Because of its prominence, it is the only derived financial indicator that is actually reported in the financial statements (it appears at the bottom of the income statement). In general terms, earnings per share, or EPS, is the amount of earnings for a particular year allocable to one share of the corporation's residual security interest, normally the common stock of the corporation. Because EPS could be manipulated by changes in the amount of outstanding shares (for example, through a stock split or reverse stock split), it has little meaning in the abstract. It is usually used in conjunction with the market price per share of the common stock. For example, EPS is one component of the calculation of the price/earnings multiple for a stock, as will be discussed below in section B.4.e.

1. EPS in a Simple Capital Structure

In a simple capital structure, EPS is calculated by dividing the earnings attributable to the common stock by the weighted average number of shares of common stock outstanding for the year. Earnings attributable to common stock is generally the net income of the corporation reduced by any dividends on preferred stock. A simple capital structure exists where there are no convertible securities, options, or other arrangements that could result in the issuance of additional common stock. It may consist of common stock only or common stock and nonconvertible preferred stock.

If the net income for the year includes separately reported items such as extraordinary items, effects of changes in accounting principles, or gain or loss from the disposal of a business (see Chapter 17), EPS is calculated and reported separately for each of these components (as well as for the net income before these items and the overall net income).

To illustrate the basic EPS calculation, assume that a corporation (Company E) has net income for the year 199x of $1,250,000. The capital structure of Company E consists of 100,000 shares of $100 par value preferred stock bearing cumulative dividends at the rate of 7% of par value (all dividends have been paid currently) and common stock. At the beginning of 199x, there were 80,000 shares of common stock outstanding. On October 1, 199x, an additional 20,000 shares of common stock were issued.

Because the numerator in the EPS calculation is the earnings attributable to the common stock, the net income of Company E for the year must be reduced by the amount of the preferred stock dividends (whether declared or not in the case of cumulative dividends). The total preferred stock dividends for the year would be $700,000 ($10,000,000 x 7%). The earnings attributable to the common stock would be $550,000 ($1,250,000—$700,000).

In this simple capital structure situation, the denominator in the EPS calculation is the weighted average number of common shares outstanding for the period. The weighted average number of common shares outstanding is computed as follows:

80,000 x 100%	80,000
20,000 x 25%	5,000
	85,000

The EPS is then calculated by dividing the earnings attributable to the common stock by the weighted average number of common shares, which in this case would be $550,000/85,000, or $5.47. The earnings per share for the current year and any prior years for which income statements are provided would be shown at the bottom of the income statement with an explanation in the footnotes regarding how the EPS was calculated.

If there is a stock split or a stock dividend, the effect of the stock split or stock dividend is applied retroactively to preserve the comparability of EPS numbers from year to year unaffected by these types of changes. To illustrate how this works, assume that in year 1, a business has net income of $1,200,000 and 500,000 shares of common stock outstanding. In year 2, the business has income of $1,500,000. No additional shares are issued in year 2 except that the company has a 2 for 1 stock split effective on July 1. In year 1, the EPS would originally be computed as follows:

$$\frac{\$1,200,000}{500,000} = \$2.40$$

In computing EPS for year 2, the weighted average number of common shares outstanding are computed by retroactively applying the stock split to the beginning of the year. Thus, the outstanding shares would be deemed to be 1,000,000 for the whole year, not 500,000 for the first half and 1,000,000 for the second half. EPS would be:

$$\frac{\$1,500,000}{1,000,000} = \$1.50$$

When year 2 financial statements are prepared and the year 1 financial statements are provided for comparative purposes, the shares outstanding in the year 1 EPS calculation are also adjusted to reflect the stock split that occurred in year 2. Thus, the year 1 EPS would now be recomputed as follows:

$$\frac{\$1,200,000}{1,000,000} = \$1.20$$

Thus, the stock split is treated as if it had occurred on January 1 of year 1. The 25% growth in EPS from year to year ($1.20 to $1.50) corresponds with the 25% growth in net income.

2. EPS in a Complex Capital Structure

The EPS calculations become more involved where the corporation has a more complicated capital structure in which there are outstanding securities, options, warrants, or other agreements that could result in the issuance of additional shares of common stock. In this situation, the corporation must take into account in computing EPS for the year the potentially dilutive effect of additional common shares that could be issued under these securities or agreements. Further, in some situations, it is necessary to calculated two EPS numbers for each year—"primary EPS" and "fully diluted EPS." Primary EPS is calculated by taking into account only certain potentially dilutive devices called "common stock equivalents." The fully diluted EPS calculation includes the effect of all potentially dilutive securities or agreements (and in some cases, uses different methods in computing the effect of the potentially dilutive securities). No options, convertible securities, or other arrangements are taken into account in computing primary or fully diluted EPS if to do so would cause an increase in the EPS (the securities and arrangements that would have this effect are called "antidilutive").

To illustrate the calculation of EPS in the complex capital structure situation, I will use a simplified example involving only outstanding stock options and convertible debt and preferred stock. The same basic set of facts used in the illustration of the simple capital structure situation in Section A.1. will be continued in this example.

a. Effect of Stock Options

Stock options (as well as warrants and other similar arrangements) are always treated as common stock equivalents. Options are therefore always taken into account in computing primary EPS unless they would have an antidilutive effect. An antidilutive effect occurs where taking into account the options would cause an increase in EPS. To calculate the effect of the options on primary EPS, a technique called the "treasury stock method" is used. The treasury stock method is a procedure for giving effect to the proceeds that would be received upon exercise of the stock options. The proceeds receivable upon exercise of the stock options are assumed to be applied in the following order:

i. The proceeds are assumed to be first used to purchase currently outstanding shares of common stock on the open market. These repurchased shares reduce the number of net additional shares assumed to be issued under the options. In computing primary EPS, these purchases are assumed to be made at the average market price for the last three months of the accounting period. The maximum number of shares that may be deemed repurchased are 20% of the outstanding shares of common stock at year-end.

ii. If there are additional proceeds because, for example, the 20% ceiling on repurchases in step i applies, the additional proceeds are next applied to reduce short term or long term debt of the company as of the first day of the year, or the first day on which the options are outstanding, if later.

iii. Any additional proceeds are assumed to be invested in governmental securities.

The effect of items ii and iii on the primary EPS calculations is an increase in the numerator (earnings applicable to common stock) because of a reduction in interest expense or an increase in interest income. This increase in the numerator offsets in part the effect of the increase in the denominator as a result of the additional shares of common stock assumed to be issued.

To illustrate application of the treasury stock method, assume that Company E has stock options outstanding giving employees the right to purchase up to 20,000 shares of common stock at a price per share of $15. The average market price of the common stock for the last three months of 199x is $20 per share. The assumed proceeds upon exercise of the options would be $300,000 (20,000 shares x $15). This could be used to purchase 15,000 shares at the $20 average market price of the stock. Since 15,000 is less than 20% of the actual outstanding shares at year-end (100,000), the effect of the options on the primary EPS calculation would be to increase the number of shares outstanding by 5,000 (20,000 option shares minus 15,000 assumed repurchased shares under the treasury stock method).

b. *Effect of Convertible Securities*

In determining the effect of convertible securities on the EPS calculation, it must first be noted that convertible securities are not always treated as common stock equivalents. The first step is therefore to determine whether the convertible securities are common stock equivalents. Convertible securities are common stock equivalents only if their effective or market yield at the date of issuance is less than ⅔ of the average Aa corporate bond yield on that date. This calculation is done only at the date of issuance and the determination on that date applies throughout the life of the convertible securities.

The effect of convertible securities on the EPS calculation is determined under the "if converted method." Under this approach, the EPS calculations are made as if the convertible securities had been converted at the later of the beginning of the current period or the date of issuance of the convertible securities. In the case of convertible debt, there would be two effects from conversion. The number of common shares deemed outstanding would be increased thus increasing the denominator. In addition, the earnings available for common shares (the numerator) would be increased because the net income would be adjusted to reflect the absence of the after-tax interest expense on the convertible debt. If the combined effect of these two changes would be to increase the EPS, the securities are antidilutive and they are not deemed converted in computing EPS. The rules are the same for convertible preferred stock. In applying the if converted method, the preferred stock dividends otherwise deducted in computing earnings available for common shares would not be deducted and this would offset the effect of the increase in the number of common shares deemed outstanding upon conversion of the preferred stock.

To illustrate, assume that Company E has outstanding convertible debt in the amount of $1,000,-000. This debt bears interest at the rate of 5% per annum and was issued at par so that the effective yield at the date of issue was also 5%. The average Aa corporate bond yield at the date of issuance was 8%. The convertible bonds are convertible into 40,000 shares of common stock. Assume also that the 7% preferred stock described in Section A.1. is convertible preferred stock that was issued at par (thus yielding 7%) and that the preferred stock is convertible into 200,000 shares of common stock. The convertible preferred stock also was issued when the average Aa corporate bond yield was 8%.

Two-thirds of the average Aa corporate bond yield of 8% would be 5.33%. Since the yield at issue on the convertible debt was 5%, the convertible debt would be treated as a common stock equivalent. The yield on the preferred stock was 7%. Since this yield exceeds the test rate of 5.33%, the convertible preferred stock would not be a common stock equivalent. Only the convertible debt would be deemed converted in determining the primary earnings per share. Both the convertible debt and the convertible preferred stock would be deemed converted in computing fully diluted earnings per share.

Before taking into account the options and convertible debt, the components of the earnings per share calculation are earnings applicable to the common stock of $550,000 and weighted average common shares outstanding of 85,000. The assumed exercise of the stock options under the treasury stock method would increase the number of shares in the denominator by 5,000. The assumed conversion of the convertible debt would increase the numerator by $30,000, assuming a tax rate of 40%. The interest expense on the convertible debt is $50,000 per year (5% of $1,000,000). Since the interest expense is deductible for tax purposes, the interest expense results in a tax savings of $20,000 (40% of $50,000). The net expense associated with the debt is $30,000. The numerator would now be $580,000. Assumed conversion of the debt would increase the common shares outstanding by 40,000. Therefore, the denominator in the primary EPS calculation would be 130,000 (85,000 plus 5,000 plus 40,000). Primary EPS would therefore be $4.46 ($580,000 divided by 130,000).

In computing fully diluted EPS, there is taken into account not only the common stock equivalents but also all other potentially dilutive securities and arrangements. In the example that we are using, the convertible preferred stock would be taken into account in computing the fully diluted EPS. If you assume conversion of the convertible preferred stock, the earnings attributable to the common stock would be increased by the amount of the preferred stock dividends, or $700,000. Thus, the total in the numerator would now be $1,280,000. The number of common shares outstanding would be increased by 200,000 to a total of 330,000. The fully diluted earnings per share would be $3.88 ($1,280,000 divided by 330,000).

In applying the treasury stock method to the options, the calculation of the assumed number of shares issued for purposes of computing fully diluted EPS could be increased. If the market price of the common stock on the last day of the accounting period is higher than the average market price of the common stock for the last three months (as used in the calculation of primary EPS) this higher price would be used in applying the treasury stock method. This would have the effect of lowering the number of shares that would be assumed to be repurchased on the open market with the proceeds from the option exercise, which would in turn increase the dilutive effect of the options.

As noted above, the primary and fully diluted EPS numbers are shown at the bottom of the income statement. If the income statement includes any extraordinary items, the effect of changes in accounting principles, or amounts attributable to the disposal of a business, primary and fully diluted EPS amounts would also be shown for these separately disclosed items.

In the example involving Company E, the bottom portion of the income statement would appear as follows:

Net Income	$1,250,000
Primary Earnings Per Share	$4.46
Fully Diluted Earnings Per Share	$3.88

B. FINANCIAL RATIOS

Earnings per share is the only example of an analytical tool that is actually computed and reported in the financial statements. The various financial ratios and calculations to be discussed in the remainder of this chapter are computed by the persons using the financial statements based on the information in the financial statements and the footnotes.

Before computing the financial ratios discussed below, most analysts undertake a careful review of the financial statements. This review is necessary to determine if any questionable accounting policies are being applied. If that is the case, the analyst will attempt to adjust the financial statements to remove the effect of the questionable practices.

Aside from questionable accounting polices, the analyst is also sensitive to the fact that many acceptable accounting practices are choices from available alternatives. Since most securities analysis involves comparison of the financial data for several companies, the existence of multiple acceptable accounting practices makes the analysis difficult since the financial statements of the different companies are not necessarily comparable. For example, one company may use LIFO in accounting for inventory and another company may employ FIFO in accounting for inventory. In this situation, the analysts will attempt to adjust the financial statements in such a way as to reflect comparable accounting policies among all the companies under review.

Finally, companies may not be directly comparable not because of different accounting policies but because of different business practices that create different accounting results even though the underlying business realities are not different in substance. An example of this situation is the choice by one company to finance its assets through leasing while another company finances its assets through debt financing. As discussed in Chapter 11, the financial statements of companies leasing assets will be significantly different from the statements of companies that purchase assets. Securities analysts will frequently "reconstruct" the financial statements of the companies employing lease financing to make the statements of all companies under review more comparable regardless of the form of financing used.

Once all of the necessary adjustments have been made to the financial statements, there are a number of financial ratios that are typically computed and used to assist in the evaluation of companies by investors and lenders. The following is a brief discussion of some of the principal financial ratios that are used by analysts. A number of these ratios are also found in negative covenants in loan agreements and other documents. Violating the test levels for one or more of these ratios may cause a default under the loan.

1. Measures of Liquidity

One group of financial ratios provide information about the liquidity of a company; that is, the ability of the company to satisfy its currently maturing obligations in the ordinary course of business. These liquidity ratios are considered in conjunction with the statement of cash flows discussed in Chapter 1, which is also highly relevant to the issue of liquidity.

a. *Current Ratio*

The current ratio is computed as follows:

$$\frac{\text{Current Assets}}{\text{Current Liabilities}}$$

The current ratio shows the relationship between the current liabilities and the current assets, which are generally viewed as the source of cash to pay the current liabilities. Current assets generally include cash, receivables, marketable securities, inventory, and short term prepayments. Current liabilities include accounts payable, accrued liabilities, and other obligations due within the coming year. It is frequently stated that a current ratio of 2:1 is an acceptable ratio. In fact, there is no single standard for this or any other financial ratio. The current ratio must be evaluated in light of the industry and the current asset mix of the company under review.

b. Quick Ratio

The quick ratio, also called the acid test ratio, is computed in a manner similar to the current ratio. The formula for the quick ratio is:

$$\frac{\text{Quick Assets}}{\text{Current Liabilities}}$$

The numerator in the quick ratio is the "quick assets" (cash, marketable securities, and receivables) that are most readily convertible into cash. The inventory and prepaid expenses are excluded from the numerator on the theory that they are further from being convertible into cash in a short time frame.

2. Measures of Leverage

The next set of ratios are measures of leverage or the overall use of debt in a corporation's capital structure and the ability of the corporation to service that debt over the long term. The long term focus distinguishes these ratios from the liquidity ratios. Utilizing leverage by borrowing increases the potential returns of the stockholders but also increases the risk for the stockholders because of the increased exposure to fixed debt service payments.

a. Debt–Equity Ratio

One of the most commonly used measures of leverage is the debt-equity ratio. This ratio measures the relative use of debt and equity in a company's capital structure. The debt component can be measured in a number of different ways by selecting different components of the total debt to be included in the calculation. Sometimes all debt is used and sometimes only long term debt is used. The general formula for the debt-equity ratio is:

$$\frac{\text{Debt}}{\text{Equity}}$$

b. Debt to Asset Ratio

A different way to express the degree of leverage in a capital structure is to look at the total debt as a percentage of the total assets of the company. This ratio is closely related to the debt-equity ratio. As in the case of the debt-equity ratio, different calculations can be made by excluding certain portions of the overall debt or by excluding certain assets from the asset component. The formula is:

$$\frac{\text{Debt}}{\text{Assets}}$$

c. *Times Interest Earned*

The times interest earned ratio (or interest coverage ratio) compares the income for the year to the amount of the interest expense for the year. It is a rough measure of how much the company's income could deteriorate without jeopardizing the ability to cover interest expense (although income is not necessarily the same as cash flow and interest expense may not all be payable currently in cash). The formula is:

$$\frac{\text{Net Income Before Interest and Taxes}}{\text{Interest Expense}}$$

Taxes are excluded from the numerator because interest expense is a deductible item in computing taxable income so that taxes do not affect the ability to pay interest.

d. *Times Fixed Charges Earned*

The times fixed charges earned ratio is similar in concept and calculation to the times interest earned formula except that certain other fixed charges are included along with interest expense. The other fixed charges that are included are usually rental expense and preferred stock dividends. Rental expense, like interest, must be paid currently to avoid a default in leases. While preferred stock dividends are not legal obligations, failing to pay preferred stock dividends would normally have a significant adverse impact on the financial markets' view of the company. The formula for this ratio is:

$$\frac{\text{Net Income Before Tax, Interest, and Rent Expense}}{\substack{\text{Interest and Rent Expense and Grossed–Up Preferred} \\ \text{Stock Dividends}}}$$

The preferred stock dividends must be "grossed-up" by taxes because preferred stock dividends are not deductible for tax purposes and more than one dollar of income must be earned to pay one dollar of dividends (at a 40% tax rate, $1.67 of income is necessary to pay $1.00 in dividends).

3. Activity Ratios

The next set of ratios are called activity ratios. They are rough measures of efficiency in the utilization of a company's assets or in selected categories of assets. The activity ratios discussed here are all turnover ratios in that they compare some flow measure (such as sales) to a stock of relevant assets, indicating how many times the stock of assets is "turned over" during the year.

a. Asset Turnover

A broad measure of activity is the ratio of total sales for the year to the total assets (usually the average of the assets at the beginning and end of the year). This ratio reflects the efficiency in the utilization of total assets. A higher turnover indicates the ability to generate a relatively high volume of sales using a given amount of assets. The formula is:

$$\frac{\text{Sales Revenue}}{\text{Average Assets}}$$

b. Receivables Turnover

Receivables turnover is a measure of the amount of receivables carried by a company in relationship to sales revenue. A high receivables turnover implies the ability to convert sales into cash on a relatively rapid basis. The formula for receivables turnover is:

$$\frac{\text{Sales Revenue}}{\text{Average Receivables}}$$

If known, the sales number in the numerator should be the credit sales only. The receivables turnover can also be used to determine the average length of time that receivables remain outstanding. A receivables turnover of 8 implies that receivables on average are outstanding for one-eighth of a year, or a little over 45 days.

c. Inventory Turnover

A third turnover measure, inventory turnover, compares the amount of inventory to the volume of goods produced and sold measured by their cost. The formula is:

$$\frac{\text{Cost of Goods Sold}}{\text{Average Inventory}}$$

If the amount of cost of goods sold is not available, this ratio is sometimes computed using sales instead of cost of goods sold. The ratio measures the rate at which inventory is consumed in the business. The higher the ratio, the faster inventory is being sold (or the lower amount of inventory that is needed to support a given volume of sales). Inventory turnover can be used to compute the number of days' sales that are held in inventory. For example, an inventory turnover of 10 implies that the business holds approximately 36.5 days' sales in inventory.

4. Measures of Profitability

The final set of ratios are measures of the degree of profitability of a business. A variety of measures are used that relate profitability to sales, investment, and market price of the company's stock.

a. Profit Margin

Profit margin reflects the portion of each sales dollar that is realized as profit of the business. The formula is:

$$\frac{\text{Net Income}}{\text{Sales}}$$

The magnitude of the profit margin indicates whether the business is a high margin business or a low margin business. The ratio also provides information about a company's relative ability to minimize expenses. Net income included in the numerator may be calculated by excluding certain nonrecurring items (*e.g.*, extraordinary gains and losses).

b. Return on Assets

Another measure of profitability is the return on assets. It is a measure of the return generated per dollar of assets invested in the business. The general formula is:

$$\frac{\text{Net Income}}{\text{Average Assets}}$$

Net income would normally be adjusted to remove nonrecurring items, as in the case of the profit margin. In sophisticated financial analysis, this return would be computed using net income before any interest or financing costs. Often, however, the simple formula set forth above is used.

When return on assets is computed under this general formula, the return on assets is equal to the profit margin multiplied by asset turnover, indicating that the return on assets is a function of the ability to maximize sales on a given amount of assets invested and the ability to minimize the amount of expenses incurred in producing the sales.

c. Return on Equity

A related measure to return on assets is return on equity, usually interpreted as common stockholders' equity. This measures the rate of return being earned by the common stockholders and therefore includes the effects, positive or negative, of employing leverage (debt) in the capital structure. The formula for return on equity is as follows:

$$\frac{\text{Net Income Minus Preferred Stock Dividends}}{\text{Average Common Stockholders' Equity}}$$

d. Earnings per Share

The computation of earnings per share has been discussed at length in Section A. In a simple capital structure, the general formula for the calculation of earnings per share is:

$$\frac{\text{Net Income Minus Preferred Stock Dividends}}{\text{Weighted Average Number of Common Shares}}$$

Earnings per share is primarily used in evaluating the earnings on common stock in relationship to the market value of the common stock, particularly in terms of the price/earnings ratio discussed below.

e. Price/Earnings Ratio

The price/earnings ratio relates the current market price of common stock to the earnings per share on that stock. Ideally, the earnings per share would be a projection or forecast of the earnings for the current year. In the absence of such a forecast, earnings per share is calculated using the most recent year's earnings per share. The general formula is:

$$\frac{\text{Market Price per Share of Common Stock}}{\text{Earnings per Share}}$$

The price/earnings ratio for traded stock is reported in the financial press. A high price/earnings ratio is generally associated with a growth stock, since the relatively high value of the stock in relation to current earnings indicates that the market is anticipating substantial growth in the earnings over time.

f. *Payout Ratio*

The payout ratio is computed as follows:

$$\frac{\text{Annual Dividends}}{\text{Net Income}}$$

This ratio indicates the extent to which current earnings are being distributed in the form of dividends or reinvested in the business. A high payout ratio is normally associated with a mature business that is not growing and is therefore not reinvesting earnings. A low payout ratio normally indicates that the business is growing and is reinvesting earnings to finance that growth.

g. *Dividend Yield*

The dividend yield is a measure of the return actually being received by stockholders in cash in relation to the value of their stock. The formula is:

$$\frac{\text{Annual Dividend}}{\text{Market Price of Stock}}$$

Dividend yield reflects only the current cash return on the stock and ignores the return attributable to retention of earnings and growth in the value of the stock.

CHAPTER 17

SPECIAL REPORTING ISSUES

This chapter will discuss three special reporting issues related to financial statements. Section A discusses certain special or nonrecurring items that must be set forth separately in the income statement. These separately disclosed items include extraordinary gains and losses, the effects of certain changes in accounting principles, and the income or loss related to certain discontinued operations of a business. Section B of this chapter discusses the requirements for certain businesses to provide disclose information regarding certain industry segments. Setting forth separately information regarding these industry segments enhances the comparability and usefulness of financial statements of diversified corporations. Finally, section C discusses accounting issues related to the preparation of interim financial statements.

A. SEPARATELY REPORTED COMPONENTS OF INCOME

Certain unusual or nonrecurring amounts, if material, must be separately reported in the income statement. The amounts that must be shown separately are any "extraordinary gains or losses," the operating results and gain or loss from certain discontinued operations, and the effect on income of certain changes in accounting methods. These items are required to be shown separately because they are likely to cause unusual distortions in the amount of net income or loss of a business from year to year. Separately stating these items permits users of financial statements to exclude them or make other adjustments in developing forecasts or projections of future income or loss of a business based on trends in past income or loss.

1. Extraordinary Items

Extraordinary items are gains and losses from events or transactions that are (i) unusual in nature and (ii) infrequent in occurrence. Whether a gain or loss is extraordinary will vary depending on the business. Examples of items that would frequently be treated as extraordinary are losses from floods or expropriations of assets by foreign governments. Gains or losses from the extinguishment of debt are always reported as extraordinary items (extinguishment of debt is discussed in Chapter 10).

To illustrate, assume that Company E realizes a gain on extinguishment of debt in the amount of $100,000. Company E has a 40% effective tax rate. The gain from the extinguishment of the debt, net of the tax attributable to that gain would be reported separately in the income statement as a $60,000 extraordinary item.

2. Discontinued Operations

Discontinued operations are the operations of a distinct business or other segment of a company that are sold or otherwise disposed of. When a decision is made to dispose of a segment, certain amounts attributable to these discontinued operations are reported separately in the income statement. The separately reported amounts are divided into two components. First, the operating income or loss for the segment for the period from the beginning of the year to the "measurement date" (the date when the company commits to a formal plan of disposal) is reported separately as "income (loss) from discontinued operations." Second, an amount called "gain or loss on disposal" is reported. This second component includes (i) the income or loss of the discontinued business for the period from the measurement date to the actual disposal date and (ii) the gain or loss realized on the actual disposition of the discontinued business. Where the disposal will not occur until after the end of the year in which the measurement date falls, an estimate of the income or loss from the measurement date to the anticipated disposal date and of the gain or loss that will be realized on the actual disposal must be made. If this estimate is a net loss, the estimated amount is included in determining net income in the year in which the measurement date occurs. If the estimated amount is a net gain, it is deferred until the year in which the actual disposal occurs and included in income in that year.

Assume, for example, that on July 1 of the current year, Company E decides to sell its Q division. As of July of the current year, the Q division has experienced an operating loss after tax of $60,000. The business continues to operate until October 1 and generates an additional after-tax loss of $30,-000. On October 1, the Q division assets are sold at a gain of $60,000, which is subject to the company's 40% tax rate. The $60,000 loss through the measurement date (July 1) is a loss from discontinued operations. The net amount of the after tax gain on the sale of the Q division assets ($36,000) and the $30,000 loss from operation of the Q division from July 1 to October 1 results in a $6,000 gain from the disposal of the discontinued operations. Both of these amounts would be reported separately from the income or loss from the continuing operations of Company E.

3. Effects of a Change in Accounting Principle

The third separately reported amount is the cumulative effect of a change in accounting principle. As defined in APB Opinion No. 20, a change in accounting principle is the decision to adopt one accepted accounting approach for a particular accounting issue in place of the accounting approach previously utilized. Such a change must be justified on the basis of improving the financial reporting. An example of a change in accounting principle would be a change in the method of pricing inventory (see Chapter 6).

For most accounting changes, it is necessary to determine the cumulative effect of the change as of the beginning of the period in which the change occurs. The cumulative effect of the change in accounting principle is the amount that retained earnings would change as of the beginning of the year in which the change is adopted if the new accounting principle had been applied in all prior periods (*i.e.*, the cumulative change in income net of tax). This cumulative effect is then reported as a separate item in the income statement. The new accounting principle is then applied prospectively in the current year and all future years.

An example of one type of change requiring cumulative effect reporting is a change in the method of depreciating previously recorded assets. For example, assume that Company E has been reporting depreciation on a $100,000 asset acquired two years ago using the double declining balance method but has determined that the asset should really be depreciated under the straight line method. The original estimated useful life of 20 years and the estimated residual value of $10,000 remain unchanged. The amount of the depreciation actually claimed in the first two years and the amount of the depreciation that would have been claimed had the straight line method been adopted initially are as follows:

Year	DDB Method	S/L Method
1	$10,000	$4,500
2	$ 9,000	$4,500

Company E has a 40% tax rate. The cumulative effect is the amount that retained earnings at the beginning of the current year (year 3 in the life of this asset) would change if the straight line method had been used from the outset. To compute this amount, you first determine the difference in the depreciation. In this case, that would be $19,000 minus $9,000, or $10,000. Since depreciation is deductible for tax purposes, you next compute the amount that taxes would have been increased because of the lower depreciation. That would be $10,000 multiplied by 40% or $4,000. The cumulative effect is the net of these two amounts or a $6,000 increase in retained earnings. This is the amount that would be separately reported as the cumulative effect of the change in accounting principle. The entry to record this change and update all of the affected accounts including balance sheet accounts would be as follows:

Accumulated Depreciation	$10,000	
Deferred Income Tax Liability		$4,000
Cumulative Effect of Change in Accounting Principle		$6,000

The adjustment to the deferred tax liability account could be in part an adjustment to the current tax liability depending on whether any change is being made to the calculation of depreciation for income tax purposes, which is a separate issue from the method of depreciation for financial accounting purposes (see Chapter 12).

In some cases, a change in accounting principle is implemented by restating the financial statements for all prior periods. In that situation, there is no cumulative effect reported as a separate amount in the income statement. There is, however, disclosure of the effect of the restatement on the income statements of all prior periods presented. APB Opinion No. 20 sets forth the rules for determining which changes in accounting principle are to be reported by restating prior years' statements.

A change in accounting principle does not include a change in any of the many estimates that are inherent in the accounting process. A change in an accounting estimate (*e.g.,* a change in the estimated useful life of depreciable property) is applied prospectively only with no restatement or cumulative effect reporting.

4. Income Statement Reporting

If any of these items requiring separate reporting exist, the income statement will first show the net income or loss before these items. The items requiring separate disclosure will next be separately stated reduced by any income tax effect associated with these items (see Chapter 12 for how to determine the tax attributable to these items). Finally, net income or loss will be computed.

The following is how the bottom portion of the income statement for Company E would appear using the examples in items 1, 2, and 3 above and assuming that Company E has after-tax net income from continuing operations of $300,000:

Income from Continuing Operations		$300,000
Results from Discontinued Operations		
Loss from Operations of Discontinued Segment Q (net of $40,000 income tax credit)	($60,000)	
Gain on Disposal of Segment Q (net of $4,000 income taxes)	6,000	(54,000)
Income Before Extraordinary Items		246,000
Extraordinary Gain on Extinguishment of debt (net of $40,000 income taxes)		60,000
Cumulative Effect on Prior Years' Income of Change in Depreciation Method (net of $4,000 income taxes)		6,000
Net Income		$312,000

B. SEGMENT REPORTING

The financial statements of diversified corporations combine all of the relevant financial information from the various businesses in which the corporation is involved. This can make comparison among different companies difficult because the amount of income contributed by, and the amount of assets related to, businesses involved in different industries will each have their own relationships and their own issues regarding risk and return analysis. Thus, a corporation may have one high margin business and one low margin business (margin generally being the difference between sales revenue and cost of goods sold (gross profit) expressed as a percentage of sales). The income statement of this corporation will show a margin that is a blend of these two businesses making analysis and comparison with other corporations difficult.

In light of this need for information regarding individual businesses, certain companies are required to include supplementary information setting forth disaggregated financial data regarding their significant business segments. Only companies with securities that are publicly traded or that are required to file financial statements with the SEC are required to report this segment information. This section will discuss this segment reporting requirement.

1. Reporting on Industry Operations

Businesses with more than one "reportable industry segment" must report certain information about each significant segment. An industry segment is a component of a company that provides a product or service, or a group of related products and services, primarily to unaffiliated customers for a profit. FASB Statement No. 14. The division of a consolidated reporting entity into segments may be based on standard industry classifications or on the company's internal profit centers, or the division may be based on the nature of the product, the nature of the production process, and the markets and marketing methods used by different parts of the business.

After the industry segments are determined, only those segments with significant operations must report information for that segment. There are three tests used to determined whether a segment is significant. If any of these tests are satisfied, the segment will be treated as a significant segment. Under a revenue test, a segment is significant if a segment's revenues are 10% or more of the combined revenues of all of the segments in the company. Under an operating profit test, a segment is significant if the absolute amount of its operating profit or loss is 10% or more of the combined operating profits of all segments that did not incur an operating loss. Under an asset test, a segment is significant if the identifiable assets of that segment are 10% or more of the combined identifiable assets of all segments. Additional tests are applicable in certain situations to expand or contract the number of segments that must report separate information.

Where segment reporting is required, the following financial information is reported for each significant segment.

    a.   The revenues related to each segment.

    b.   The operating profit or loss of each segment. Operating profit or loss is determined by subtracting from revenues operating expenses that include traceable expenses that relate to the specific revenues of the segment and other operating expenses that are allocable on some reasonable basis among the segments. General corporate expenses, interest expense, taxes, and other general items are not allocated to the individual segments for this purpose.

c. Identifiable assets of a reportable segment. The assets reported include both tangible and intangible assets used by the segment. The assets reported are those used exclusively by the segment and a reasonably allocated portion of assets that are used by two or more segments. General corporate assets and other nonoperating assets are not allocated to a segment.

d. Additional items reported for each segment. These items include the depreciation, depletion, and amortization expense included in computing operating profits for each segment, the capital expenditures of each segment, the types of products and services from which revenue is derived, and the accounting policies relevant to each segment.

Where industry segment information is required to be reported, it may be reported within the body of the financial statements with supporting notes. Alternatively, it may be provided entirely in the notes to the financial statements or in a separate schedule that is included as an integral part of the financial statements. The third option is used by most companies reporting segment information.

2. Reporting on Foreign Operations and Export Sales

Companies with international operations are required to report separately certain information related to foreign operations and export sales. Foreign operations are those revenue producing operations that are located outside the United States. Significant foreign operations that must report information related to their activities include those foreign operations that generate revenue of at least 10% of the company's total revenues or have identifiable assets of at least 10% of the total company assets. Furthermore, if a particular foreign geographic area accounts for more than 10% of total company revenues or assets, additional information must be disclosed related each significant geographic area.

Where reporting regarding foreign operations is necessary, the information that is separately reported includes the revenues related to domestic and foreign operations as well as the operating profit or loss and the identifiable assets of those operations. This information must be set forth separately for each significant geographic area. In addition, if the domestic operations make 10% or more of their sales to unaffiliated customers in foreign countries, the amount of export sales must be separately reported either in the aggregate or by geographic areas.

3. Information About Major Customers

Finally, certain businesses are required to report information regarding revenue generated by sales to a single customer. This is necessary where a single customer accounts for at least 10% of a company's revenues. A single customer may include a group of entities under common control, the federal government, a state government, a local government, or a foreign government. The information required to be disclosed is the amount of revenue generated from each such significant customer and the identity of the industry segment or segments that are making those sales.

C. INTERIM FINANCIAL STATEMENTS

Most of the information set forth in this nutshell relates to the financial statements that are prepared on an annual basis. These are full financial statements subject to all of the rules included in GAAP with all required notes and supplementary disclosures. Many companies report certain financial information on an interim basis (typically quarterly) in addition to their primary annual financial statements. These interim financial statements are normally not audited and the level of detail included in these financial statements is significantly less than the annual financial statements.

APB Opinion No. 28 sets forth rules to be followed in presenting interim financial information where such financial information is presented. Certain special procedures must be followed in determining the amount of revenues and expenses to be assigned to each quarterly or other interim period for which interim financial statements are prepared. Revenues are generally assigned to interim periods based on the same rules and procedures that are used in determining revenue for the annual accounting period. Expenses that are associated directly with product sales or for the provision of services are matched with the related revenues in a manner similar to that in annual financial statements. For expenses that are not directly associated with product sales, the method of assigning expenses to interim periods must be consistent with the methods used for annual financial reporting. Gains and losses that occur in a particular period are reported in the interim period in which they occur and not allocated or apportioned among the interim periods.

Special procedures are applied in connection with inventory reporting. First, companies may use certain estimating procedures to determine their inventory for purposes of presenting interim financial information. Companies using the LIFO method to account for inventory may avoid recognition of additional income associated with temporary liquidations of old LIFO layers if those temporary liquidations are expected to be replaced by the end of the year.

Income taxes are also handled specially. In determining the income tax rate to be applied to the financial reporting income, the company uses an estimated effective tax rate that it believes will apply for the entire year.

The information that is presented in interim financial statements is usually summarized information that is less detailed and complete than that set forth in the regular annual financial statements. APB Opinion No. 28 sets forth as a minimum the information that must be set forth. The minimum information that must be reported includes sales or gross revenues, income taxes, extraordinary items, cumulative effects of changes in accounting principles, and net income for each period. The statements must also disclose the primary and fully diluted earnings per share for each period presented, the amounts of seasonal revenues, costs, and expenses, significant changes in estimates of income taxes, results of discontinued operations, material unusual or infrequent items, contingent items, changes in accounting principles or estimates, and significant changes in financial position. In addition, companies are encouraged to provide condensed balance sheets and cash flow data for interim periods. Segment information required to be set forth in annual financial statements is not required to be disclosed in interim reports.

CHAPTER 18

CORPORATE FINANCE—
VALUATION

A significant use of financial accounting information is in connection with the valuation of business enterprises and the valuation of the individual securities issued by businesses. The information from the financial statements may be used directly in the valuation process or the accounting information may be used indirectly in projecting such items as earnings or cash flow or in determining the risk associated with the securities of the business. Risk is reflected in the discount rate or required rate of return that is a central element of many valuation techniques used in the area of corporate finance.

Section A of this chapter will describe methods used to value the principal securities issued by a corporation (bonds, preferred stock, and common stock). Section B will then introduce the concept of a corporation's "cost of capital." Section C will then review some of the methods used to value an entire business enterprise.

A. VALUATION OF SECURITIES

Securities analysts and other users of financial information frequently use that information to determine the value of the individual securities issued by a business. For example, an analyst may compute the "intrinsic value" of outstanding securities of a business to determine whether to purchase or sell the securities of that business and, if so, at what price to purchase or sell the securities. Another need for a valuation of securities arises when a business uses its securities to acquire assets. The value of the securities needs to be determined for purposes of recording the acquisition of assets and issuance of the securities in the noncash exchange transaction. This section will review some of the common methods for determining the values of three basic types of securities—bonds, preferred stock, and common stock.

1. Valuation of Bonds

The valuation of bonds is heavily dependent on the determination of the appropriate discount rate to be used in determining value. The discount rate is the rate of return (interest) that the market would expect to earn on the particular bond issue. Once that rate of return is determined, the valuation process is relatively simple.

a. Mechanics of Bond Value Calculations

A bond generally represents a stream of cash flows that will be paid in fixed amounts at fixed dates. The value of the bonds is determined by computing the present value of the stream of cash flows promised under the bond indenture using the required or market rate of interest as the discount rate. The procedures for determining present value are set forth in Appendix A.

To illustrate the valuation of bonds, assume that bonds with a face amount of $1,000,000 are issued with a term to maturity of twenty years, at which time the full face amount of the bonds is payable. The bonds have a stated or coupon interest rate of 10% per annum, payable semi-annually. The required rate of return on this bond issue is 12% (the determination of the required rate of return will be discussed below).

This bond has two cash flow components. One component is an annuity of $50,000 (the coupon interest payment) that is payable for forty semi-annual periods. The second component is a terminal cash flow equal to the principal or face amount of the bonds payable in a lump sum of $1,000,000 at the end of twenty years (or forty semi-annual compounding periods). The sum of the present values of these two cash flow components gives the market value of the bonds based on the current market yield of 12%. Using the appropriate present value factors [from a financial calculator], the current market value of the bonds would be:

$$
\begin{array}{rcl}
\$ \ \ \ 50,000 \times 15.0463 &=& \$752,315 \\
\$1,000,000 \times .09722 &=& \underline{\$ \ 97,220} \\
&& \underline{\underline{\$849,535}}
\end{array}
$$

Note that the market value of the bond issue is less than its face or principal amount. That results from the fact that the required market interest rate is greater than the coupon rate actually payable on the bonds. The excess of the principal amount payable at maturity over the current market value of the bonds (the bond discount) compensates the purchaser of the bonds for the coupon rate that is lower than the current market interest rate.

Similar calculations are used to value most bonds regardless of the nature of their cash flows. For example, zero coupon bonds that pay no stated interest are valued by discounting the single terminal cash flow (the face amount payable at the date of maturity) to its present value using the appropriate market interest rate as the discount rate.

b. Determining Market Interest Rates

The market interest rates to be used in valuing bonds are determined by several factors. The primary determinants of the market interest rates for a particular bond issue for a particular company are discussed in this section. This nutshell does not discuss the determinants of the overall level of interest rates in the economy since these factors are not specific to the particular bond issue.

(i) Credit Risk. The credit risk associated with a bond issue is a key factor in determining the appropriate market interest rate. Credit risk is the risk that the obligor under the bonds will not be able to make the cash payments required by the bonds when those payments are due. U.S. treasury securities are generally regarded as being risk-free in terms of credit risk. Other borrowers (bond issuers) must add a risk premium to the U.S. trea-

sury rates to compensate for the additional risk that holders bear in holding these securities rather than government securities. In addition to the effect of the issuer's overall financial condition (use of leverage, quality of assets, liquidity, etc.), the risk premium will be affected by such factors as collateral securing the bonds. Thus, bonds secured by a mortgage on the issuer's real estate or a security interest in equipment or other property will normally have a lower interest rate as compared to unsecured bonds (sometimes called debentures).

(ii) Term to Maturity. The length of the maturity of the bond issue is also a determinant of the appropriate interest rate. The longer the term to maturity, the greater the interest rate risk. Interest rate risk is the risk of changes in the value of the bonds as a result of changes in the level of market interest rates. This factor generally adds a premium to the market rate for longer term debt. Closely related to the term to maturity is the size of the stated or coupon interest rate. A higher stated interest rate results in less interest rate risk because more of the total cash to be received on the bonds is received earlier as compared to a low coupon bond issued at a discount where relatively more of the total cash to be received will be received at the maturity date. Financial analysts have a concept called duration that actually provides a measure of the relative speed at which the cash is received.

As a practical matter, the bond markets generally provide a basis for estimating the appropriate market interest rate for a particular bond. If the bond issue is publicly traded, of course, the trading price will normally establish the market value of the bonds. For nontraded bonds, the procedure is generally to determine the market interest rate for the most comparable publicly traded bonds and then apply that market rate of interest to the bonds in question with appropriate adjustment for any particular features associated with the bonds being valued. In determining comparability, analysts look at the factors described above including term to maturity and credit risk. Credit risk can be evaluated in part by looking at the ratings that are assigned to many bonds by bond rating agencies such as Standard & Poors and Moodys. For unrated bonds, the analyst must determine how the bonds being analyzed would be rated if they were rated. The analysts can then look at the market interest rates of bonds with similar ratings and terms to maturity. Comparison also must take into account the specific features of the bonds including the existence of any collateral or other security for the bonds.

c. Bonds With Additional Features

If the bonds in question have other features, this will affect the valuation of the bonds. For example, a right of the issuer to call the bonds or the right of the holder to put the bonds at a fixed price prior to maturity will affect the valuation. A call feature normally increases the required market rate of interest and lowers the value of the bonds as compared to similar bonds with no call feature. This results because the call feature may result in the bonds being redeemed prior to maturity at a time when the market interest rates are lower and the opportunity for reinvestment is not attractive. Some bonds are convertible into stock of the issuer. This convertibility feature adds an additional element of value to the bonds beyond the present value of the stated interest and principal payments. Thus, actual bond valuation must take into account these and other special features associated with the bonds being analyzed.

2. Valuation of Preferred Stock

Valuation of straight preferred stock bearing a fixed rate of dividend is similar in many respects to the valuation of bonds. The discounting process varies depending on whether or not the preferred stock is redeemable.

a. Nonredeemable Preferred Stock

In the case of nonredeemable preferred stock, the expected cash flow stream that is discounted is a perpetual cash flow in the amount of the preferred dividend payable on the preferred stock. In this situation, the value of the preferred stock is the fixed dividend payment divided by the appropriate market rate of return. For example, assume that a preferred stock investment is being considered. The preferred stock has a par value of $500,000 and bears a 6% cumulative annual dividend, payable quarterly. The expected cash flow stream is quarterly payments of $7,500 in perpetuity. If the appropriate market discount rate for this preferred stock is 8%, the value of the stock would be computed by dividing $7,500 by 2%, which would produce a value of $375,000.

b. Redeemable Preferred Stock

If the preferred stock is mandatorily redeemable at some fixed date in the future, the valuation of the preferred stock would proceed in the same manner as the valuation of bonds. The present value of the expected dividends for the period up to the redemption date would be computed and added to the present value of the amount payable on the date of redemption. The sum of these two amounts would be the market value of the preferred stock.

c. Rate of Return for Preferred Stock

Determining the appropriate market rate of return for preferred stock is similar to determining the market interest rate for debt with two primary changes. Because preferred stock generally ranks below debt in the event of liquidation and because companies are generally not legally obligated to pay dividends on preferred stock to avoid the possibility of bankruptcy, the required rate of return on preferred stock is generally higher than the market rate of debt for a given issuer. The amount of this differential depends on the perceived risk of the issuer with respect to payment of its preferred stock dividends. On the other hand, corporate holders of preferred stock are generally allowed to exclude at least 70% of their dividends on preferred stock in computing their taxable income making the preferred stock dividends partially tax-exempt in the hands of the corporate holders. Because of this partial tax exemption, the market rate of return for preferred stock is reduced as compared to otherwise comparable investments that are fully taxable. The net effect of these two factors will vary in each situation.

As in the case of bonds, it is often possible to determine an appropriate rate of return for preferred stock by looking at the market rates of return on the preferred stocks of comparable issuers that are publicly traded. Analysts may also employ rules of thumb or guidelines for the amount of a premium to be added to the market interest rate on the debt of an issuer to determine the appropriate market rate of return on the preferred stock.

d. *Preferred Stock With Additional Features*

The valuation of preferred stock will also be affected by other features that may be associated with the preferred stock. The preferred stock may be participating preferred stock with some right to participate in distributions in excess of the basic fixed dividend rate on the stock. The preferred stock may be convertible into common stock of the issuer, in which case some additional value attributable to the conversion feature will be added to the basic value of the preferred stock ignoring the conversion feature. The preferred stock may be "puttable" meaning that the holder has the right under certain circumstances to require the stock to be redeemed, subject to limitations under applicable law. These and other special features must be taken into account when valuing preferred stock.

3. Valuation of Common Stock

The third principal security issued by the typical corporation is common stock. This is also the most difficult of the three basic securities to value because of the absence of any fixed cash flows associated with an investment in common stock. For companies that pay or are expected to pay reasonably regular dividends, valuation models have been developed to value common stock.

a. *Constant Dividends*

In a situation where a company is paying a regular dividend on the common stock and that dividend is expected to remain constant into the foreseeable future, the valuation process is identical to the valuation process for nonparticipating, nonredeemable preferred stock. The expected dividend is divided by the required or market rate of return for the stock (the determination of which is discussed below) to produce the value of the stock. For example, if a common stock is paying a quarterly dividend of $1.50 and the appropriate rate of return for this stock is 10%, the value of the common stock would be computed by dividing the dividend ($1.50) by the rate of return (2.5% on a quarterly basis). Thus, the value of the common stock would be:

$$\frac{\$1.50}{.025} = \$60$$

b. Dividends Growing at a Constant Rate

Many companies do not expected to pay a level dividend on their common stock forever. For example, the goal of many companies is to achieve growth through reinvestment of earnings and other actions and to increase the rate of dividends payable on the common stock. In the situation where a fixed rate of growth in the amount of dividends paid is projected, a valuation formula or model has been developed. Under that model, the value of common stock is computed by the following formula:

$$\frac{D}{k - g}$$

Where D is the expected dividend for the coming year, k is the required rate of return on the stock and g is the expected rate of growth in the dividends. For example, if the dividend for the coming year is expected to be $2.00, the required rate of return is 10%, and it is anticipated that the dividends will grow by 5% per year, the value of this stock would be $2/(.1—.05), or $40.00. This is the same value that would be computed by calculating the projected dividends into the future based on the assumed growth rate and then discounting all of the future dividends to present value using the required rate of return.

c. Present Value Analysis

Both of the formulas described above are particular applications of a general approach to valuing common stock in which the value is simply the present value of all of the cash flows expected to be received from the investment in the stock. These cash flows could be dividends or they could be dividends plus an expected amount to be received as the result of an eventual sale or liquidation of the stock. When the common stock does not fit either of the situations described above (constant projected dividends or dividends with a constant growth rate), valuing common stock requires additional present value calculations. For example, there are situations where a high and possibly variable growth rate is expected to apply for several years, after which point the growth in dividends is expected to level off at a long term, sustainable level. Neither of the common stock valuation models set forth above will fit this situation. In this case, the common stock valuation proceeds in two stages. During the variable growth period, the analyst must estimate the amount of dividends expected to be paid in each of the years during this initial period. Once the long term normal growth period begins, the analyst determines the stock value as of the start of this period using the constant growth model set forth in the previous paragraph. The stock price so computed becomes the terminal cash value as of the beginning of the normal or constant growth period. The analyst then discounts the cash flows so computed using the present value procedures described in Appendix A and the appropriate market rate of return for the stock as the discount rate.

To illustrate, assume that a company anticipates the following dividends per share on common stock for the next five years:

Year	Dividend
1	$0.00
2	$ .50
3	$ .50
4	$2.00
5	$2.75

Beginning in year six, the company expects to pay a dividend of $3.00 per share and expects that dividend to increase thereafter at a constant rate of 8% per year. The required rate of return on this stock is 12%.

To value this stock, we first note that as of the beginning of year six, the stock can be valued using the constant growth model. The value of the stock at the beginning of year six would be:

$$\frac{3.00}{.12 - .08} = \$75$$

The value of the common stock now becomes a five year present value calculation. Using the appropriate present value factors from Table 2 in Appendix A, the stock would be valued as follows (the assumed value of the stock at the beginning of year six ($75) is treated as an additional end of year five cash flow):

Year	Cash Flow	PV Factor	PV
1	$ 0	.8929	$ 0
2	$ .50	.7972	.3986
3	$ .50	.7118	.3559
4	$ 2.00	.6355	1.271
5	$77.75	.5674	44.11
			$46.14

The value of the common stock is the sum of the present values of the expected cash flows, or $46.14.

d.   Price/Earnings Multiples

Another approach for valuing common stock is to determine the approximate value of a stock based on price/earnings multiples. Under this approach, the analyst will determine the expected normalized earnings for the coming year (or the next four quarters). The analyst will then determine the appropriate price/earnings multiple for this company based on the price/earnings multiples of comparable companies whose stocks are publicly traded. The value for the common stock is then the estimated earnings for the next four quarters multiplied by the appropriate price/earnings multiple. To illustrate, assume the estimated earnings per share for Company J for the next four quarters are $2.30. Based on an analysis of similar companies, the appropriate price/earnings multiple is determined to be 9. The value of this stock under the price/earnings multiple approach would be $2.30 multiplied by 9, or $20.70.

e.   Determining the Required Rate of Return

A critical input in these common stock valuation models is the appropriate discount rate (rate of return) or the appropriate price/earnings multiplier to be used. One approach to determining the required rate of return for a common stock is to add certain components to compute an appropriate discount rate. Analysts may determine, for example, that the rate of return for a common stock should be the long term market interest rate in some appropriate segment of the long term debt market plus an appropriate risk premium based on the perceived level of risk associated with the stock under consideration. The appropriate risk premium would be based on the analyst's review of historical relationships between the rates of return in the long term bond markets and the rates of return in the equity markets for common stocks with different levels of risk. For example, an analyst might determine that the required rate of return on a company's common stock should be four percentage points higher than the market interest rate on long term debt of the company. If the company's long term debt has a market yield of 8.5%, the required return for the common stock would be $12.5%.

A more sophisticated variation of this approach is to use a model called the capital asset pricing model to determine appropriate rates of return. The theoretical and conceptual basis for the capital asset pricing model is beyond the scope of this nutshell. A simplified application of this model will, however, illustrate its use in determining common stock values. Analysts determine the expected rate of return for a "market portfolio of stocks" consisting, for example, of all of the stocks in the Standard &

Poors 500 index. This rate of return for a broad based market index is composed of two elements, a risk free interest rate and a risk premium. The expected rate of return for individual stocks is determined to bear a relationship to the rate or return for the market as a whole. This relationship is stated as follows:

$$RR_S = RF + (RR_M{-}RF) \times \beta$$

In this formula, RR_S is the expected rate of return for security S that we are trying to compute. RF is the current risk free interest rate component for common stocks. RR_M is the current expected rate of return for the market portfolio. A stock's beta (β) is determined by the risk of the stock in question in relationship to the risk associated with a portfolio of stocks of many companies. Risk is measured in terms of the projected or historical variability of returns on the stock and for the market as a whole. β is a computed relationship between the market rate of return and a particular security's rate of return. For example, a β of 2 means that the security in question requires a risk premium that is twice that of the market portfolio. Individual analysts and financial reporting services have developed their estimates of β for a number of stocks.

To illustrate the use of the capital asset pricing method in determining rates of return, assume that the rate of return for a broad based segment of the stock market is currently 12%, which consists of a risk-free rate of 4% plus a risk premium of 8%.

Assume that company L has been determined to have a β of 2.4. The appropriate rate of return for this stock would be the sum of (i) the risk free rate of 4% plus (ii) a risk premium of 8% x 2.4 (19.2%), or 23.2%.

B. COST OF CAPITAL

A concept related to the valuation of securities is the "cost of capital" for a company. One of the primary uses of a company's cost of capital is in capital budgeting. Capital budgeting is the analysis of whether a particular long term project or investment should be undertaken by a company, (*e.g.*, should the company construct an additional warehouse to better service customers in a particular region). In a capital budgeting situation, a company will often use a discounted cash flow technique to determine whether the proposed project has a positive net present value. This is accomplished by discounting the expected cash flows that will result from a project and then comparing that present value amount with the cost of the project. If the discounted cash flows from the project exceed its cost, the project has a positive net present value. Cost of capital plays a role in the capital budgeting process because it is the cost of capital that is usually used as the discount rate in the present value calculations.

1. Determining a Company's Cost of Capital

A company's cost of capital is generally computed as the weighted average cost of capital for each of the components of its capital structure. The cost for each component is the market rate of return required by each of the suppliers of capital as discussed above in connection with valuation of securities. The weighting factors may be determined by the actual percentage of the company's capital supplied from each source or it may be based on the percentage that each component would represent in the ideal or target capital structure for the company.

To illustrate, assume that Company P has determined that its cost of debt is 9%, its cost of preferred stock is 10%, and its cost of common stock is 15%. Interest on debt is deductible in computing income tax so that the cost of debt to Company P is really the cost of the debt after taking in account the deductibility of interest. If the applicable tax rate is 40%, the after-tax cost of the debt capital is 9% x (1–.4), or 5.4%. The target capital structure for Company P would have 40% debt, 20% preferred stock, and 40% common stock. The weighted average cost of capital for Company P would be:

Debt	5.4% × 40%	2.2%
Preferred Stock	10% × 20%	2.0%
Common Stock	15% × 40%	6.0%
		10.2%

For Company P, the cost of capital to be used in net present value calculations or other computations requiring a cost of capital would be 10.2%.

This analysis of cost of capital is simplified in some respects. For example, companies may compute a separate cost of capital for retained earnings and a cost of capital for new equity raised through issuance of additional common stock. The theory underlying the separate calculations is that transaction costs are incurred in raising additional equity and such transaction costs are not incurred in retaining and reinvesting earnings. The foregoing does illustrate, however, the basic approach to computing cost of capital.

2. Use of Cost of Capital in Capital Budgeting

To illustrate the use of cost of capital, assume that Company P is reviewing a proposed project that would produce a cash flow stream of $150,000 per year for ten years. At the end of ten years, there would be an additional terminal cash flow of $300,000. The initial cost of the project is $1,000,-000. If Company P applies discounted cash flow analysis to evaluate this project, it would first compute the net present value of the expected cash flows using its cost of capital as the discount rate. The present value of an annuity of $1 for ten years at a discount rate of 10.2% is 6.092. The present value of $1 at the end of ten years at a 10.2% discount rate is .379. Therefore, the present value of the expected cash flows to Company P is:

$150,000 × 6.092   = $ 913,800
$300,000 × .379   = $ 113,700
                         $1,027,500

Since the cost of this project is $1,000,000, it has a positive net present value of $27,500, which means that undertaking this project would provide positive returns to its common shareholders (*i.e.,* after paying back the debt holders and the preferred stockholders with their required rates of return, the remaining return to the common stockholders would be more than their required 15%).

C. VALUATION OF A BUSINESS

The discussion in section A. of this chapter deals with the valuation of the individual securities of a company. In many cases, however, there is a need to determine the value of an entire business. This section will discuss approaches to valuing a business.

1. Discounted Cash Flow Analysis

One approach to the valuation of a business employs discounted cash flow analysis similar in many respects to the capital budgeting process discussed in section B. The following is a brief overview of the procedures for valuing a business using the discounted cash flow approach.

a. *Estimate the Cash Flows for a Projection Period*

The initial step is the estimation of the future cash flows of the business for an appropriate number of years (typically ten (10) years). When valuing individual securities, the cash flows that are analyzed and discounted are the projected cash flows on the particular securities being valued. When valuing a business, the cash flows that are analyzed are the expected cash flows of the whole business. These cash flows are determined before the payment of any cash to suppliers of capital such as creditors so that the cash flows are sometimes referred to as unleveraged free cash flows. These estimates are based on the analyst's judgment as to the future prospects of the business. The unleveraged free cash flows from operations are approximately equivalent to the amount shown as cash flow from operations in the Statement of Cash Flows discussed in Chapter 1 except that interest expense is not taken into account.

The initial step in the calculation of the unleveraged free cash flows is to calculate the estimated or projected "free cash flows" for the projection period. The free cash flows are computed as (i) the projected net income after tax, plus (ii) the noncash charges deducted in computing net income (*e.g.*, deferred taxes and depreciation expense), less (iii) the projected capital expenditures necessary to produce the projected net income, less (iv) the projected increase in the net working capital necessitated by the business (other than cash and short-term investments).

The free cash flows are converted into the unleveraged free cash flows by adding back to the free cash flows the interest expense included in determining net income multiplied by the difference between one and the applicable tax rate. The adjustment for the tax rate reflects the fact that taxes are reduced by the payment of interest. If the interest were not incurred, there would be an increase in the taxes for the year. The unleveraged free cash flows are the cash flows that would be available after all operating needs have been met. These unleveraged free cash flows are the amounts that would be available to service any debt and pay any residual to the owners.

b.   Terminal Cash Flow

The next step is to determine the terminal cash flow, or the amount of cash for which the business could be sold at the end of the projection period. The terminal cash flow is difficult to determine since it involves an estimate of the value of the business at the end of the projection period but this terminal cash flow is being used as an input in the determination of the value of the business at the current time.

Analysts use different techniques to estimate this terminal cash flow value. The terminal value may be based on the projected book value of the business taking into account the projected income, capital expenditures, and changes in working capital, and distribution of all free cash flow to the owners over the projection period. Another procedure used to estimate the terminal cash flow is an earnings based value computing by multiplying the estimated earnings (unleveraged) for the final year in the cash flow projection period by an appropriate price/ earnings multiple to compute a terminal value for the business. A third calculation might involve a calculation of a terminal value of the business based on an appropriate multiplier applied to the free cash flow for the final year in the projection period.

From these amounts, the analyst will determine a subjective estimate of the terminal cash value for the firm.

The procedures for determining the terminal value are somewhat rough and circular (if you can so easily determine the value of a business in ten years, why is it so difficult to determine it now). The reason why this does not cause more concern is due to the effect of present value. At a discount rate of 12%, the present value factor at the end of ten years is approximately .32. Therefore, the final valuation of the business in question will not be very sensitive to changes in the terminal value.

c. Determination of Discount Rate

The next step is the determination of an appropriate discount rate to be used in discounting the cash flows. A typical approach would be to use the weighted cost of capital for the business computed in the manner described in section B. above. The weights would be based on the perceived optimal capital structure for the business under consideration. The individual cost components used in calculating the weighted average cost of capital would be determined in the manner described in sections A. and B.

d. Computation of the Value of the Firm

The next step is to compute the value of the business. This value is calculated by discounting the annual cash flows for the projection period and the terminal cash flow component to present value using the weighted average cost of capital as the appropriate discount rate. Note that the value of the whole firm is being computed, not the value of the equity of the firm. Accordingly, it is the unleveraged free cash flows that are discounted in the calculation.

If desired, a value of the equity of the business under consideration could be derived as a by-product of the calculation of the value of the firm. The value of the equity would be computed by subtracting from the value of the firm the value of the firm's present debt. The value of the debt would be computed in the same manner as described above in section A. 1.

e. Example

An example of the application of the discounted cash flow approach to valuing a business will assist in understanding the procedure. Table I presents the information necessary to compute the unleveraged free cash flows of a business. Part A includes a 10–year projection of net income and also includes information regarding projected capital expenditures and working capital needs.

Part B computes the unleveraged free cash flows. The computation begins with the projected net income and then adds back the depreciation (the only noncash expense or revenue item assumed to exist in this case). This produces the assumed cash flow from operations. The next step is to deduct from the cash flow from operations the nonoperating cash necessary for capital expenditures and working capital. This gives the free cash flows. Finally, the interest expense (net of the tax benefit from deducting interest) is added back to produce the unleveraged free cash flows.

TABLE I

COMPUTATION OF UNLEVERAGED FREE CASH FLOWS

Years	1	2	3	4	5	6	7	8	9	10
Part A:										
Operating Income	$200,000	$208,000	$216,300	$225,000	$234,000	$243,400	$253,100	$263,200	$273,700	$284,600
Depreciation Expense	($40,000)	($41,200)	($42,400)	($43,700)	($45,000)	($46,400)	($47,800)	($49,200)	($50,700)	($52,200)
Interest Expense	($50,000)	($51,800)	($53,600)	($55,500)	($57,400)	($59,400)	($61,500)	($63,700)	($65,900)	($68,200)
Income Before Tax	$110,000	$115,000	$120,300	$125,800	$131,600	$137,600	$143,800	$150,300	$157,100	$164,200
Income Tax (40%)	($44,000)	($46,000)	($48,120)	($50,320)	($52,640)	($55,040)	($57,520)	($60,120)	($62,840)	($65,680)
Net Income	$66,000	$69,000	$72,180	$75,480	$78,960	$82,560	$86,280	$90,180	$94,260	$98,520
Other Information:										
Capital Expenditures	$45,000	$46,400	$47,800	$49,200	$50,700	$52,200	$53,800	$55,400	$57,100	$58,800
Change in Noncash Working Capital	$30,000	$31,200	$32,400	$33,700	$35,000	$36,400	$37,900	$39,400	$41,000	$42,600
Part B:										
Net Income	$66,000	$69,000	$72,180	$75,480	$78,960	$82,560	$86,280	$90,180	$94,260	$98,520
Depreciation Expense	$40,000	$41,200	$42,400	$43,700	$45,000	$46,400	$47,800	$49,200	$50,700	$52,200
Cash Flow from Operation:	$106,000	$110,200	$114,580	$119,180	$123,960	$128,960	$134,080	$139,380	$144,960	$150,720
Capital Expenditures	($45,000)	($46,400)	($47,800)	($49,200)	($50,700)	($52,200)	($53,800)	($55,400)	($57,100)	($58,800)
Increase in Noncash Working Capital	($30,000)	($31,200)	($32,400)	($33,700)	($35,000)	($36,400)	($37,900)	($39,400)	($41,000)	($42,600)
Free Cash Flows	$31,000	$32,600	$34,380	$36,280	$38,260	$40,360	$42,380	$44,580	$46,860	$49,320
Interest (Net of Tax)	$20,000	$20,720	$21,440	$22,200	$22,960	$23,760	$24,600	$25,480	$26,360	$27,280
Unleveraged Free Cash Flows	$51,000	$53,320	$55,820	$58,480	$61,220	$64,120	$66,980	$70,060	$73,220	$76,600

The next step is to compute a terminal value for the business at the end of ten years. In this case, it is assumed that the business would be sold at the end of ten years for a price equal to a multiple of ten times the year 10 net income before interest. The income before interest in year 10 would be $98,250 plus $27,280, or $125,530. The implied price at the end of year 10 would be $1,255,300.

The next step is the computation of the cost of capital. Using the procedures set forth in Section B, the weighted average cost of capital is computed as follows:

	Cost	Weight	Weighted Cost
Debt (After Tax)	6%	50%	3%
Equity	12%	50%	6%
			9%

The final step is the computation of the present value of the cash flows. The computation would be as follows:

Year	Cash Flow	PV Factor	Present Value
1	$ 51,000	.91743	$ 46,789
2	$ 53,320	.84168	$ 44,878
3	$ 55,820	.77218	$ 43,103
4	$ 58,480	.70843	$ 41,429
5	$ 61,220	.64993	$ 39,789
6	$ 64,120	.59627	$ 38,233
7	$ 66,980	.54703	$ 36,640
8	$ 70,060	.50187	$ 35,161
9	$ 73,220	.46043	$ 33,713
10	$1,331,900	.42241	$562,608
			$922,343

2. Multiples Analysis

Another less precise approach to determining the value of a business is to use various multiples to estimate the value of the business. These multiples could be derived from reviewing the amounts paid for other businesses in acquisition transactions for which there is available public information. By examining these other transactions, the analyst can determine what types of multiples are being paid for reasonably comparable businesses. These multiples can then be applied to the business under review.

Several types of multiples can be used. A multiple based on book value of a company may be used. This multiple would be based on the relationship between the price paid for other comparable businesses and the book value of those businesses at the time of the acquisition. For most industries, book value multiples are extremely unreliable because of the use of historical costs in accounting for inventory and property, plant, and equipment. Different businesses may have widely disparate book values solely as the result of historical cost accounting.

Other more reliable multiples would be based on the relationship between the price paid for comparable businesses and the earnings or cash flow of those businesses. The earnings multiple analysis would be similar to the use of price/earnings ratios to compute the value of the common stock of a company as discussed in section A. 3. above. In order to apply a meaningful earnings multiple analysis, the earnings for the comparable companies must be "cleaned up." This clean up process involves converting the companies under consideration to common bases of accounting where multiple acceptable accounting approaches exist (*e.g.*, inventory accounting) and eliminating from the earnings any unusual or nonrecurring items that would distort the comparisons. Earnings multiples can be based on net income or they may be based on some partial earnings number such as operating earnings before or after interest expense. Cash flow multiples are similar to earnings multiples except that the multiples are based on an appropriate cash flow number such as free cash flows. Cash flow multiples are more relevant to some industries that others.

3. Asset Values

Another approach for valuing a business is to value the business based on the sum of the values of its individual assets. The value of the assets could be computed on the basis of their replacement values or on the basis of liquidation values, depending on the differences between these two amounts and the purpose for which the business is being valued.

One problem with asset valuation approaches is that it is difficult to determine directly the value of the goodwill or going concern value of a business. Goodwill or going concern value is usually based in large part on the earning power of the business as a whole. There is normally not a market for these types of assets. Their value is usually computed as a residual amount. The goodwill or going concern value is the difference between the value of the business as a whole and the aggregate of the values of the assets that are directly capable of valuation.

Because of this circularity problem, it is difficult to determine the value of a business for which good-will or going concern value is significant without using an earnings or discounted cash flow approach to valuation. Accordingly, these types of values are generally used in special situations or as a check on the values determined under one of the procedures described above. Thus, the liquidation value of a business might be viewed as the minimum value of a business. Replacement value, on the other hand, may be viewed as a type of maximum value for the business.

*

APPENDIX
TIME VALUE OF MONEY

This appendix will discuss the concept of the time value of money (also known as present value and future value analysis or discounting). Time value of money concepts are employed extensively in the areas of accounting and corporate finance. This appendix will introduce the concepts of present and future value for those who are not familiar with them and will serve as a convenient review for those who are familiar with these concepts.

The underlying purpose of time value of money concepts is to reflect the fact that $1 available today is not the same as $1 that is available at some time in the future. Aside from the theoretical basis for this fact, the difference in value can be illustrated quite easily. Assume that you are offered the choice between receiving $1 today or $1 at the end of one year. If you elect to receive the $1 today, the dollar can be put to work. It can be used to pay down interest-bearing debt and thereby reduce interest expense. Alternatively, you can invest the $1 and earn additional income on the $1. In either event, you will be better off by taking the $1 today as opposed to $1 at the end of one year because at the end of one year, you will not only have the original $1 but you will also have the interest expense saved or the income earned on the $1. Thus, $1 today is more valuable than $1 at a later date.

In order to compare meaningfully cash flows that occur at different times, it is necessary to have a way of expressing these dollar amounts on an equivalent basis. This can be done by converting dollars today to an appropriate equivalent at a future date (called future value analysis) or by converting dollars in the future to a current equivalent value (called present value analysis or discounting).

The computations in this appendix are all based on "compound interest." Compound interest must be distinguished from simple interest. Simple interest means that interest is payable or accrues only on the original principal balance regardless of how often interest is paid. Thus, if a loan provides for 6% simple interest on a $100 principal balance with all interest accruing and payable at the end of two years, the interest for the first year would be $6 ($100 x 6%) and the interest for the second year would also be $6 ($100 x 6%). The total interest would be $12.

Where compound interest applies, interest is computed on the original principal balance plus any interest that has accrued and not been paid in prior periods. Thus, if the loan example in the prior paragraph provides that interest compounds annually, the interest would be computed as follows. Interest in the first year would still be $6. The interest in the second year would be 6% of the original principal plus the first year's accrued interest. Thus, the interest for year 2 would be 6% of $106, or $6.36 and the total interest with annual compounding is $12.36.

1. Future Value of $1

The future value of $1 is the future equivalent value of $1 today. One dollar available today will increase to a greater amount in the future as a result of the ability to earn interest on the $1 by investing it until the future date. Thus, future value is the sum of the original principal amount plus the interest that accrues on that original amount over a designated period of time.

To illustrate, assume that you have $100 today and you want to know the future equivalent value of that $100 at the end of three years. To compute the future value, you need to know the relevant interest rate to use in the calculations. In this illustration, it is assumed that you can earn 6% interest on investments over the three-year period. At the end of the first year, the original $100 will have grown to $106. This amount is computed by multiplying the original $100 by the sum of 1 plus the appropriate interest rate expressed as a decimal. Thus the calculation is $100 x 1.06 = $106.

For the next year, the amount available to invest is not only the original $100, but the additional six dollars of interest earned in the first year as well. As discussed above, the ability to earn additional interest on interest from prior periods is referred to as compounding. Accordingly, at the end of the second year, the original $100 will have grown in value to $106 x 1.06, or $112.36. Similarly, at the end of the third year, the original $100 will have grown in value to $112.36 x 1.06, or $119.10.

From these calculations, it can be seen that the appropriate factor to compute the future value of $1 at the end of three years assuming an annual interest rate of 6% is 1.191 ($119.10/$100). This factor can be computed directly by multiplying 1.06 x 1.06 x 1.06, which can also be expressed as 1.06^3. More generally, the formula used to compute future value factors is $(1 + r)^n$ where r is the appropriate interest rate per period and n is the number of periods for which the money will be invested. The known present value (PV) multiplied by this factor equals the unknown future value (FV). Expressed as a formula, future value is computed as follows:

$$FV = PV \times (1+r)^n$$

Aside from performing the mathematical calculation each time a future value factor is needed, there are two primary sources for future value factors. Many books have future value tables that give the future value factors for a number of different interest rates and different time periods. The interest rates are listed on the top or side margin and the time periods are listed on the other margin. The appropriate factor for use in a calculation is taken from the intersection in the table of the interest rate and the number of time periods (called compounding periods). A future value factor table is included at the end of this appendix (Table 1). As can be seen, the future value factor for 6% interest for three periods is 1.191. A principal limitation of the table approach is that the factors are only provided for certain discrete interest rates and numbers of compounding periods. Other factors can be estimated by interpolation between the closest factors given in the table.

The other primary source for future value factors are calculators or computers. Most calculators and many computer software packages include built-in formulas for calculating the appropriate future value factor for any interest rate and any number of periods.

In many cases, interest compounds or is payable on a basis other than annually. When that is the case, the procedures described above are applied except that the interest rate used in the calculations is the annual interest rate divided by the number of compounding periods during the year and the number of periods used in the calculations is the number of years multiplied by the number of compounding periods during the year. After making these adjustments, the calculations proceed in the same manner as set forth above. To illustrate, if the 6% interest in the example above is compounded quarterly, the future value would be computed using an interest rate of 1.5% (6% divided by 4) for twelve periods (three years multiplied by 4). Mathematically, the future value factor would be 1.015^{12}, or 1.1956. Note that the effect of compounding on a more frequent basis than annually is to increase the future value factor.

2. Present Value of $1

The present value of $1 is the present equivalent value of $1 that is not available until some time in the future. It is the amount that would have to be invested now so that at the end of the time period at issue, the amount invested plus accrued interest would equal the known future value. The $1 that is available in the future is not worth as much as $1 available today because if you had the $1 available today, you would be able to earn interest on the $1 by investing it until the future date.

To illustrate, assume that you are offered $100 at the end of three years and you want to know the present equivalent value of that $100 (that is, how much you would be willing to receive today in lieu of the $100 at the end of three years). To compute the present value, you need to know the relevant interest rate to use in your calculations. In this illustration, assume that you can earn 6% interest on investments over the three year period. To compute present value, it is helpful first to review the future value calculation. From the analysis of future value in Section 1, we know that the future value of $1 after three years assuming a six per cent interest rate is $1 x 1.06^3. If FV equals the future value and PV equals the present value, then FV = PV x 1.06^3. If you rearrange this expression, then PV = FV/1.06^3. Accordingly, if the future value (the amount available in three years) is $100, the present value equivalent is $100/$1.06^3$, or $83.96. Thus, if you had $83.96 available to invest today and you invest it for three years at 6% interest, the total investment at the end of three years would be $83.96 x 1.06^3, or $100. We therefore say that the present value equivalent of $100 available at the end of three years is $83.96.

More generally, the formula used to compute present value factors is $1/(1 + r)^n$ where r is the appropriate interest rate per period and n is the number of periods for which the money will be invested. As noted above in connection with future value calculations, many books have present value factor tables that give the present value factors for a number of different interest rates and compounding periods. The appropriate present value factor is taken from the intersection in the table of the interest rate and the number of compounding periods. A present value factor table is included at the end of this appendix as Table 2. The present value factor in Table 2 for 6% interest and three periods is .8396.

As in the case of future value factors, most calculators and many computer software packages include built-in formulas for calculating the appropriate present value factor for any interest rate and any number of periods.

Where interest compounds on a basis other than annually, the same procedures are applied except that the interest rate is the annual rate divided by the number of compounding periods during the year and the number of periods to use is the number of years multiplied by the number of compounding periods per year. After making these adjustments, the calculations proceed in the same manner as set forth above. Thus, if the 6% interest in the example above is compounded quarterly, the present value would be computed using an interest rate of 1.5% (6% divided by 4) for twelve periods (three years multiplied by 4). Mathematically, the present value factor would be $1/(1.015)^{12}$ or .8364. Note that the effect of compounding more frequently than annually has the effect of decreasing the present value factor.

3. Future Value of an Annuity of $1

In some cases, a future value analysis involves a stream of equal periodic payments rather than just a single cash flow. A string of equal periodic payments is called an annuity. An example of an annuity would be where a parent decides to make a contribution of $1,000 to a child's college investment fund at the end of each of the next ten years. This creates a ten year annuity of $1,000. In order to determine the amount that will be in the child's college fund at the end of the ten year period, we need to compute the future value of a ten year annuity.

To calculate the future value of this annuity, assume that the relevant interest rate is six per cent. The annuity can be analyzed as ten separate amounts of $1,000 each. The sum of the future values of these ten amounts will be the future value of the annuity. The $1,000 invested at the end of the first year will earn interest for nine years. Therefore, using the procedures for calculating future value as discussed in Section 1, the future value of the first $1,000 payment at the end of the ten-year period will be $1,000 x 1.06^9, or $1,689.48. The $1,000 contribution at the end of the second year will only be invested for eight years. The future value of the second contribution at the end of ten years will therefore be $1,000 x 1.06^8, or $1,593.85. This process is repeated for each payment until the last payment at the end of the ten year period. The last payment will not be invested at all so that the future value of the last payment will be $1,000. The total of the future values of each $1,000 payment would be $13,180.79. This is the future value of an annuity of $1,000 per year for ten years at an interest rate of 6% per year.

Note that in the problem in the preceding paragraph, each payment of $1,000 is being multiplied by a future value factor. The separate future values are then added to give the future value of the entire annuity. An alternative approach to making this calculation would be to add the appropriate future value factors for each period in the annuity and then multiply this sum of future value factors by $1,000. Mathematically, this will produce the same result as the calculation of the separate future values for each $1,000 payment and adding those future values.

Future value tables for annuities are prepared just as in the case of future values and present values of $1. The factors in these tables represent the future value of an annuity of $1 for the number of periods indicated and at the interest rate indicated. A sample table of future value factors for annuities is included at the end of this appendix as Table 3. Calculators and computer software also have functions that calculate the future value of an annuity.

The annuity illustrated above called for payments to made at the end of each year during the annuity period. This is called an ordinary annuity or an annuity in arrears. If the payments in the annuity are to be made at the beginning of each of the years in the annuity period, this is referred to as an annuity due or an annuity in advance. As compared to an annuity in arrears, an annuity in advance gets one additional year's interest on each of the annuity payments. For example, the first payment of a ten year annuity in arrears earns interest for nine years but the first payment in a ten-year annuity in advance earns interest for ten years. The last payment in an annuity in arrears does not earn any interest but the last payment in an annuity in advance earns interest for one year. Most tables for the future value of an annuity give the future value for an annuity in arrears. When using such tables to determine the factor for an annuity in advance, the procedure is to look up in the table the factor for the period one greater than the actual number of payments in the annuity and then subtract one from that factor. This can be illustrated using the factors in Table 3. Assume that you want to determine the future value of a ten year annuity in advance at an interest rate of 8%. The future value factor for an eleven-year annuity in arrears at an interest rate of 8% is 16.64549. Subtracting one from that factor gives 15.64549, the appropriate factor for a 10–year annuity in advance at an interest rate of 8%. Similar adjustments must be made when using a calculator or computer software function, unless the calculator or software has separate functions for annuities in advance.

4. Present Value of an Annuity of $1

In many situations, it is necessary to determine the present value of an annuity. For example, a proposed investment may be projected to produce an annual cash flow for a number of years. If the cash flow each year is projected to be equal in amount, the returns on this investment constitute an annuity. To determine whether this investment should be made, the present value of the annuity would be computed. The present value of the annuity is the sum of the present values of the separate payments making up the annuity. As in the case of the future value of the annuity, you can alternatively add up the present value factors for each year in the annuity and multiply the constant annuity payment by the sum of these present value factors.

Tables are available that give the factors for the present value of an annuity of $1 for selected interest rates and selected terms for the annuity. Based on the term of the annuity and the applicable interest rate, you determine the appropriate factor from the table and multiply that factor by the amount of the annuity payment. Table 4 at the end of this appendix gives the present value factors for annuities at a variety of interest rates and for a variety of periods. Alternatively, special functions in calculators or computer software can be used to calculate the present value of an annuity based on any interest rate and any number of periods for the annuity.

The factors in the present value tables discussed above are normally based on the present value of an annuity in arrears. Adjustments must be made to calculate the present value of an annuity in advance. As compared to an annuity in arrears, the payments on an annuity in advance are discounted for one less period (since each payment occurs one period earlier as compared to an annuity in arrears). The last payment of a ten-year annuity in arrears is discounted for ten periods while the last payment of a ten year annuity in advance is discounted for only nine years. The first payment in an annuity in arrears is discounted for one year while the first payment of an annuity in advance is not discounted at all. To determine the appropriate present value factor for an annuity in advance from the tables for the present value of an annuity in arrears, you select from the tables the appropriate factor for one period less than the number of periods in the annuity and then add one to that factor. This can be illustrated using the factors in Table 4. The factor for the present value of a ten-year annuity in advance at an interest rate of 12% would be the present value factor for a nine-year annuity in arrears at a 12% interest rate (5.32825) plus one, or 6.32825. Similar adjustments must be made when using a calculator or a computer software application unless they provide separate functions specifically for annuities in advance.

The formula for computing the present value of an annuity can be rearranged to produce different results. For example, assume that you have $100,-000 to invest. You want to know the amount that you would have to receive as an annuity for fifteen years to earn an interest rate of 14%. In the illustrations above, the annuity factor is multiplied by the annuity amount to compute the present value of the annuity. In this case, since the present value of the annuity is known, you can divide this amount by the annuity factor to compute the annuity that would have to be received to produce the desired 14% return. The factor for the present value of a 15–year annuity at an interest rate of 14% from Table 4 is 6.14217. Dividing this into the present value gives the necessary annuity amount of $16,280.89 ($100,000/6.14217).

5. Irregular Cash Flows

The discussion above relates to determining present or future values for a single amount or for simple annuities with an equal payment in each of the annuity periods. Most present value and future value problems do not present such simple cash flow patterns. This section will discuss how to compute present and future values for more complicated cash flow streams.

One type of problem that is encountered frequently is a computation of the present value of a cash flow stream that includes an annuity for the life a project and then a terminal cash flow at the end of the project. For example, the market value of a bond is the present value of the stream of stated interest payments on the bond (an annuity) plus the present value of the principal amount of the bond at the date of maturity. To compute the present value in this situation, you simply compute the present value of the stated interest payments using the procedures for the present value of an annuity and then add to that amount the present value of the principal amount determined using the procedures for computing the present value of a single cash flow.

To illustrate, assume that a ten-year, $1,000,000 bond is issued with a stated interest rate of 8% payable semi-annually. The actual yield on the bond is 10%. The market value of this bond is the sum of two components. The present value of the semi-annual interest payment of $40,000 is determined using the factor for the present value of an annuity for 20 periods at a rate of 5%. From Table 4, this factor is determined to be 12.46221 and the present value of the interest payments is $498,-488.40. The second component is the present value of a single amount at the end of 20 periods at an interest rate of 5% (using 20 periods reflects the semi-annual compounding on the bond). The present value factor for $1 received at the end of 20 periods at a rate of 5% is .35894 and the present value of the $1,000,000 principal amount is $358,-940. The total market value of the bond is thus $857,428.40 ($358,940 + $498,488.40).

A second type of problem occurs where none of the cash flows are equal. There are multiple cash flows presented in the problem and the amounts of cash flow to be received or paid during each period vary. In this type of problem, the present or future value must be computed separately for each cash flow and the sum of these separate present or future value calculations would be the present or future value of the uneven stream.

The third type of frequently encountered problem in future value/present value problems arises when the relevant stream of cash flows involves an annuity but the initial period of the annuity is not the current period. Computing a present or future value in this type of problem involves multiplying the annuity by both an annuity factor and a single sum factor. For example, a business might be reviewing a project that involves a stream of cash flows that is structured as an annuity but that does not begin until some time in the future. Assume that such a project generates a cash flow of $100,-000 per year for twelve years beginning at the end of year five. The present value of this annuity (assuming a 10% discount rate) would be determined in two steps. First, the $100,000 annuity is multiplied by the present value of an annuity factor for twelve periods at 10%. From Table 4 this factor is determined to be 6.81369 and the present value of the annuity is $681,369. This, however, is the present value at the end of year four. To determine the present value as of the present date, you must multiply the present value of the annuity by the present value of $1 at the end of four years at a 10% discount rate. This rate from Table 2 is .68301 and the present value of the annuity at the current time would be $465,381.84 ($681,369 x .68301).

Table 1

Future Value of $1

Interest Rates	2.0%	3.0%	4.0%	5.0%	6.0%	7.0%	8.0%
Number of Compounding Periods							
1	1.02000	1.03000	1.04000	1.05000	1.06000	1.07000	1.08000
2	1.04040	1.06090	1.08160	1.10250	1.12360	1.14490	1.16640
3	1.06121	1.09273	1.12486	1.15762	1.19102	1.22504	1.25971
4	1.08243	1.12551	1.16986	1.21551	1.26248	1.31080	1.36049
5	1.10408	1.15927	1.21665	1.27628	1.33823	1.40255	1.46933
6	1.12616	1.19405	1.26532	1.34010	1.41852	1.50073	1.58687
7	1.14869	1.22987	1.31593	1.40710	1.50363	1.60578	1.71382
8	1.17166	1.26677	1.36857	1.47746	1.59385	1.71819	1.85093
9	1.19509	1.30477	1.42331	1.55133	1.68948	1.83846	1.99900
10	1.21899	1.34392	1.48024	1.62889	1.79085	1.96715	2.15892
11	1.24337	1.38423	1.53945	1.71034	1.89830	2.10485	2.33164
12	1.26824	1.42576	1.60103	1.79586	2.01220	2.25219	2.51817
13	1.29361	1.46853	1.66507	1.88565	2.13293	2.40985	2.71962
14	1.31948	1.51259	1.73168	1.97993	2.26090	2.57853	2.93719
15	1.34587	1.55797	1.80094	2.07893	2.39656	2.75903	3.17217
16	1.37279	1.60471	1.87298	2.18287	2.54035	2.95216	3.42594
17	1.40024	1.65285	1.94790	2.29202	2.69277	3.15882	3.70002
18	1.42825	1.70243	2.02582	2.40662	2.85434	3.37993	3.99602
19	1.45681	1.75351	2.10685	2.52695	3.02560	3.61653	4.31570
20	1.48595	1.80611	2.19112	2.65330	3.20714	3.86968	4.66096
21	1.51567	1.86029	2.27877	2.78596	3.39956	4.14056	5.03383
22	1.54598	1.91610	2.36992	2.92526	3.60354	4.43040	5.43654
23	1.57690	1.97359	2.46472	3.07152	3.81975	4.74053	5.87146
24	1.60844	2.03279	2.56330	3.22510	4.04893	5.07237	6.34118
25	1.64061	2.09378	2.66584	3.38635	4.29187	5.42743	6.84848
26	1.67342	2.15659	2.77247	3.55567	4.54938	5.80735	7.39635
27	1.70689	2.22129	2.88337	3.73346	4.82235	6.21387	7.98806
28	1.74102	2.28793	2.99870	3.92013	5.11169	6.64884	8.62711
29	1.77584	2.35657	3.11865	4.11614	5.41839	7.11426	9.31727
30	1.81136	2.42726	3.24340	4.32194	5.74349	7.61226	10.06266
35	1.99989	2.81386	3.94609	5.51602	7.68609	10.67658	14.78534
40	2.20804	3.26204	4.80102	7.03999	10.28572	14.97446	21.72452
45	2.43785	3.78160	5.84118	8.98501	13.76461	21.00245	31.92045
50	2.69159	4.38391	7.10668	11.46740	18.42015	29.45703	46.90161

Table 1—Continued

Future Value of $1

Interest Rates	10.0%	12.0%	14.0%	16.0%	18.0%	20.0%
Number of Compounding Periods						
1	1.10000	1.12000	1.14000	1.16000	1.18000	1.20000
2	1.21000	1.25440	1.29960	1.34560	1.39240	1.44000
3	1.33100	1.40493	1.48154	1.56090	1.64303	1.72800
4	1.46410	1.57352	1.68896	1.81064	1.93878	2.07360
5	1.61051	1.76234	1.92541	2.10034	2.28776	2.48832
6	1.77156	1.97382	2.19497	2.43640	2.69955	2.98598
7	1.94872	2.21068	2.50227	2.82622	3.18547	3.58318
8	2.14359	2.47596	2.85259	3.27841	3.75886	4.29982
9	2.35795	2.77308	3.25195	3.80296	4.43545	5.15978
10	2.59374	3.10585	3.70722	4.41144	5.23384	6.19174
11	2.85312	3.47855	4.22623	5.11726	6.17593	7.43008
12	3.13843	3.89598	4.81790	5.93603	7.28759	8.91610
13	3.45227	4.36349	5.49241	6.88579	8.59936	10.69932
14	3.79750	4.88711	6.26135	7.98752	10.14724	12.83918
15	4.17725	5.47357	7.13794	9.26552	11.97375	15.40702
16	4.59497	6.13039	8.13725	10.74800	14.12902	18.48843
17	5.05447	6.86604	9.27646	12.46768	16.67225	22.18611
18	5.55992	7.68997	10.57517	14.46251	19.67325	26.62333
19	6.11591	8.61276	12.05569	16.77652	23.21444	31.94800
20	6.72750	9.64629	13.74349	19.46076	27.39303	38.33760
21	7.40025	10.80385	15.66758	22.57448	32.32378	46.00512
22	8.14027	12.10031	17.86104	26.18640	38.14206	55.20614
23	8.95430	13.55235	20.36158	30.37622	45.00763	66.24737
24	9.84973	15.17863	23.21221	35.23642	53.10901	79.49685
25	10.83471	17.00006	26.46192	40.87424	62.66863	95.39622
26	11.91818	19.04007	30.16658	47.41412	73.94898	114.47546
27	13.10999	21.32488	34.38991	55.00038	87.25980	137.37055
28	14.42099	23.88387	39.20449	63.80044	102.96656	164.84466
29	15.86309	26.74993	44.69312	74.00851	121.50054	197.81359
30	17.44940	29.95992	50.95016	85.84988	143.37064	237.37631
35	28.10244	52.79962	98.10018	180.31407	327.99729	590.66823
40	45.25926	93.05097	188.88351	378.72116	750.37834	1469.77157
45	72.89048	163.98760	363.67907	795.44383	1716.68388	3657.26199
50	117.39085	289.00219	700.23299	1670.70380	3927.35686	9100.43815

TIME VALUE OF MONEY

Table 2

Present Value of $1

Interest Rates	2.0%	3.0%	4.0%	5.0%	6.0%	7.0%	8.0%
Number of Compounding Periods							
1	0.98039	0.97087	0.96154	0.95238	0.94340	0.93458	0.92593
2	0.96117	0.94260	0.92456	0.90703	0.89000	0.87344	0.85734
3	0.94232	0.91514	0.88900	0.86384	0.83962	0.81630	0.79383
4	0.92385	0.88849	0.85480	0.82270	0.79209	0.76290	0.73503
5	0.90573	0.86261	0.82193	0.78353	0.74726	0.71299	0.68058
6	0.88797	0.83748	0.79031	0.74622	0.70496	0.66634	0.63017
7	0.87056	0.81309	0.75992	0.71068	0.66506	0.62275	0.58349
8	0.85349	0.78941	0.73069	0.67684	0.62741	0.58201	0.54027
9	0.83676	0.76642	0.70259	0.64461	0.59190	0.54393	0.50025
10	0.82035	0.74409	0.67556	0.61391	0.55839	0.50835	0.46319
11	0.80426	0.72242	0.64958	0.58468	0.52679	0.47509	0.42888
12	0.78849	0.70138	0.62460	0.55684	0.49697	0.44401	0.39711
13	0.77303	0.68095	0.60057	0.53032	0.46884	0.41496	0.36770
14	0.75788	0.66112	0.57748	0.50507	0.44230	0.38782	0.34046
15	0.74301	0.64186	0.55526	0.48102	0.41727	0.36245	0.31524
16	0.72845	0.62317	0.53391	0.45811	0.39365	0.33873	0.29189
17	0.71416	0.60502	0.51337	0.43630	0.37136	0.31657	0.27027
18	0.70016	0.58739	0.49363	0.41552	0.35034	0.29586	0.25025
19	0.68643	0.57029	0.47464	0.39573	0.33051	0.27651	0.23171
20	0.67297	0.55368	0.45639	0.37689	0.31180	0.25842	0.21455
21	0.65978	0.53755	0.43883	0.35894	0.29416	0.24151	0.19866
22	0.64684	0.52189	0.42196	0.34185	0.27751	0.22571	0.18394
23	0.63416	0.50669	0.40573	0.32557	0.26180	0.21095	0.17032
24	0.62172	0.49193	0.39012	0.31007	0.24698	0.19715	0.15770
25	0.60953	0.47761	0.37512	0.29530	0.23300	0.18425	0.14602
26	0.59758	0.46369	0.36069	0.28124	0.21981	0.17220	0.13520
27	0.58586	0.45019	0.34682	0.26785	0.20737	0.16093	0.12519
28	0.57437	0.43708	0.33348	0.25509	0.19563	0.15040	0.11591
29	0.56311	0.42435	0.32065	0.24295	0.18456	0.14056	0.10733
30	0.55207	0.41199	0.30832	0.23138	0.17411	0.13137	0.09938
35	0.50003	0.35538	0.25342	0.18129	0.13011	0.09366	0.06763
40	0.45289	0.30656	0.20829	0.14205	0.09722	0.06678	0.04603
45	0.41020	0.26444	0.17120	0.11130	0.07265	0.04761	0.03133
50	0.37153	0.22811	0.14071	0.08720	0.05429	0.03395	0.02132

Table 2—Continued

Present Value of $1

Interest Rates	10.0%	12.0%	14.0%	16.0%	18.0%	20.0%
Number of Compounding Periods						
1	0.90909	0.89286	0.87719	0.86207	0.84746	0.83333
2	0.82645	0.79719	0.76947	0.74316	0.71818	0.69444
3	0.75131	0.71178	0.67497	0.64066	0.60863	0.57870
4	0.68301	0.63552	0.59208	0.55229	0.51579	0.48225
5	0.62092	0.56743	0.51937	0.47611	0.43711	0.40188
6	0.56447	0.50663	0.45559	0.41044	0.37043	0.33490
7	0.51316	0.45235	0.39964	0.35383	0.31393	0.27908
8	0.46651	0.40388	0.35056	0.30503	0.26604	0.23257
9	0.42410	0.36061	0.30751	0.26295	0.22546	0.19381
10	0.38554	0.32197	0.26974	0.22668	0.19106	0.16151
11	0.35049	0.28748	0.23662	0.19542	0.16192	0.13459
12	0.31863	0.25668	0.20756	0.16846	0.13722	0.11216
13	0.28966	0.22917	0.18207	0.14523	0.11629	0.09346
14	0.26333	0.20462	0.15971	0.12520	0.09855	0.07789
15	0.23939	0.18270	0.14010	0.10793	0.08352	0.06491
16	0.21763	0.16312	0.12289	0.09304	0.07078	0.05409
17	0.19784	0.14564	0.10780	0.08021	0.05998	0.04507
18	0.17986	0.13004	0.09456	0.06914	0.05083	0.03756
19	0.16351	0.11611	0.08295	0.05961	0.04308	0.03130
20	0.14864	0.10367	0.07276	0.05139	0.03651	0.02608
21	0.13513	0.09256	0.06383	0.04430	0.03094	0.02174
22	0.12285	0.08264	0.05599	0.03819	0.02622	0.01811
23	0.11168	0.07379	0.04911	0.03292	0.02222	0.01509
24	0.10153	0.06588	0.04308	0.02838	0.01883	0.01258
25	0.09230	0.05882	0.03779	0.02447	0.01596	0.01048
26	0.08391	0.05252	0.03315	0.02109	0.01352	0.00874
27	0.07628	0.04689	0.02908	0.01818	0.01146	0.00728
28	0.06934	0.04187	0.02551	0.01567	0.00971	0.00607
29	0.06304	0.03738	0.02237	0.01351	0.00823	0.00506
30	0.05731	0.03338	0.01963	0.01165	0.00697	0.00421
35	0.03558	0.01894	0.01019	0.00555	0.00305	0.00169
40	0.02209	0.01075	0.00529	0.00264	0.00133	0.00068
45	0.01372	0.00610	0.00275	0.00126	0.00058	0.00027
50	0.00852	0.00346	0.00143	0.00060	0.00025	0.00011

Table 3

Future Value of Annuity of $1

Interest Rates	2.0%	3.0%	4.0%	5.0%	6.0%	7.0%	8.0%
Number of Compounding Periods							
1	1.00000	1.00000	1.00000	1.00000	1.00000	1.00000	1.00000
2	2.02000	2.03000	2.04000	2.05000	2.06000	2.07000	2.08000
3	3.06040	3.09090	3.12160	3.15250	3.18360	3.21490	3.24640
4	4.12161	4.18363	4.24646	4.31012	4.37462	4.43994	4.50611
5	5.20404	5.30914	5.41632	5.52563	5.63709	5.75074	5.86660
6	6.30812	6.46841	6.63298	6.80191	6.97532	7.15329	7.33593
7	7.43428	7.66246	7.89829	8.14201	8.39384	8.65402	8.92280
8	8.58297	8.89234	9.21423	9.54911	9.89747	10.25980	10.63663
9	9.75463	10.15911	10.58280	11.02656	11.49132	11.97799	12.48756
10	10.94972	11.46388	12.00611	12.57789	13.18079	13.81645	14.48656
11	12.16872	12.80780	13.48635	14.20679	14.97164	15.78360	16.64549
12	13.41209	14.19203	15.02581	15.91713	16.86994	17.88845	18.97713
13	14.68033	15.61779	16.62684	17.71298	18.88214	20.14064	21.49530
14	15.97394	17.08632	18.29191	19.59863	21.01507	22.55049	24.21492
15	17.29342	18.59891	20.02359	21.57856	23.27597	25.12902	27.15211
16	18.63929	20.15688	21.82453	23.65749	25.67253	27.88805	30.32428
17	20.01207	21.76159	23.69751	25.84037	28.21288	30.84022	33.75023
18	21.41231	23.41444	25.64541	28.13238	30.90565	33.99903	37.45024
19	22.84056	25.11687	27.67123	30.53900	33.75999	37.37896	41.44626
20	24.29737	26.87037	29.77808	33.06595	36.78559	40.99549	45.76196
21	25.78332	28.67649	31.96920	35.71925	39.99273	44.86518	50.42292
22	27.29898	30.53678	34.24797	38.50521	43.39229	49.00574	55.45676
23	28.84496	32.45288	36.61789	41.43048	46.99583	53.43614	60.89330
24	30.42186	34.42647	39.08260	44.50200	50.81558	58.17667	66.76476
25	32.03030	36.45926	41.64591	47.72710	54.86451	63.24904	73.10594
26	33.67091	38.55304	44.31174	51.11345	59.15638	68.67647	79.95442
27	35.34432	40.70963	47.08421	54.66913	63.70577	74.48382	87.35077
28	37.05121	42.93092	49.96758	58.40258	68.52811	80.69769	95.33883
29	38.79223	45.21885	52.96629	62.32271	73.63980	87.34653	103.96594
30	40.56808	47.57542	56.08494	66.43885	79.05819	94.46079	113.28321
35	49.99448	60.46208	73.65222	90.32031	111.43478	138.23688	172.31680
40	60.40198	75.40126	95.02552	120.79977	154.76197	199.63511	259.05652
45	71.89271	92.71986	121.02939	159.70016	212.74351	285.74931	386.50562
50	84.57940	112.79687	152.66708	209.34800	290.33590	406.52893	573.77016

Table 3—Continued

Future Value of Annuity of $1

Interest Rates	10.0%	12.0%	14.0%	16.0%	18.0%	20.0%
Number of Compounding Periods						
1	1.00000	1.00000	1.00000	1.00000	1.00000	1.00000
2	2.10000	2.12000	2.14000	2.16000	2.18000	2.20000
3	3.31000	3.37440	3.43960	3.50560	3.57240	3.64000
4	4.64100	4.77933	4.92114	5.06650	5.21543	5.36800
5	6.10510	6.35285	6.61010	6.87714	7.15421	7.44160
6	7.71561	8.11519	8.53552	8.97748	9.44197	9.92992
7	9.48717	10.08901	10.73049	11.41387	12.14152	12.91590
8	11.43589	12.29969	13.23276	14.24009	15.32700	16.49908
9	13.57948	14.77566	16.08535	17.51851	19.08585	20.79890
10	15.93742	17.54874	19.33730	21.32147	23.52131	25.95868
11	18.53117	20.65458	23.04452	25.73290	28.75514	32.15042
12	21.38428	24.13313	27.27075	30.85017	34.93107	39.58050
13	24.52271	28.02911	32.08865	36.78620	42.21866	48.49660
14	27.97498	32.39260	37.58107	43.67199	50.81802	59.19592
15	31.77248	37.27971	43.84241	51.65951	60.96527	72.03511
16	35.94973	42.75328	50.98035	60.92503	72.93901	87.44213
17	40.54470	48.88367	59.11760	71.67303	87.06804	105.93056
18	45.59917	55.74971	68.39407	84.14072	103.74028	128.11667
19	51.15909	63.43968	78.96923	98.60323	123.41353	154.74000
20	57.27500	72.05244	91.02493	115.37975	146.62797	186.68800
21	64.00250	81.69874	104.76842	134.84051	174.02100	225.02560
22	71.40275	92.50258	120.43600	157.41499	206.34479	271.03072
23	79.54302	104.60289	138.29704	183.60138	244.48685	326.23686
24	88.49733	118.15524	158.65862	213.97761	289.49448	392.48424
25	98.34706	133.33387	181.87083	249.21402	342.60349	471.98108
26	109.18177	150.33393	208.33274	290.08827	405.27211	567.37730
27	121.09994	169.37401	238.49933	337.50239	479.22109	681.85276
28	134.20994	190.69889	272.88923	392.50277	566.48089	819.22331
29	148.63093	214.58275	312.09373	456.30322	669.44745	984.06797
30	164.49400	241.3327	356.7868	530.3117	790.9480	1181.8816
35	271.0244	431.6635	693.5727	1120.7130	1616.6516	2948.3411
40	442.5926	767.0914	1342.0251	2360.7572	4163.2130	7343.8578
45	718.9048	1358.2300	2590.5648	4965.274	9531.577	18281.310
50	1163.9085	2400.0182	4994.5213	10435.649	21813.094	45497.191

TIME VALUE OF MONEY

Table 4

Present Value of Annuity of $1

Interest Rates	2.0%	3.0%	4.0%	5.0%	6.0%	7.0%	8.0%
Number of Compounding Periods							
1	0.98039	0.97087	0.96154	0.95238	0.94340	0.93458	0.92593
2	1.94156	1.91347	1.88609	1.85941	1.83339	1.80802	1.78326
3	2.88388	2.82861	2.77509	2.72325	2.67301	2.62432	2.57710
4	3.80773	3.71710	3.62990	3.54595	3.46511	3.38721	3.31213
5	4.71346	4.57971	4.45182	4.32948	4.21236	4.10020	3.99271
6	5.60143	5.41719	5.24214	5.07569	4.91732	4.76654	4.62288
7	6.47199	6.23028	6.00205	5.78637	5.58238	5.38929	5.20637
8	7.32548	7.01969	6.73274	6.46321	6.20979	5.97130	5.74664
9	8.16224	7.78611	7.43533	7.10782	6.80169	6.51523	6.24689
10	8.98259	8.53020	8.11090	7.72173	7.36009	7.02358	6.71008
11	9.78685	9.25262	8.76048	8.30641	7.88687	7.49867	7.13896
12	10.57534	9.95400	9.38507	8.86325	8.38384	7.94269	7.53608
13	11.34837	10.63496	9.98565	9.39357	8.85268	8.35765	7.90378
14	12.10625	11.29607	10.56312	9.89864	9.29498	8.74547	8.24424
15	12.84926	11.93794	11.11839	10.37966	9.71225	9.10791	8.55948
16	13.57771	12.56110	11.65230	10.83777	10.10590	9.44665	8.85137
17	14.29187	13.16612	12.16567	11.27407	10.47726	9.76322	9.12164
18	14.99203	13.75351	12.65930	11.68959	10.82760	10.05909	9.37189
19	15.67846	14.32380	13.13394	12.08532	11.15812	10.33560	9.60360
20	16.35143	14.87747	13.59033	12.46221	11.46992	10.59401	9.81815
21	17.01121	15.41502	14.02916	12.82115	11.76408	10.83553	10.01680
22	17.65805	15.93692	14.45112	13.16300	12.04158	11.06124	10.20074
23	18.29220	16.44361	14.85684	13.48857	12.30338	11.27219	10.37106
24	18.91393	16.93554	15.24696	13.79864	12.55036	11.46933	10.52876
25	19.52346	17.41315	15.62208	14.09394	12.78336	11.65358	10.67478
26	20.12104	17.87684	15.98277	14.37519	13.00317	11.82578	10.80998
27	20.70690	18.32703	16.32959	14.64303	13.21053	11.98671	10.93516
28	21.28127	18.76411	16.66306	14.89813	13.40616	12.13711	11.05100
29	21.84438	19.18845	16.98371	15.14107	13.59072	12.27767	11.15841
30	22.39646	19.60044	17.29203	15.37245	13.76483	12.40904	11.25778
35	24.99862	21.48722	18.66461	16.37419	14.49825	12.94767	11.65457
40	27.35548	23.11477	19.79277	17.15909	15.04630	13.33171	11.92461
45	29.49016	24.51871	20.72004	17.77407	15.45583	13.60552	12.10840
50	31.42361	25.72976	21.48218	18.25593	15.76186	13.80075	12.23348

Table 4—Continued

Present Value of Annuity of $1

Interest Rates	10.0%	12.0%	14.0%	16.0%	18.0%	20.0%
Number of Compounding Periods						
1	0.90909	0.89286	0.87719	0.86207	0.84746	0.83333
2	1.73554	1.69005	1.64666	1.60523	1.56564	1.52778
3	2.48685	2.40183	2.32163	2.24589	2.17427	2.10648
4	3.16987	3.03735	2.91371	2.79818	2.69006	2.58873
5	3.79079	3.60478	3.43308	3.27429	3.12717	2.99061
6	4.35526	4.11141	3.88867	3.68474	3.49760	3.32551
7	4.86842	4.56376	4.28830	4.03857	3.81153	3.60459
8	5.33493	4.96764	4.63886	4.34359	4.07757	3.83716
9	5.75902	5.32825	4.94637	4.60654	4.30302	4.03097
10	6.14457	5.65022	5.21612	4.83323	4.49409	4.19247
11	6.49506	5.93770	5.45273	5.02864	4.65601	4.32706
12	6.81369	6.19437	5.66029	5.19711	4.79322	4.43922
13	7.10336	6.42355	5.84236	5.34233	4.90951	4.53268
14	7.36669	6.62817	6.00207	5.46753	5.00806	4.61057
15	7.60608	6.81086	6.14217	5.57546	5.09158	4.67547
16	7.82371	6.97399	6.26506	5.66850	5.16235	4.72956
17	8.02155	7.11963	6.37286	5.74870	5.22233	4.77463
18	8.20141	7.24967	6.46742	5.81785	5.27316	4.81219
19	8.36492	7.36578	6.55037	5.87746	5.31624	4.84350
20	8.51356	7.46944	6.62313	5.92884	5.35275	4.86958
21	8.64869	7.56200	6.68696	5.97314	5.38368	4.89132
22	8.77154	7.64465	6.74294	6.01133	5.40990	4.90943
23	8.88322	7.71843	6.79206	6.04425	5.43212	4.92453
24	8.98474	7.78432	6.83514	6.07263	5.45095	4.93710
25	9.07704	7.84314	6.87293	6.09709	5.46691	4.94759
26	9.16095	7.89566	6.90608	6.11818	5.48043	4.95632
27	9.23722	7.94255	6.93515	6.13636	5.49189	4.96360
28	9.30657	7.98442	6.96066	6.15204	5.50160	4.96967
29	9.36961	8.02181	6.98304	6.16555	5.50983	4.97472
30	9.42691	8.05518	7.00266	6.17720	5.51681	4.97894
35	9.64416	8.17550	7.07005	6.21534	5.53862	4.99154
40	9.77905	8.24378	7.10504	6.23350	5.54815	4.99660
45	9.86281	8.28252	7.12322	6.24214	5.55232	4.99863
50	9.91481	8.30450	7.13266	6.24626	5.55414	4.99945

*

INDEX

References are to Pages

ACCOUNTING PRINCIPLES BOARD
Defined, 49
Opinions, 49

ACCOUNTING RESEARCH BULLETINS, 50

ACCOUNTS
Permanent, 41
Revenues and Expenses, 39–41
Temporary, 41–42

ACCOUNTS PAYABLE
Defined, 98
Imputing Interest on, 100
Purchase Discounts on, 98–99
Reporting Basis, 98–99

ACCOUNTS RECEIVABLE
See Receivables

ACCRUAL METHOD OF ACCOUNTING
Defined, 25
Annual Reporting, Effect of, 60

ACCRUED EXPENSES, 27–28

ACCRUED INTEREST EXPENSE
Issuance of Bonds Between Interest Dates, 189–190

407

ACCRUED LIABILITIES
Accounting for, 103–104
Defined, 4, 103

ACCRUED REVENUES, 26

ACQUISITIONS
See Business Combinations

ADDITIONAL PAID–IN–CAPITAL, 22

ADJUSTING ENTRIES
Defined, 24

AICPA
See American Institute of Certified Public Accountants

ALLOWANCE FOR DOUBTFUL ACCOUNTS
See Bad Debts

**AMERICAN INSTITUTE OF CERTIFIED PUBLIC ACCOUN-
TANTS**
Code of Professional Conduct, 50
Enforcement of GAAP, 50

AMORTIZATION
Bond Discount or Premium, 164–170
Expense Related to Intangible Assets, 155–156

ASSET TURNOVER, 332–333

ASSETS
Defined, 2–3
Return on, 334–335

AUDITS
Reports, 14–15

BAD DEBTS
Aged Receivables Analysis, 91–92
Allowance for Doubtful Accounts, 89–92
Computing, 89–92
Percentage of Sales Method, 90–91

BALANCE SHEET, 1–2
Example, 2, 45
Format, 6

BALANCE SHEET EQUATION
Defined, 5

BOND ISSUANCE COSTS, 193–194

BONDS AND DEBT INVESTMENTS
Acquisition, 161, 164–167
Bond Discount or Premium, 164–170
Interest Revenue, 162–170
Recognition of Changes in Value, 170–172
Valuation, 354–359

BUSINESS COMBINATIONS
Defined, 298
Determining Accounting Methods to Apply, 300–306
Goodwill, 308–309
Pooling of Interests Method of Accounting, 300, 311–313
Purchase Method of Accounting, 299–300, 306–311
Stock Acquisitions, 314

BUSINESS, VALUATION OF, 372–381

CAPITAL ASSET PRICING MODEL
Common Stock Valuation, 367–369

CAPITAL BUDGETING, 371–372

CAPITAL EXPENDITURES
Improvements to Fixed Assets, 149–151

CAPITAL LEASES
Defined, 209–210, 214
Lessee Accounting, 211–214
Lessor Accounting, 215–217

CAPITAL STOCK, 22

CAPITALIZATION
Defined, 35
Interest, 136–138

CASH
Accounting For, 82–85
Cash Equivalents, 82–83
Internal Controls, 84–85
Petty Cash, 84
Restricted Cash, 83

CASH DISCOUNTS ON RECEIVABLES, 86–88

CASH RECEIPTS BASIS FOR REVENUE RECOGNITION, 73–74

CHANGES IN ACCOUNTING PRINCIPLES, 341–344

CLOSING ENTRIES, 43–44

CLOSING THE BOOKS, 42–44

COMMON STOCK
Valuation, 362–369

COMPLETED CONTRACT METHOD OF ACCOUNTING
See Long Term Contracts

COMPUTER SOFTWARE COSTS, 157–158

CONSERVATISM, 61–63

CONSOLIDATED FINANCIAL STATEMENTS
Generally, 179–183

CONTINGENT LIABILITIES
Accounting for, 108–111
Conservatism, 62
Defined, 4

CONTRA ACCOUNTS
Accumulated Depreciation, 139–140
Allowance for Doubtful Accounts, 90
Defined, 36

CONTRIBUTIONS TO CAPITAL
Cash, 257–258
Noncash Property, 258–259

CONVERTIBLE DEBT
Generally, 201–204
Effect on Earnings Per Share, 322–326

CONVERTIBLE STOCK
Effect on Earnings Per Share 322–326
Issuer Accounting 274–275

COPYRIGHTS, 154

CORPORATIONS
See Stockholders' Equity

COST
Defined, 77

COST-BENEFIT ANALYSIS, 64

COST OF CAPITAL, 369–372

COST OF GOODS SOLD
Example, 37–38
Lower of Cost or Market, Effect of, 127–128
Periodic Inventory Systems, 114–116
Perpetual Inventory Systems, 116–118

COST METHOD
Accounting for Investments in Stock, 172–176

CREDITS
See Journals

CURRENT ASSETS
　See also Cash; Inventory; Marketable Securities; Prepaid
　　　Expenses; Receivables
Defined, 6, 81

CURRENT LIABILITIES
　See also Accounts Payable; Accrued Liabilities; Deferred
　　　Revenues; Deposits
Defined, 6, 81–82

CURRENT RATIO, 328–329

CUSTOMERS
Reporting on Major Customers, 349–350

DEBITS
See Journals

DEBT EQUITY RATIO, 330

DEBT SECURITIES
See Bonds and Debt Investments; Long Term Debt

DEBT TO ASSET RATIO, 330

DEFERRED CHARGE
See Deferred Expenses

DEFERRED EXPENSES
　See Prepaid Expenses
Defined, 3
Intangible Assets, 154

DEFERRED INCOME
See Deferred Revenues

DEFERRED REVENUES
Defined, 4, 104
Examples, 31–33

DEFERRED TAXES
See Income Tax Accounting

DEFINED BENEFIT PENSION PLANS, 244–253

DEFINED CONTRIBUTION PENSION PLANS, 241–243

DEPLETION, 147–148

DEPOSITS, 105–106

DEPRECIATION
Accumulated Depreciation, 139–140
Computing, 140–141
Declining Balance Method, 144–146
Defined, 138–139
Example, 35–36
Salvage Value, 140–141
Straight Line Method, 141–142
Sum-of-the-Years'-Digits Method, 142–144
Units of Production Method, 146–147
Useful Life, 140

DISCONTINUED OPERATIONS, 340–341

DISPOSAL OF A SEGMENT
See Discontinued Operations

DIVIDEND INCOME
Cost Method, 173
Equity Method, 177–178

DIVIDENDS
Cash Dividends, 264–265
Dates Related to Dividend Accounting, 263–264
Payout Ratio, 337
Property Dividends, 265–266
Stock Dividends, 266–267
Stock Rights, 267–268
Stock Splits, 268–269
Yield Ratio, 337

DOUBLE-ENTRY BOOKKEEPING, 18

EARNINGS PER SHARE
Generally, 10, 336
Complex Capital Structures, 319–326
Defined, 315
Simple Capital Structures, 316–319

EQUITY METHOD
Accounting for Investments in Stock, 176–178

ERRORS
See Prior Period Adjustments

EXCHANGES OF ASSETS, 132–135

EXPENSES
Defined, 8, 77–78

EXTRAORDINARY ITEMS, 339

FINANCIAL ACCOUNTING, 1

FINANCIAL ACCOUNTING STANDARDS BOARDS
Conceptual Framework, 55–56
Defined, 48
Interpretations, 48
Statements on Accounting Standards, 48

FINANCIAL RATIOS
See also entries for individual ratios
Generally, 328–327

FINANCIAL STATEMENT ANALYSIS, 326–328

FINANCIAL STATEMENTS
See also Balance Sheet; Income Statement; Statement of
Owners' Equity; Statement of Cash Flows
Generally, 1
Annual Reporting Basis, 59–61
Consolidated Financial Statements, 179–183
Footnotes, 13–14
Interim, 350–352
Supplemental Disclosures, 14

FIRST IN, FIRST OUT (FIFO) METHOD
See Inventory

FIXED ASSETS
See Property, Plant, And Equipment

FOOTNOTES
Generally, 10–11
Leases, 221
Other Post–Retirement Plans, 255
Retirement Plans, 252–253
Stock Options and Stock Appreciation Rights, 281

FOREIGN SEGMENT REPORTING, 348–349

FRANCHISES, 154

FULLY DILUTED EARNINGS PER SHARE, 320–321, 325–326

FUTURE VALUES
Computing, 385–387, 390–393
Tables, 399–400, 403–404

GAAP
See Generally Accepted Accounting Principles

GAINS
Defined, 7

GENERALLY ACCEPTED ACCOUNTING PRINCIPLES
Defined, 46–47
Sources, 47–51

GOING CONCERN ASSUMPTION, 58–59

GOODWILL
Generally, 59
Accounting for, 58–159
Business Combinations, 308–309

HISTORICAL COST
Accounting Basis, 57–58
Property, Plant, and Equipment, 131

INCOME STATEMENT
Changes in Accounting Principles, 341–344
Defined, 7
Discontinued Operations, Reporting on, 340–341
Example, 7, 45
Extraordinary Items, 339
Multiple Step Format, 9
Separately Stated Items, Reporting, 344–345

INCOME STATEMENT—Cont'd
Single Step Format, 9

INCOME TAX ACCOUNTING
  Generally, 53–54
Balance Sheet Reporting, 236–237
Deferred Tax Assets, 228–229
Deferred Tax Liabilities, 226–228
Deferred Taxes, 223–237
Intraperiod Tax Allocation, 237–239
Net Operating Losses, 233–234
Permanent Differences Defined, 223
Permanent Differences, Disclosing the Effects of, 239–241
Temporary Differences, Accounting for, 223–237
Temporary Differences Defined, 222, 225–226
Valuation Allowances on Deferred Tax Assets, 234–236

INDUSTRY SEGMENT REPORTING, 346–348

INDUCED CONVERSIONS, 203–204

INFLATION
Accounting For, 58

INTANGIBLE ASSETS
Amortization Expense, 155–156
Copyrights, 154
Deferred Charges, 154
Defined, 153
Franchises, 154
Goodwill, 159–158
Identifiable, 153–158
Internally Created, 156–158
Patents, 153–154
Purchased, 155–156
Trademarks, Service Marks, and Trade Names, 154
Unidentifiable, 158–159

INTEREST
Capitalization of Interest on Self–Constructed Assets, 136–138
Expense on Long Term Debt, 188–193
Imputing on Accounts Payable, 100
Imputing on Receivables, 95–96
Revenue on Bonds, 162–170

INTEREST RATES
Determinants, 356–358

INTERIM FINANCIAL STATEMENTS, 350–352

INTERNAL CONTROLS, 84–85

INVENTORY
Average Cost Method, 123–124
Cost Flow Assumptions, 119
Defined, 112
Dollar Value LIFO, 122–123
First in, First Out (FIFO) Method, 120–121
Last in, Last Out (LIFO) Method, 121–123
LIFO Tax Conformity Requirement, 54
Lower of Cost or Market, 62, 125–128
Manufacturing Companies, 128–129
Periodic Inventory System, 37–38, 114–116
Perpetual Inventory System, 38, 116–118, 124–125
Quantities, Determining, 113–118
Retail Inventory Method, 125
Specific Identification, 119
Turnover Ratio, 333–334

INVESTMENTS
See also Bonds and Debt Investments; Stock Investments
Cash Value of Life Insurance, 184–185
Land, 183–184
Sinking Funds, 185

JOURNALS
Debits and Credits, 18–19, 20–21
Defined, 17–18
Entries, 18–19
General, 19
Special, 19

LAND
Held for Investment, 183–184

LAST IN, LAST OUT (LIFO) METHOD
See Inventory

LEASES
Classifying, 208–209
Comparison with Debt Financing, 206–208
Disclosures in Footnotes, 221
Leverages Leases, 217–218
Real Estate, 218

LEASES—Cont'd
Sale/Leasebacks, 218–220
See also Capital Leases; Operating Leases

LEDGERS
Defined, 19–20

LEVERAGED LEASES, 217–218

LIABILITIES
See also Current Liabilities; Long Term Debt
Contingent, 108–111
Defined, 3–4
Estimated, 106–108

LIFE INSURANCE
Cash Value as an Investment, 184–185

LONG TERM CONTRACTS
Accounting For, 71–72
Completed Contract Method, 71–72
Percentage of Completion, 72

LONG TERM DEBT
Convertible Debt, 201–204
Currently Callable, 102–103
Currently Maturing Amounts, 101–102
Discount, 191–192
Early Retirement, 194–197
In–Substance Defeasance, 196–197
Issuance, Accounting for, 187–193
Issue Costs, 193–194
Premium, 192–193
Restructuring, 197–201
Stock Warrants Issued With, 204–205
Types of Debt, 186–187

LOSSES
Defined, 8

MARKET VALUES
Recognizing Revenues Based on Changes In, 74–76

MARKETABLE SECURITIES
Accounting For, 85–86

MATCHING CONCEPT
Direct Matching of Expenses, 78–79

MATCHING CONCEPT—Cont'd
Expense Recognition Generally, 61
Immediate Write-off, 79
Systematic and Rational Allocation, 79–80

MATERIALITY
Effect on Accounting Methods, 63–64

NATURAL RESOURCES
Depletion, 147–148

NET OPERATING LOSSES
See Income Tax Accounting

NOTES PAYABLE
Generally, 100–101
Discount Interest, 101

NOTES RECEIVABLE
Generally, 94–95
Imputing Interest on, 95–96

OPERATING CYCLE
Defined, 81

OPERATING LEASES
Defined, 210, 214
Lessee Accounting, 210–211
Lessor Accounting, 214–215

ORGANIZATION COSTS
Corporations, 261

OWNERS' EQUITY
Defined, 4–5
Revenues and Expenses, 39–41
Statement of, 10

PARTNERSHIPS
Admissions of New Partners, 288–294
Contributions to Capital, 282–283, 290–294
Income and Loss Allocation, 283–288
Retirements of Partners, 294–297
Transfers of Partnership Interests, 288–290

PATENTS, 153–154

PAYOUT RATIO, 337

PENSION PLANS
See Retirement Plans

PERCENTAGE OF COMPLETION METHOD ACCOUNTING
See Long Term Contracts

POOLING OF INTERESTS ACCOUNTING
See Business Combinations

POSTING, 20–21

PREFERRED STOCK
Valuation, 359–362

PREPAID EXPENSES
Defined, 96
Examples, 33–35, 96–97

PREPAID REVENUES
See Deferred Revenues

PRESENT VALUE
Computing, 388–390, 393–395
Irregular Cash Flows, 395–398
Tables, 401–402, 405–406
Use in Bond Valuation, 355–356
Use in Business Valuation, 375–378
Use in Common Stock Valuation, 363–366

PRICE EARNINGS (P/E) RATIO
Calculation, 336
Common Stock Valuation, 366

PRIMARY EARNINGS PER SHARE, 319, 321, 324–326

PRIOR PERIOD ADJUSTMENTS, 269

PROFIT MARGIN, 334

PROPERTY, PLANT, AND EQUIPMENT
  See also Depreciation
Acquisition, Accounting for, 131–138
Capital Expenditures After Acquisition, 149–151
Defined, 130
Disposals, 151–152
Exchange Transactions, 132–135
Multiple Asset Acquisitions, 135–136
Repairs, 149–150
Self–Constructed Assets, 136–137

PURCHASE ACCOUNTING
See Business Combinations

PURCHASE DISCOUNTS
Accounts Payable, 98–99

QUICK RATIO, 329

REAL ESTATE
Leases, 218

REALIZATION REQUIREMENT
See Revenue Recognition Principle

RECEIVABLES
Assignment, 92–94
Bad Debts, 89–92
Cash Discounts, 86–88
Defined, 86
Imputing Interest on, 95–96
Related Parties, 96
Reporting Basis, 89
Sales of, 93–94
Trade Receivables, 86–88
Turnover Ratio, 333

REGULATORY AGENCIES
Financial Statements Filed With, 52–53

REPAIRS
Related to Fixed Assets, 149–150

RESEARCH AND DEVELOPMENT, 157

RESTRUCTURING OF LONG TERM DEBT, 197–201

RETAINED EARNINGS
Appropriations, 270
Defined, 262
Dividends and Other Distributions, 263–269
Income or Loss for the Year, 262–263
Prior Period Adjustments, 269

RETIREMENT OF LONG TERM DEBT, 194–197

RETIREMENT PLANS
Defined Benefit Plans, 244–253
Defined Contribution Plans, 241–243
Disclosures Required, 252–253

RETIREMENT PLANS—Cont'd
Minimum Liability, 250–252
Pension Expense, 242, 245–249
Post–Retirement Benefits Other than Pensions, 253–255
Reporting Assets and Liabilities Related to, 242–243, 249–252

RETURN ON ASSETS, 334–335

RETURN ON EQUITY, 335

REVENUE RECOGNITION PRINCIPLE
   Generally, 61
Completion of Production, 74
Cost Recovery Method, 73–74
Earnings Process Complete, 67
Installment Method, 73
Long Term Contracts, 71–72
Market Values, Recognizing Changes In, 74–76
Realization Requirement, 67
Sales of Goods, 68–69
Services, 69–71

REVENUES
Defined, 7

REVERSING ENTRIES, 29–30

SALE/LEASEBACKS, 218–220

SALES OF FIXED ASSETS, 151–152

SALES OF GOODS
Revenue Recognition, 68–69
Right of Return, 68–69
Warranties, 68

SEC
See Securities and Exchange Commission

SECURITIES AND EXCHANGE COMMISSION
Regulation of Accounting Standards, 51–52

SEGMENT REPORTING
Customers, 349–350
Foreign Operations, 348–349
Industry Segments, 346–348

SERVICE MARKS, 154

SERVICES
Revenue Recognition, 69–71

SINKING FUNDS
Investment in, 185

SOFTWARE COSTS, 157–158

SOURCE DOCUMENTS, 16–17

STATEMENT OF CASH FLOWS
Cash flow from financing activities, 12
Cash flow from investing activities, 12
Cash flow from operations, calculating, 11–12
Defined, 10–11
Example, 13

STATEMENT OF FINANCIAL POSITION
See Balance Sheet

STATEMENT OF OWNERS' EQUITY, 10

STATEMENT OF RESULTS OF OPERATIONS
See Income Statement

STOCK APPRECIATION RIGHTS (SARs)
Accounting for, 279–281
Defined, 278–279

STOCK DIVIDENDS
Accounting by Investors, 175–176
Distributed, 266–267

STOCK, INVESTMENTS IN
Changes in Value, Recognition of, 174–175
Common Stock Valuation, 362–369
Consolidated Financial Statements, 179–183
Cost Method, 172–176
Equity Method, 176–178
Preferred Stock Valuation, 359–362
Stock Dividends, 175–176
Stock Splits, 175–176

STOCK OPTIONS
Accounting for, 276–278
Defined, 275–276
Effect on Earnings Per Share, 320–322

STOCK SPLITS
Accounting by Investors, 175–176
Accounting by Issuer, 268–269

STOCK SUBSCRIPTIONS, 259–260

STOCK WARRANTS
Exercise, 205
Issued with Long Term Debt, 204–205
Lapse, 205

STOCKHOLDERS' EQUITY
Cash Contributions, 257–258
Noncash Property Contributions, 258–259
Retained Earnings, 262–273
Stock Issuance Costs, 260–262
Stock Subscriptions, 259–260
Treasury Stock, 270–273

SUBSIDIARIES
In Consolidated Financial Statements, 179–183

T-ACCOUNTS, 20

TIMES FIXED CHARGES EARNED, 331–332

TIMES INTEREST EARNED, 331

TRADE NAMES, 154

TRADEMARKS, 154

TREASURY STOCK
Cost Method, 270–272
Defined, 270
Par Value Method, 272–273

TRIAL BALANCE, 42–43

VALUATION
Bonds, 353–359
Businesses, 372–381
Common Stock, 362–369
Preferred Stock, 359–362

WARRANTS
See Stock Warrants

WORK–IN–PROCESS INVENTORY, 128–129

WRITEDOWNS OF ASSETS
Generally, 76

†